Kevin Smith

MASTERING BUSINESS NEGOTIATION

MASTERING BUSINESS NEGOTIATION

A Working Guide to Making Deals and Resolving Conflict

Roy J. Lewicki

Alexander Hiam

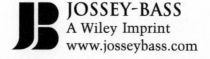

JOSSEY-BASS
A Wiley Imprint
www.josseybass.com

Published by Jossey-Bass
A Wiley Imprint
989 Market Street, San Francisco, CA 94103-1741   www.josseybass.com

Portions of this book previously appeared in the volume *The Fast Forward MBA in Negotiating and Deal Making* (New York: Wiley, 1991).

Jossey-Bass books and products are available through most bookstores. To contact Jossey-Bass directly call our Customer Care Department within the U.S. at 800-956-7739, outside the U.S. at 317-572-3986, or fax 317-572-4002.

Jossey-Bass also publishes its books in a variety of electronic formats. Some content that appears in print may not be available in electronic books.

Library of Congress Cataloging-in-Publication Data
Lewicki, Roy J.
  Mastering business negotiation : a working guide to making deals and resolving conflict / Roy J. Lewicki, Alexander Hiam.
    p. cm.
  Includes bibliographical references and index.
  ISBN-13: 978-0-7879-8099-3 (cloth)
  ISBN-10: 0-7879-8099-4 (cloth)
  1. Negotiation in business. I. Hiam, Alexander. II. Title.
  HD58.6.L496 2006
  658.4'052—dc22   2006013043

Printed in the United States of America
FIRST EDITION

HB Printing   10 9 8 7 6 5 4 3 2 1

Contents

Preface   vii

1	The Negotiation Imperative	1
2	The Flexibility of the Master Negotiator	19
3	Getting Ready to Negotiate	40
4	The Art of the Master Competitor	73
5	Executing a Competitive Negotiation	92
6	Mastering the Art of Collaboration	127
7	Mastering the Art of Compromise	159
8	Mastering Accommodation and Avoidance Strategies	185
9	Three (or More) Is a Crowd: Mastering Multiparty Negotiations	202
10	Mastering the Framing Process in Negotiation	219
11	Mastering the Power and Influence Process	238
12	Mastering Personal Negotiations	263

The Authors   293

Index   295

PREFACE

This is a book about negotiating effectively. We don't have a lot to tell you before you start reading this book—just a few key points to explain our approach:

- We teach a lot of people who work in businesses, so our approach is pragmatic and practical. We want you to achieve mastery of negotiation so that you can succeed, and help your organization succeed, in the world of work. Negotiation is also important to your personal life, and the last chapter of the book gives special attention to all of the personal negotiations in your life.
- We don't make this stuff up. This book is grounded in lots of solid research. It's amazing how many aspects of negotiation have been studied and how much is proven and known about effective negotiation and conflict resolution processes. It's also amazing how impenetrable and useless this research is to the busy executive or other business-oriented reader. Our role is to find the pearls of useful wisdom and interpret them for you so you don't have to spend a decade studying the literature.
- We've written on this subject before. Roy coauthored the best-known textbook on negotiating, as well as a book of readings, cases, and role-play materials that is the staple of many business school courses. Alex has written a variety of popular books and workshop binders, as well as assessment tools that thousands of government and corporate training departments use. And together, we've written two earlier "popular" books on negotiating. We hope this experience adds up to the ability to write a useful, interesting book. We're at a point in our careers where the chance to write a great book seems really appealing. We hope this is the best book we've ever written, and we aim to make it the most useful book

you'll ever read on the subject. We don't know if we've succeeded, but it's certainly an exciting goal to shoot for, and that always helps.

That's it, really. Oh, except that we need to address some possible confusion around terms.

You may wonder if negotiation is different from bargaining or haggling or from broader processes of conflict management and conflict resolution. There are a lot of terms floating around. The answer is that these are, at best, different flavors of the same thing. *Negotiation* is the proper term to describe this process, while *bargaining* and *haggling* are often used to describe the more competitive dynamics of the process. *Conflict management* and *conflict resolution* encompass a broader set of processes that may include negotiation and the involvement of third parties such as mediators and arbitrators. But the basic skills and techniques of the master negotiator that we outline in this book are the key to resolving conflicts, handling difficult conversations, protecting oneself against a competitive adversary, or negotiating a good business deal. They also help immensely with a variety of more informal day-to-day negotiations on the job: selling, buying, team building, product development, project management, hiring, correcting poor performance, and much more.

Negotiation is the master practice that allows you to move in and out of business situations with confidence and success. Being an effective master negotiator is a critical key to business success. We hope you partake of our insights, and attain the skills to make you a Master Negotiator!

We thank Neil Maillet of Jossey-Bass for his helpful guidance and feedback as we completed the manuscript for this book. We also thank Beverly Miller and Steve Stenner for their excellent assistance in copyediting and manuscript preparation.

May 2006

Roy J. Lewicki
Columbus, Ohio

Alexander Hiam
Amherst, Massachusetts

MASTERING BUSINESS NEGOTIATION

CHAPTER ONE

THE NEGOTIATION IMPERATIVE

Negotiating is a bit like breathing. You don't have to do it, but the alternatives aren't very attractive.

Negotiation is the daily give-and-take of social interactions. Once your eyes and ears are tuned to the language of negotiation, you realize that everybody negotiates constantly—all day long.

Some of those many daily negotiations are trivial and may not deserve care and conscious thought (and they certainly don't get it). But many do. The strange thing is, people rarely realize they are negotiating. They think they are just talking or maybe not even talking, just reading each other's body language and nonverbal signals and responding. Other times they think they are disagreeing, or making a point, or making an offer, or trying to close a deal, or finding out what's wrong, or helping someone out, or calling in a favor, or making a sale, or buying something, or fighting their way through rush-hour traffic. People use a lot of different terms to describe these things they do, because they rarely recognize that they are engaged in negotiations.

One of the most interesting recent developments in the field is the rise in popularity of the term *crucial conversations* or *difficult conversations* to describe many person-to-person negotiations. These are conversations in which the stakes are high, people have different points of view, and there are strong emotions attached to those points of view. This effort to create a new term for negotiating may seem strange to people who have studied and practiced negotiation for many years, but it's not. It's just another manifestation of an interesting social phenomenon: most people don't recognize when they are negotiating. Lacking this awareness, they aren't able to take advantage of the treasure trove of information and insight offered by the research on negotiation and how to do it well.

When you have those crucial conversations, they will go a lot better if you realize that most, if not all, of them are negotiations, and you therefore apply the tools and techniques available to you as a negotiator. Many other conversations that may seem casual will also go better and be less likely to escalate into conflict or hurt feelings if you realize that they may be negotiations too.

Then there are the formal negotiations, where you know you are working out a deal, the stakes are high, and you want to get a good result. Although it's obvious that negotiation is in the air, most people still fail to take advantage of the wealth of research about how negotiation works. We aim in this book to give you a significant advantage in all negotiations, from informal daily negotiations to formal important deals that have to go well. From your preparations (both mental and investigative) to your conduct, response to tactics, and clarity about style, strategy, and goals, there is a great deal we can help you refine in the pursuit of mastery over the many negotiations you encounter in business and in life as well.

Is negotiation as prevalent in business as in life in general? What's true at home and among friends is even truer at work. We work in ever more interdependent ways. Nobody can accomplish anything alone, which means we often help each other at work— and just as often get in each other's way or run into conflicts and problems.

That's why the business that negotiates better generally grows and prospers faster than others. And that's why individuals who master negotiation are rated as high in emotional intelligence by their peers, tend to be promoted more rapidly, are more productive, and emerge as natural leaders. Whether it's sales, administration, customer service, engineering, management, or any other area of business, negotiation skills play a surprisingly large role in career success.

NEGOTIATING BY DAY

Think back on the events of a recent day. Did you negotiate? Did you win? It may be hard to say, since so many of our daily negotiations may go unrecognized. Following a fictional character through her day will help you answer those questions.

Helen, we will call her, awoke to the alarm clock at 6:45 A.M. She waited a moment, but Jim, her husband, did not stir, so she climbed over him to turn off the alarm. She found this irritating, especially with her bad back. Jim's son from his prior marriage, Noel, was staying with them for the week while his mom traveled. Helen went to his door and called to him before heading down to the kitchen to pack his lunch for school. Then she went back upstairs to get ready for work. But the bathroom door was closed and the shower water was running. Was it Noel or Jim? No, Jim was no longer in bed. It must be Noel. But that meant no time for her to shower before work, since it was her turn to drive the car pool to work and she had to leave home early to pick up everyone else. She wished she had remembered Noel was coming when they discussed the car pool schedule at work; it would have been more convenient for her to drive next week. As she stood in front of her closet, she debated whether to wear her new red skirt, which she had just bought, or the older gray one. After looking to see what blouses were clean, she decided that the red skirt would have to wait until she had time to do some ironing.

Helen has not gotten very far in her day and already she has ended up on the wrong side of *five* negotiations. Did you take note of them? She accommodated Jim's irritating habit of sleeping through the alarm (rather than nudging him and waking him up). She generously packed a lunch for his son, and by so doing she lost her opportunity to take a shower before rushing to her car pool. To Helen, all three interactions with her family are probably losses, and there's no point losing in any situation unless you gain something in the future from it. These sacrifices were not likely to be noticed and reciprocated. And her fourth loss—agreeing to drive in an inconvenient week—also accomplishes nothing in the long term. It is an example of suboptimal results due to incomplete information, a remarkably common problem for most negotiators. Finally, her "negotiation" with herself over which skirt to wear led to her decision to wear the older skirt because she had nothing ironed to go with the new red one. But let's not dwell on this, as Helen's workday is likely to hold many more negotiation situations for her.

Helen left the house a little late, and a little irritated at Jim, who had driven off without offering an apology. Perhaps that is why she was driving faster than usual on the freeway and why she was pulled over by a state trooper. Even worse, she forgot how outspoken Fred, her coworker who was riding in the front seat, could be—or she certainly would have told him to keep his mouth shut! The police officer had clocked her at only five miles over the speed limit and seemed ready to let her off with a warning when Fred started arguing with him.

Fred is a senior manager at her company and often loses his temper quickly. He was angry this morning since he had an early staff meeting and he told the officer in no uncertain terms how inconvenient the situation was for him. Now Helen had a speeding ticket to pay, and Fred was going to be even later for that meeting.

What mistake did Helen make this time? Another common one: she failed to plan and control others' communication in her negotiation with the police officer. She should have managed Fred even if he is her boss. Many negotiations turn sour when the wrong thing is said, the timing is bad, or the wrong person gets involved.

The importance of planning the communications was brought home to Helen later that morning when her project team met. Her team is charged with cutting costs in the assembly of one of her company's products. They had begun to work with suppliers to reduce prices, and one of the suppliers was resisting the changes they proposed. Then Helen had called an old friend at the supplier company, who was able to get his firm to agree to a concession. Just as a solution was in sight, however, her friend took a new job and left the company. Now the supplier refused to sign the new contract. Her boss was impatient and wanted her to disband the current team and start all over again. But Helen knew this would hurt her relationships with the team members—all of them key personnel from the main functional areas of her firm. She suspected that these business relationships with team members were more important than the small price cut her boss wanted her to obtain from the supplier. But how could she get her boss to see it that way? She was not sure what to do, but she knew she had some difficult negotiations ahead of her.

THE NEGOTIATION IMPERATIVE

Even before taking her lunch break, Helen has had to cope with many negotiations. Some seem trivial, some are minor but irritating, and others are important to her career or personal success.

These situations and similar ones we all face daily are important to consider for four reasons.

First, we care about the results. We care because we have one or more *goals* that we hope to accomplish, and our goals often conflict with other people's goals. The traffic cop wants to meet his quota for tickets, but we want to minimize travel time and cost. Our boss wants a quick, forced solution to a problem, but we have to live with our associates afterward, so preserving our relationships is more important. If people openly shared all their goals, they might be more easily achieved. And, in fact, as we will soon see, aligning our goals is a useful negotiating strategy in contexts where collaboration is feasible and important. But we will also see that openly sharing goals can be a wasteful, even damaging, strategy in other situations.

Second, in negotiation, we have *emotional* as well as rational goals. This is perfectly natural, since negotiation is a human activity, and humans are both rational and emotional. When we let our emotions take over and drive the negotiations without recognizing them or planning how to offset them with tough rational thinking, we are bound to negotiate out of control. All of us have said things we wished we hadn't, or fired off an angry e-mail that we wished we could call back through cyberspace. Emotional outbursts can be extremely damaging in negotiation—but emotions can also be very powerful and critical to winning a point. It takes a carefully planned strategy to prevent passions or gut instincts from spoiling the outcome.

Third, our rational and emotional goals lead us to work with the other party to pursue specific *outcomes* in the negotiation. The outcome is the result of the way that the parties resolve conflicts in their broader goals; it is what they agree to do as a result of their discussions. The outcome may be more supportive of our goals; it may favor the other but be very disappointing to us; it may actually be neutral; or it may favor neither of us. The outcome is the traditional focus of negotiators, and therefore it is helpful to keep it in context, but only as one of the four main concerns of strategic negotiation.

Fourth, we often have a *relationship* with the other people involved in the negotiation. All negotiations affect the relationship in which they occur, and the importance of the relationship with that other party must therefore be considered carefully in the

development of any negotiating strategy. Thus, we might negotiate differently if we are buying a used car from a dealer lot, from
a neighbor down the street, or from our aging grandmother who
has decided it is time to stop driving. The critical idea to keep in
mind is that the more important it is to maintain a good relationship, the more likely it is that we may make sacrifices on pursuing
the desired outcome. While we might negotiate aggressively with
the used car dealer, we might give Grandma more than the car is
worth just to please her. Helen accepted a negative outcome in
some of her negotiations because she wished to maintain a good
relationship with that person; for example, she didn't poke Jim and
tell *him* to turn off the alarm clock.

Many people plan and execute negotiation strategies without
considering their impact on the key relationship. If your relationship with the other party is one you value and want to keep strong
by maintaining open communications, high trust, and positive feelings, be careful what you do.

These four concerns are the cornerstones of a careful, planned
approach to negotiation (see Exhibit 1.1).

Like Helen, we all face many negotiations in which there are
important goals we need to try to achieve. Some are *tangible*:
money, time, materials, and so on. Others are *intangible*: establishing a broader principle, maintaining a precedent, or looking
strong and tough to other people. Based on these tangible and
intangible goals, we formulate a few specific desired outcomes—
which, if we negotiate well, we may actually manage to accomplish.

Add up what's at stake in many negotiations, and you've got a
collection of goals, desired outcomes, and relationships that need
tending to and thinking about—every day, and both at home and
at work. It is imperative to recognize that your goals, desired outcomes, and relationships will not sort themselves out without your
careful attention. You need to negotiate. And you need to become
a skilled negotiator in order to accomplish your bigger-picture
goals, such as forming and maintaining healthy personal and business relationships, achieving outstanding business results, and
advancing your career.

This, then, is the negotiation imperative: *recognize the many times
each day you have to negotiate and influence others. In doing so, treat these
as opportunities to advance your personal goals, help your business pros-*

EXHIBIT 1.1. THE FOUR MAIN CONCERNS OF NEGOTIATION

Be clear about your goals.

Be aware of emotional goals.

Specify desired outcomes that are consistent with goals.

Pay attention to the importance of the relationship with the other
    party.

---

*per, and build stronger supportive relationships in a widening business and
professional network.*

At the beginning of this chapter, we compared negotiating to
breathing and said that it was a natural part of social interaction;
nobody can avoid it, and most of us do it unconsciously. That's true
as far as it goes, but the comparison is flawed in one respect: unlike
breathing, we are not born with an innate knowledge of how to
negotiate well.

People spend much of their childhood learning to negotiate.
We are convinced that negotiation begins when a baby learns to get
a caregiver's attention—to be fed, to have a diaper changed, or just
to be picked up and cuddled. Young children learn how to get their
needs met from parents. They learn how to share with sisters and
brothers. Some learn to be bullies, some learn to be passive, and
some learn how to work out differences so that each party benefits.
Parents, teachers, and older siblings serve as role models who may
or may not be experts themselves. We don't get formal instruction
in the art and science of negotiating when in school, although parents and teachers give us a lot of informal guidance on how to get
along and play well with others. Eventually most of us piece
together a patchy, partial understanding of negotiating, usually
related to a preferred approach to handling conflict (more about
this later). But we usually never *question* the adequacy or com-
pleteness of this approach until we are not meeting our goals and
the approach is not successful at getting us the outcomes we want.

Some people compare negotiating to the martial arts, because
there are so many who try but so few who achieve mastery. This is
a helpful comparison in its own way, because it reminds us that
there is much to learn and much need of practice if we hope to be

able to master exceptional negotiating skills. Learning to negotiate well requires constant practice and a consistent willingness to step back, examine how things were done effectively and ineffectively, and specify improvements that need to be made in the next negotiation.

But negotiation is not a martial art; it's a social art, and it is not always (or even usually) practiced to inflict damage on the other side. Part of the negotiation imperative is the necessity of conducting negotiations that are constructive, not destructive. Great negotiators create great solutions, and it's always harder to create than to destroy. Whether you are negotiating to win against a tough competitor or to engineer a friendly collaboration with a coworker or family member, your goal is always to create a constructive solution that moves everyone ahead and truly resolves the conflict.

In this book, we take a productive, well-managed approach to negotiations—both the occasional formal ones and the far more frequent informal negotiations that fill our days and affect the quality of our lives and work. This approach suggests that first, we must clarify our goals and the goals of those with whom we must negotiate. Second, it means substituting a careful, rational plan for the impulsive, emotion-based approach we often tend to take to such situations. And third, it means optimizing outcomes, or relationships—or if you are really good, optimizing both.

THE GREAT GAME OF NEGOTIATION

As long as we are exploring comparisons, a good way to think about negotiation is that it is a game. Thinking about negotiation in this way has lots of advantages:

- We can understand the game. It is not a random process. Most negotiations can be analyzed after they are over, and, with increasing understanding comes the ability to predict and control what happens.
- The game has a predictable sequence of activities. Many people who do not understand negotiation see it as a chaotic, almost random series of events. While it is true that it may be difficult to accurately predict exactly what a party will do next at any given point, the entire negotiation sequence generally follows a clear,

understandable pattern. As you read this book, you will learn to better predict and control how parties move from disagreement toward agreement.

- There are players in the game. As we can see from the earlier example, there can be only one player (when Helen negotiates with herself about which skirt to wear), or there can be two players (her negotiations with Fred and Jim), or there can be multiple players (her negotiations with her team). Who the other players are and what they do have a great deal of impact on how we should plan and execute our strategy. Certainly that's obvious, but we say it because in this book, we intend to help you understand and manage the other players better than most other people do. We are not going to deal with self-negotiation, but we are going to deal with all kinds of negotiations with others.

- The game has rules. There are do's and don'ts for what can be done in negotiation. In some negotiations, these rules are clear; they may even be written in a contract or set of procedures. For example, in your "negotiations" with the Internal Revenue Service each spring, the rules state that you have to report accurately how much income you earned and what you owe the government. You can't simply make an opening offer and hope the government accepts it. In other negotiations, the rules are informal and may even be unclear. In this book, we will identify some of the most important informal rules—the do's and don'ts—that will help you plan your game strategy.

SABOTAGING OURSELVES: WHAT INEXPERIENCED NEGOTIATORS DO

Many inexperienced negotiators think of the negotiation process as akin to entering a long, dark tunnel. They are moving into a process that they don't understand, and they have no idea what is going to happen. Feeling out of control—often because they fear conflict or confrontation—these people do a number of foolish things. Truth is, all of us have fallen into one or more of these traps, so let's take a good look at how people most often go wrong:

- Sometimes we have no clear objective or desired outcome other than to "get something," "do better than the last time we negotiated," or "get this done quickly." Negotiators who do this seldom achieve good outcomes because they had no clear objectives to begin with—unless the other party is also equally unclear and unprepared. To quote the Cheshire Cat in *Alice in Wonderland*, "If you don't know where you're going, any road will get you there!"

• Sometimes we formulate a desired outcome or objective and cling to it desperately, refusing to compromise or modify their objective based on what the other party wants. This plan usually winds up in angry exchanges or a standoff with no satisfactory resolution. (We call this *digging in*. We don't recommend it.)

• Sometimes we may formulate a desired outcome or objective but then surrender it too quickly in order to get the conflict resolved. This usually leaves us with a deal we regret later; most negotiators who do this have a lot of regret that maybe they could have done better. (We call this *caving in* and don't recommend it either.)

• Or we may change our desired outcome or objective midway through the discussion, leading the other side to believe that we may not have a strategy, don't understand what is going on, don't know what we want, or, worst, are intentionally being difficult. This often happens when our own mind wasn't made up, or because the other's behavior led us to believe we would never get what we wanted. When we do this, we often anger the other party, which can lead to the breakdown of talks or a settlement that makes little sense down the road. (We call this error *zigzagging* and will specify ways that negotiators can avoid doing this.)

You can avoid these common errors, and many more, by preparing carefully for the negotiation and by walking through it step by step. Usually there is a recognition period in which you become aware of and concerned about a conflict of interest. Instead of leaping to a premature effort to close or resolve, the master negotiator explores the conflict at this stage, sounds out the other party, gathers information, and explores his or her own feelings and needs as well. Next, the master negotiator selects an appropriate style and approach to reach the goals most productively. In this book, we stress collaborating and competing as the dominant strategies to pursue, but there are other alternatives, and we'll show you how to use all of these strategies later in this book.

Notice that we've suggested a variety of actions in the beginning of your negotiation, all of which precede the normal give-and-take of offers or disputes. In this book, we'll help you slow down the initial steps of your negotiations to allow a little more breathing room and time for thought and insight. Negotiating should be a careful process. Don't rush it.

NEGOTIATING TO WIN

Sometimes we encounter eager negotiators in our classes and workshops who ask us if we can teach them to "win" every negotiation. If you have a competitive streak, negotiation is indeed a competitive game, and winning is close to your heart. To people who ask us if we can help them win their negotiations, we say yes, *but*:

We don't mean to split semantic hairs, but it depends on how you define winning. This takes us back to the metaphor of negotiation as a game. In most games, there are winners and losers, which is what makes them exciting to watch. But in negotiation, winning can mean different things. It may mean getting a better outcome than your opponent, but it may also mean getting the outcome you desire and helping the other party get its goals met. If the two parties have different goals, both may be able to "win." Or it may mean strengthening the relationship with the other party. The more you can define winning as a way to help both parties achieve their goals and strengthen their relationship, the more productive your negotiations will be.

You also don't want to win every negotiation. Sometimes it's wiser to avoid a conflict. Sometimes it's better to split the difference and go on to something more important. And sometimes it's a good idea to cooperate with the other parties instead of trying to "kill" them. So, yes, we can teach you the techniques you need to go for the big win, but you have to use them appropriately—not every time you negotiate.

And even when you decide it's right to compete and try to outmaneuver the competitor, remember this secret of great competitive negotiators: always leave something on the table. You don't have to clear the field to win a battle, and you don't have to win every aspect of every negotiating point to win the negotiation. People who don't allow the other side dignity in defeat are resented and cultivate revenge down the road. Nobody wants to do business with them. And the deals they cut are resented too and tend not to stick. If you want a durable win—a deal or agreement or under-standing that the other party can and will live with—then leave a little something on the table for them.

We'll show how complex this becomes in a real negotiation. One of us (Alex) just sold his office building and moved his busi-ness to larger quarters. The buyers played a tough competitive nego-tiating game during the course of the sale, so Alex did too.

At first, it wasn't clear the buyers were going to be tough nego-tiators. They opened with an attractive offer: just a small amount below the asking price. Then Alex offered to split the difference between his asking price and their offer, and they quickly accepted.

Next, they insisted on an early closing date to consummate the sale. This wasn't a major problem for Alex, so he accepted, even though it gave him just a few weeks to move out of the building. He already had a new building lined up and could push the date of his move up without too much inconvenience.

The other shoe fell at the end of the one-week inspection period the buyers had built into their offer. They brought forward a laundry list of "severe" problems with the building, including a bad roof, siding that needed immediate replacement, and struc-tural problems with the foundation. They demanded a big reduc-tion: about 10 percent off Alex's original listing price.

If these problems were real, Alex would not have been sur-prised. However, the building was in good repair, except that the roof shingles were within a few years of their twenty-year life. Alex asked his own contractor to take a look, who agreed that the build-ing was in very good shape. Armed with the information from the contractor that did not support the buyers' claims, Alex decided he needed to "play hardball" in this negotiation.

First, he decided to do some additional research on the buy-ers. Asking around, he learned that they were under pressure to close the deal rapidly because they had a buyer lined up for their old building and needed to move. This convinced Alex that they were serious about closing a deal, and not just playing games. He also learned that the buyers had a reputation for being tough negotiators. From these two pieces of information, he surmised that they were perhaps regretting how quickly they'd negotiated the sale price and now wanted to see if they could nibble any more concessions in their favor before closing.

Alex decided to send an emotional signal to the buyers through his agent. Instead of responding with a counteroffer, Alex asked his agent to let the buyers know that he was upset with their behavior and would think about whether he wanted to complete the sale over the coming weekend (it was Thursday afternoon). Then he put the matter out of his mind for a few days.

By midday Monday, Alex's agent was on the telephone, sounding desperate. "They want to hear *something*," she said to Alex on his cell phone. "Their agent says you have to reply today, since the closing date is only two weeks away." This sounded promising to Alex. Probably by putting the time pressure on them plus his showing that he might not be interested, he was now building a feeling of urgency on the buyers' end.

Late Monday, before he left the office, Alex called his realtor and left a message on her voice mail saying that his inspector said their claim about the roof was reasonable and that he would be willing to add 25 percent of the estimated cost of replacing the roof to the deal. This would bring the final price down to about 98 percent of Alex's original asking price. It was a small but significant concession. It illustrated the principle that a negotiator needs to leave something on the table rather than going for the jugular. These buyers might have been desperate enough to back down completely, but it would have been risky to push that hard. It was better to give them something they could feel good about. But Alex also wanted to avoid further nibbles, so he said his offer was firm and final and delivered it with as much time pressure as he thought he could get away with.

Alex intentionally made his counteroffer late in the day and used his agent's office voice mail instead of her cell. He complied with their request that he respond that day, but he did so in a way that would make it likely they'd have to wait until Tuesday morning to learn about his Monday offer. He wanted them to be good and worried about the deal by the time they heard his terms.

On Tuesday morning, Alex's counteroffer was accepted, and the papers were drawn up and signed by the end of the day. In the end, Alex sold the building at the price of the buyer's first offer,

which seemed reasonable to him since it was only a few percentage points beneath his original asking price. In fact, he would have
been willing to go another percent or two down but was hoping he
wouldn't have to.

Let's take a look at how Alex handled this situation. Alex
resorted to competitive negotiating tactics to avoid being "nibbled," the term used to describe a negotiating tactic in which one
party attempts to take another slice of the deal after the other party
thinks that terms have been agreed to. Alex also used emotional
signaling to change the frame of the negotiation from a rational
debate about the numbers to one in which the buyers needed to
be concerned about the personal impact their behavior was having on the seller. He did this because there are unwritten rules
about what's fair in the inspection period, and he wanted the buyers to recognize that their violation of these rules could create negative feelings and break down the trust needed to close a deal.

Finally, Alex resorted to the oldest but best trick in the book:
he used time pressure. Remember that the buyers used this tactic
first by not being upfront about their need to close the deal
quickly. Once Alex learned that the buyers had a ticking clock, he
realized he could take the upper hand, no matter how aggressively
they tried to negotiate. Alex did not have the same time pressure
to sell that they had to buy. He preferred not to have to wait for
another buyer, as it would mean he'd have holding costs on his old
building, but he was willing to walk away if he had to because his
agent assured him the property was appealing and would generate
more offers in the future if this deal didn't go through.

Throughout this negotiation, both parties were uncertain
about the other side's feelings and actions. Why did they do that?
What are they thinking? How low will they go? How high will they
go? Are they serious about walking away, or just trying to play me?
These are the kinds of questions that we always have in a competitive negotiation. Like a poker player, the competitive negotiator
keeps his or her cards close to the chest.

Alex took advantage of the information barrier by using an
emotional signal and a temporary withdrawal from the negotiation
to raise doubts in the buyers' minds. The buyers were dealing with

Alex through two intermediaries: their agent and Alex's agent. They couldn't be sure about his state of mind. How upset was he? Was he still committed to the deal? Had they gone too far and spoiled the negotiation? These sorts of uncertainties are always greater where there is less information, and they can be a problem in negotiations. Sometimes they can also be a useful weapon. The buyers were probably quite relieved by the time they finally received a substantive counteroffer and not willing to risk their deal again by playing games with it.

This story illustrates several things we warn negotiators who want to win. First, recognize that parties may have different definitions of winning. For the buyers, it was more about getting a new building quickly; for Alex, it was getting his price and not making further improvements. Second, don't forget to leave something on the table so the other side can walk away with dignity and live with the terms of the deal too. Even when you have the other party on the run, don't humiliate them or strip them clean. Finally, sometimes you can't achieve a good deal, and you have to recognize this and be willing to walk away.

What if Alex's buyers had not been able to afford his building but were hoping to bring him down to a much lower price level? Then no amount of negotiating could have bridged the gap. Alex didn't know whether there was truly an overlap between his selling range (the least he was willing to take) and their buying range (the most they were willing to pay) until the ink dried on the check. He hoped the buyers could afford to pay what he wanted them to, and he negotiated on the assumption they could. But what if their original offer had actually been way beyond their means? Then they might have used their phony inspection report as an excuse to back out of the deal, and Alex would have had to wait for another offer.

You never really know if there is a deal to be made until you try. If you keep trying and the other party just seems to get further away instead of closer, then you may need to abandon the effort and look for an alternative. You don't have to play every competitive negotiating game to its final whistle. Sometimes you find you are on the wrong playing field and with the wrong competitor, and the smartest thing to do is to clear out as gracefully as you can.

NEGOTIATING TO A WIN-WIN SOLUTION

There are people and organizations you can't really afford not to negotiate with. If your boss disagrees with you about an important issue, it's a good idea to try to negotiate through to a solution that makes both of you happy instead of playing a high-stakes game. Competing with your boss has only two likely outcomes: you score a victory that leaves your boss angry and looking for payback opportunities, or you lose and feel defeated and unappreciated and start polishing your résumé. Actually, you better work on your résumé either way, because bosses generally don't like to be treated to competitive negotiating tactics.

When we have important ongoing relationships with people, it's generally appropriate not to play a competitive game and instead play an alternative game: a collaborative, compromising, or even avoiding or accommodating negotiating game. We'll say something about collaborating here and more about the other strategies in Chapter Two.

Collaboration is the opposite of competition in most ways: you share information instead of concealing it, you focus on the other side's concerns over your own, and you sit side by side instead of negotiating at arm's length. Collaboration requires rich, ongoing communication, and it relies on joint problem solving. Good collaborators sound very different from good competitors. They talk more, they listen more, they ask a lot more questions, and they make a lot fewer declarations. They also are more forgiving about waffling and take-backs, since they want to get at the real underlying issues and understand that these may not be apparent to the other side at first.

The negotiating game is very different when the goal is to make sure both sides win. It's not like the games we watch on TV or most of the games we played as children. In this book, we'll be sharing a lot of ideas and techniques for win-win negotiating, because it is the lifeblood of business success in most organizations. Anyone you work with is a candidate for win-win negotiating, including coworkers, team members, employees, bosses, suppliers, customers, regulators, and boards of directors.

When we write a book, we at first compete with the publisher as we bargain to sign a favorable contract with a publishing house that we think will handle the book competently and sell it well. For these competitive negotiations, we usually use a literary agent and keep the communications tightly controlled. We want the publishers to worry that they may lose us to one of their competitors. We want them to offer us as big an advance and as favorable a royalty rate as we can wring out of them—well, almost; we always try to leave something on the table so that they find the deal livable in the future too.

But you can't develop and market a new product by continuing to compete with the parties you just signed the contract with. It takes collaboration to write and produce a book that sells well. So as soon as the contract is signed, we put it in the back of a file cabinet and generally forget all about it. We thank the agent who helped us and send him packing. And we begin to communicate openly and honestly with the editors involved in the project. Our behavior changes because now we need to do team building and stop competing against the publisher. We have to reach out and learn to work together, sharing concerns, ideas, suggestions, and needs in order to create a good new product together. Like most other projects in the world of business, writing a book requires a win-win, not just a win. If anybody loses, the project will fail.

The master negotiator moves from the competitive to the collaborative negotiation with ease. He or she must also know how to compromise, avoid, or accommodate with grace as the situation demands. Flexibility is the greatest asset of the master negotiator. All other skills are secondary, although they are nevertheless important in their own right. So before we get into any more of the particulars of negotiating tactics and skills, we want to work with you on your flexibility as a negotiator.

What style or approach do you tend to use instinctively? We all have a tendency toward one style or another, and understanding this built-in bias is the first step toward true mastery. Just as the samurai of old trained by practicing swordplay with either hand, the master negotiator today needs to be equally facile in every style and type of negotiation.

But are you left-handed or right-handed by nature? Or, to put it into the context of negotiating, which are your naturally stronger and weaker negotiating styles? As you read this book and learn about the details of each style, ask yourself which one or ones you tend to be most comfortable with. Here are two fundamental questions to help you make this determination:

• Do you tend to avoid conflict (a flight response) or wade right in and enjoy dealing with it (a fight or engagement response)? People who don't mind engagement in conflict-oriented situations tend to be naturally drawn to competing or collaborating. Others favor avoiding or, if pressed, find it easiest to compromise because this style is ritualized and simpler than competing or collaborating.

• Do you tend to feel competitive and want to win, or do you focus more on the other party and how to help them? People who respond competitively tend to be most comfortable with the competing style, and secondarily with compromising. Others find it hard to compete because they are naturally more collaborative in nature and may simply accommodate when pressed.

There are entire assessment instruments to determine your negotiating style (such as Assessing Behavior in Conflict, which one of us, Alex, designed, and many others as well). But you probably will get a clear sense of your own habits and patterns as you read about each style. Whatever your natural tendencies, remember that one of your goals on the road to greater negotiating mastery is to learn to be more flexible, and willing to switch out of your own comfort zone if necessary. Master negotiators are prepared to play and win any game, not just the ones that occur on their home turf.

CHAPTER TWO

THE FLEXIBILITY OF THE MASTER NEGOTIATOR

Style flexibility is one of the hallmarks of the master negotiator. To master every negotiating situation and resolve varied conflicts, you need to adjust your approach to each. This is a little like dressing for the correct sport before you go onto the playing field. Don't show up with shin guards and cleats for a tennis tournament (or show up for a soccer game in white shorts and carrying a can of green tennis balls). And make sure you know how to play both tennis and soccer well enough that you can win either depending on which you find yourself playing!

Athletes may not be able to switch games easily and still be the best at both, but master negotiators should be able to. That's because we're playing the bigger negotiating game, and it sometimes requires us to suit up for one type of negotiation, and other times another. Getting ready for negotiation is more like staying in shape to play either tennis or soccer; although there may be some difference in the unique skills, both require a strong degree of basic athletic conditioning.

Here's an example of the need for flexibility. The CEO of a regional furniture manufacturer is examining his schedule for the day. It looks like this:

9:00   Meet with a delegation from the mayor's office to discuss their request for company sponsorship of new playing fields for the town's youth sports.

10:00   Conference call with the company's attorney and lawyers who are representing a laid-off employee who has claimed age discrimination.

12:00   Lunch with sales staff at a local restaurant to celebrate their success at exceeding their quarterly sales goals.

1:15   Following lunch, meet with the sales manager, who has asked for an increase in the commission rate for sales-people and is waiting for a response.

1:45   Review proposals from several bidders to upgrade an important piece of equipment in the plant.

3:00   Talk with the head of another furniture company, who wants to explore the idea of a merger.

In the great game of negotiation, you should always take a moment to think about what type of negotiation you are entering. Don't just start negotiating. If you haven't determined what the game is, you'll often find yourself playing the wrong game.

The executive whose calendar we peeked at above will have to use several different types of strategies during the day. In the first meeting, with a representative of the mayor's office, it's probably a good idea to be friendly and open. A good long-term relationship with the community is clearly important. Nevertheless, this isn't one of those deals of a lifetime that are worth a lot of time and attention. If the mayor's office asks for a modest donation, it's probably appropriate to just accommodate the request with a yes and move on to the next item on the agenda. If the request is for more than our executive can comfortably accommodate, then he might suggest a compromise and offer some smaller amount. He could also offer to help find other local companies that might provide sponsorships.

In the next meeting, a conference call with the attorneys involved in an employee dispute, the executive will need to take a different tack. He probably wants to be quite open with the company's attorney in private, but when talking to the attorneys for the former employee, careful competition is probably the best approach. He should be guarded about what he says, since he does not want to say anything that makes the company more legally liable or damages the company's ability to challenge the lawsuit. Nor should he make any commitments or give any firm answers in a meeting like this. "Taking it under advisement" is the best approach. Whatever the other side asks, threatens, or offers should be discussed in private with the firm's lawyer (putting the call on hold or talking after the call) and before giving a firm response. But he'll need to sound concerned and should be sure the former employee's attorneys feel they can trust him to consider whatever offer they make and get back to them fairly promptly.

The celebratory lunch with the sales staff should be handled in a positive, friendly style. But the CEO has to keep in mind that there is, in the background, a proposal for higher sales commissions and that the salespeople are probably aware of this and eager to get his response. He'll probably want to avoid the topic if it comes up during lunch and wait until his meeting with the sales manager before discussing it.

Before he meets with the sales manager, the CEO needs to study the numbers, perhaps consult his finance and accounting staff, and think about how much more commission the firm can afford to pay. He should know what his negotiating range is, so as not to get talked into a bigger raise than is in the firm's best interests. It would probably be helpful to know what comparable companies in the area are paying their salespeople. He also needs to think about and perhaps learn more about whatever issues are behind the sales manager's proposal. If sales force motivation or performance is slipping or it is proving hard to hire or retain competent salespeople, a raise might make sense. But in this case, performance is up, and salaries are already better than the regional average, so what needs fixing? He might try to reframe this negotiation. Perhaps the salespeople really need some form of special recognition for their good work, but it doesn't need to be a raise. If he can shift the sales manager to a creative discussion of how to reward the top salespeople without spending a lot more money, this could become a collaborative meeting.

In reviewing proposals from potential vendors, one of the things the CEO needs to look for is the style of each proposal. Some may be framed as competitive negotiations, in which the vendors are trying to capture a contract on terms that secure the best profit margins for themselves. Others may be framed more collaboratively, by asking questions and giving choices in an effort to find win-win ways of working together. The CEO will probably be most drawn to these more collaborative proposals, providing they are priced in the same general range as the more competitive, arms-length ones.

The final meeting of the afternoon, with the CEO of a furniture company who has floated the idea of a merger, should probably be treated as a very early-stage discussion with the goal of learning more. Maybe Matchstick has some kind of problem, such as falling sales or heavy debt. Why else would this CEO have come to him? He should be cautious about this conversation, ask a lot of questions, and just try to find out more about the other executive's motives for starting the conversation. If it sounds serious after the first meeting, then it might be best approached by involving financial experts and consultants who handle mergers, but now he just needs to do a basic evaluation of the proposal and get a sense as to whether it's serious and worth further attention.

How would you handle each of these negotiations? Would you handle each one the same way? Would you recognize that every agenda item is a negotiation and that each requires a different strategy and approach? Which of these would you find the easiest and handle the best? Which might cause you the most stress or give you the most trouble?

Like the CEO in the example, you no doubt have to deal with many, varied negotiations. Your flexibility is essential to your ability to master each of the negotiating situations comfortably and competently.

There are many ways to negotiate. You'll become master of five negotiation styles by the end of this book, as well as learn to adjust your approach to how negotiations are framed, how you build trust, and many other factors, such as which strategy or style to use.

DETERMINING THE IMPORTANCE OF OUTCOME AND RELATIONSHIP

To choose the right strategy, you need to address these two important factors:

- The outcome. What might you win or lose on the substantive issues in negotiation?

- The relationship. How will the negotiation process, and the specific outcome settlement, affect your relations with the other player now and in the future?

Outcome and relationship. Outcome and relationship. That's your mantra as a negotiator. Every time you approach the beginning of a negotiation, think about the outcome, and think about the relationship. This is such an important point that we illustrate it with an example.

Imagine you are negotiating to rent an office for a year. The office is in a desirable building and a good location, and you really like it. The agent representing the landlord has quoted a painfully high rent figure, but you gather there is some room for movement if you press her on the point. You learned from another tenant in the building that the landlord is in a hurry to rent this unit and has had trouble finding someone appropriate.

Let's look at this case from an outcome-and-relationship perspective. How important is outcome to you? Fairly important. On a one-to-five scale, for example, it might rate a four, since you want this unit and you will probably take it if the price comes down.

How important is the relationship with the agent? Well, you aren't dealing direct with the landlord, and the whole thing seems to be done on a professional rather than personal basis. Furthermore, you may not need to deal with this agent again, and even if you do, the rental rate you negotiate now will set a precedent. So on a one-to-five scale, relationship probably only gets a two.

What you have then is a situation in which outcome is fairly important and relationship is not very important. To help you visualize this, put outcome and relationship on a two-dimensional graph (Figure 2.1). Importance of the outcome is represented on the horizontal dimension (left to right), and importance of the relationship is represented on the vertical dimension (bottom to top). Knowing that outcome is important and relationship is not in this example of renting an office, Figure 2.1 reveals that the best strategy is a high-outcome, low-relationship one. You'll want to work hard for a low rent and other favorable terms. We can also guess that the other party, the landlord's agent, will feel the same way. She will probably be ready and willing to adopt this same strategy. But even if she comes across as very friendly and collaborative, your analysis tells you this situation requires a tough-minded pursuit of good outcome terms, so that is what you will do.

Make reference to both axes in Figure 2.1, and you can plot your outcome and relationship concerns to select an optimal style for each of the problems at the beginning of this chapter. For example, if you are meeting with the lawyers representing a former employee who performed poorly and you never expect to hire again, then you are going to rate relationship concerns fairly low. If the employee is pursuing potentially expensive claims that you feel are unjustified and that portray your firm in a bad light, then you will rate the outcome as important. Low relationship and high outcome plot to the compete style and no other. That's the best style to use in this negotiation. (See the sidebar for the style choices in this negotiation.)

We have given you the once-over-quickly version of how to choose your negotiating style, but it's important enough that we want to go through it a little more carefully now. Let's start with examining the relationship.

FIGURE 2.1. CONSIDERING OUTCOME AND RELATIONSHIP CONCERNS

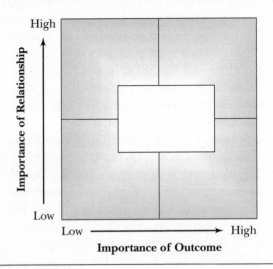

Negotiation Style Choices in This Situation

- Avoid: Inappropriate here because you feel the outcome is important and you need to deal with this conflict. And besides, once lawyers get involved, you cannot very well ignore the conflict. It will not ignore you.
- Accommodate: Also inappropriate because you are more concerned about sticking up for your firm's interests than letting a former employee have her way.
- Compromise: You might accept a compromise if the other party appears ready to make a reasonable offer, but right now, she probably is not.
- Collaborate: Nothing about the former employee's approach to you suggests she wants to collaborate, and besides, your firm's interests are more important than her interests in your mind right now, so a win-win approach does not seem like the most important goal to you now.
- Compete: Because the claims against your firm are potentially costly, you will probably want to respond firmly, using the compete style. Counterclaims based on her poor performance and an assertion of the due process used to dismiss her may undermine her claim and save your firm a potentially costly settlement.

Examining Relationship Concerns

How important is your past and especially your future relationship with the other party? How have the two of you gotten along in the past, and how important is it for the two of you to get along, work together, and like each other in the future? Perhaps it is very important. Perhaps it does not matter at all. Perhaps it is somewhere between these extremes. If maintaining a good relationship with the other party is important to you, then you should negotiate differently than if the relationship is unimportant.

How do you think about the importance of the relationship? Whether it's mostly a personal relationship or one that involves your companies, there are potentially a lot of factors to consider.

This list of relationship factors will help you think about the nature and importance of the relationship more carefully rather than just relying on intuition or off-the-cuff judgments:

- Is there a past relationship with this other person? If so, what did you learn about the other person or organization?
- Has that past relationship generally been positive or negative (that is, have the two of you have gotten along well or poorly in the past)?
- Is there likely to be a future relationship between you and the other party?
- How committed is each party to the relationship? How hard are you and the other person willing to work to keep the relationship strong and productive? If commitment has been low historically on either side, then be suspicious about the future.
- How much interdependence is there in the relationship—that is, how much does each of you need this particular other person to have your needs met, as opposed to having other ways to get your needs met? If you depend on each other to any significant degree, then rate this relationship high on your importance scale.
- How much free and open communication is there between the parties (if communication is poor, rate the relationship lower)? Can the communication be improved?
- How much can the other party affect your reputation among current and future business contacts? In business, people learn a lot about others through informal comments and gossip. While you may expect very little direct contact with the other party, if he or she can have a major positive or negative impact on your reputation, you ought to worry about how you treat him or her in the current negotiation.

For example, if you are negotiating the purchase of some new vehicles at auction for your company's fleet, you may never have met the seller before and do not expect to have a continuing relationship. Therefore, your relationship concerns are low. However, if your business buys vehicles from the same company that maintains them for you and you expect to work with this person on deals in the future—or this person can affect your reputation—your relationship concerns are high, and this will affect negotiations.

In the case of a party with whom you have an ongoing relationship, it may be congenial, or, if earlier negotiations have been hostile, it may be antagonistic. If it is a congenial relationship, you may wish to keep it that way and avoid escalating emotions. In contrast, if the relationship has a history of hostility, you may prefer not to negotiate, or you may want to lower the emotional level in the negotiations. Lowering the emotional level is important if you expect the relationship to continue in the future.

How do you take the emotions down a notch where you fear they are contaminating an important relationship? One simple way is to tell the other party you want to improve relations. Take time away from the specific negotiations to get to know the other person better. Talk about subjects on which you have common interests. Spend time talking with the other about how he sees you and what you can do to increase his trust and confidence in you. If he is upset, find out why and what you may have done to make things worse. Apologize and offer to change or improve your behavior. You may wish to offer small concessions, which you hope will be seen as goodwill gestures and will help rebuild the level of trust. But at the same time, try to repair the relationship with comments and dialogue that do not necessarily require you to make any major sacrifices on pursuing your negotiation goals.

Negotiating has a powerful impact on any relationship—for good or for bad, depending on how you choose to handle the negotiation. Be careful not to poison good relationships by choosing overly competitive negotiating games. Here are some things to watch out for when the relationship is important:

- Don't take back concessions or go back on commitments; it always upsets or angers the other party.
- Signal clearly before doing anything that might upset the other party by giving advance warning and a chance to anticipate what you will do. Or better yet, if possible ask for permission before taking the action.
- Communicate more. Share more information, ask more questions, and make more opportunities for informal, friendly chats. Listen carefully to the other party's concerns. The quantity of communication is often too low in busy business

relationships, and if there isn't a steady flow of communication, relationships tend to suffer.
- If you make a mistake or do something that offends the other
  party, address the situation quickly: accept responsibility for
  your actions and the consequences, and apologize with sincerity.
- If you have to assert and do something the other party doesn't
  like, offer compensation or benefits in other areas. Most business (and personal) relationships can stand a lot of give-and-
  take as long as the overall balance is maintained.
- If you have a problem or are feeling pressured, ask the other
  party for help instead of closing down and acting on your own.
  If this person values the relationship too, he or she should be
  willing, even happy, to try to help you out. In other words, collaborate to solve problems instead of competing.

Negotiators who value their relationships pick up the telephone or ask for a meeting when they have a problem rather than
making demands or acting unilaterally. But it can be hard to follow this advice when you feel pressured by circumstances.

Whether the relationship is important is one of the keys to how
you should act in any negotiation. But it is not the only key. Next,
think about the importance of the outcome—whatever is at stake
or on the table in this business negotiation.

MANAGING OUTCOME CONCERNS

How important is it for you to achieve a good outcome in this
negotiation? Do you need to win on all points to gain the advantage? Or is the outcome of only moderate importance? Or, perhaps, does the outcome not really matter at all?

It's hard at first to accept that there might be times when the
outcome is unimportant in a business negotiation. Why negotiate
if the outcome doesn't matter? Yet often we find ourselves involved
in relatively unimportant negotiations that threaten to take up too
much of our time and energy. The squeaky wheel of a loud,
assertive, and demanding negotiator may be receiving a lot of
attention, while more important things don't get the attention they
deserve. And sometimes the matter is very important to the other

party but not to you, and you have to avoid getting caught up in becoming overly concerned about her perspective to the exclusion of considering your own.

Here's a common example. A supervisor spends a lot of time focusing on a particularly difficult employee who performs below standards, complains a lot, and refuses to take responsibility for his actions. Many supervisors find themselves caught up in dealing with such a problematic employee. Perhaps without realizing it, they are negotiating with this employee frequently. How do we redo something that was done poorly? How do we handle the employee's excuses, complaints, or claims against other employees? How do we treat this employee's poor performance and maintain standards for other employees? All of this can take a lot of the manager's energy and time and keep her from attending to her own work and maintaining department productivity.

Yet poor performers are worthy of far less attention than good performers, who are doing the bulk of the work and carrying the department, office, or business on their shoulders. The manager who is caught up in dealing with a poor performer would probably do better to limit her time on this problem and remember to spend more time working with and managing the good performers, so that they don't become disillusioned and stop performing well or, worse, leave. Managers need to look at the future performance potential of each employee and give more negotiating time and supervisory attention to those with the greatest potential, not the least. Rating the importance of each negotiating situation with your employees will help you follow this rule.

How does your rating of the importance of the outcome affect your negotiating style? For another example, let's return to the example of your buying vehicles for your company. When we first presented this example, we recognized that the relationship would affect your competitiveness over pricing to some extent.

If you are buying a vehicle at auction, price may be the most important factor, and you may have absolutely no interest at all in the relationship. But if you are buying a van from a long-term vehicle supplier and want to keep a good relationship with the supplier, then you might not press quite as hard to get a good price. That's what we decided when we looked at the impact of your relationship. But what about the importance of the outcome? Clearly, you don't want to spend too much when buying vehicles for your company. For example, if you are planning to buy a number of vans and this first purchase may set a price precedent, then you'll want to work hard to establish a favorable precedent by getting a low price. You'll probably want to let the supplier know you may buy a lot more vehicles in order to push him or her toward offering the best possible price to you. But the supplier can't afford to lose money either, so negotiating for multiple vehicles might be different from just buying one.

Or maybe service is of paramount concern, and you want to press hard for a good service contract or an extended warranty. A company that uses vans to do deliveries doesn't want to worry about breakdowns, so a service contract that guarantees rapid roadside service, quick turnaround on repairs, and loaner vehicles when yours are in the shop is important. If there is any way to reduce business costs on an ongoing basis, then the outcome is paramount, and you need to assert your business interests strongly.

Does the negotiation affect your ongoing costs of business? This is often the most important question to ask before choosing your negotiating style. Here are some examples of negotiations that affect ongoing costs of business and therefore warrant a high level of concern about the outcome and an assertive approach to the negotiation:

• Salary negotiations, which usually spill over by affecting salary levels of multiple employees, not just the one you're negotiating with. Even if salaries are meant to be confidential, employees often compare notes and know pretty well who is making what.

• Per-unit costs of anything purchased repeatedly. Even a dollar saved can make a big difference if multiplied by thousands of transactions. Keep a sharp eye out for this multiplier effect, and negotiate hard whenever it applies. If you are a restaurant and negotiating with a laundry for cleaning tablecloths and napkins, twenty-five cents a tablecloth can make a big difference over a year.

• Agreements that reach into the future. If you are negotiating a one-year lease, your level of concern for the outcome may not need to be as high as for a ten-year lease. Assert strongly when the time frame is longer than a year. If you can't win the concessions you want, try to switch the time frame to something shorter. There's nothing worse than being locked into an unfavorable or expensive deal or contract for a long period of time. This problem often appears to be the smoking gun behind corporate bankruptcies. For example, many of the big automakers and airlines negotiated away huge commitments for retirement and health care benefits that are now draining all the available cash from the company. If you are uncertain about the future, negotiate a current deal that can be revisited at some defined time in the future.

- Fixed and other ongoing costs, since you have to pay them no matter how well or poorly your business does. If you are paying too much for your basic utilities, for example, you won't be able to make a profit when times are tough and sales are slow. Of course, all costs are important, but fixed and other repeated costs—rent and utilities, for example—are strategically more important than one-time costs and should be approached with great care in any business negotiation. Unfortunately, most managers do just the opposite: they tend to ignore or give little attention to fixed costs, often assuming these can't be negotiated. (*Everything* can be negotiated. If you haven't negotiated your telephone rates, utility costs, or rents lately, take another crack at them.) And it's all too easy to focus on the one-time or special deal, and ignore the routine costs that pile up and drive your profit and loss.

Choosing a Negotiating Strategy

By considering the relative importance of both outcome and relationship, you are able to adapt your game to each negotiating situation. Untrained negotiators, and those who have taken a simplistic course in competitive tactics, generally use the same approach in every conflict situation. Yet each deal is different and each opponent may be different; you will get better results by flexing your style to suit the situation.

Refer now to Figure 2.2. Like Figure 2.1, the vertical axis represents your degree of concern for the relationship, and the horizontal axis represents your degree of concern for the outcome. But it adds five different negotiation styles in the five boxes:

FIGURE 2.2. HOW TO SELECT A NEGOTIATION STRATEGY

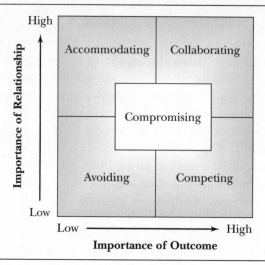

- *Avoiding (lose-lose).* In this strategy, shown in the lower left of the diagram, the priorities for both the relationship and the outcome are low. Neither aspect of the negotiation is important enough for you to pursue the conflict further. You implement this strategy by withdrawing from active negotiation or avoiding negotiation entirely.

- *Accommodating (lose to win).* This strategy is represented in the upper left of the diagram, where the importance of the relationship is high and the importance of the outcome is low. In this situation, you back off your concern for the outcome to preserve the relationship; you intentionally "lose" on the outcome dimension in order to "win" on the relationship dimension.

- *Competing (win-lose).* The lower right of the diagram represents high concern for the outcome and low concern for the relationship. You use this strategy if you want to win at all cost and have no concern about the future state of the relationship.

- *Collaborating (win-win).* The upper right part of the diagram defines a strategy where there is a high priority for both the relationship and the outcome. In this strategy, the parties attempt to maximize their outcomes while preserving or enhancing the rela-

tionship. This result is most likely when both parties can find a resolution that meets the needs of each.[1]

• *Compromising (split the difference).* In the middle is an area we
call a compromising, or "satisficing," strategy. It represents a combination approach that is used in a variety of situations. For example, it is often used when the parties cannot achieve full
collaboration but still want to make some progress toward achieving outcome goals or take some actions to preserve the relationship. It is also often used when the parties are under time pressure
and need to come to a resolution quickly, or do not have the
energy to work toward a fully collaborative agreement. Each party
will give in a bit to find a common ground.

MATCHING AND MESHING STYLES

So far we've focused on how to choose the best negotiating game
by considering two key factors: how important the outcome is to
be gained from this negotiation, and how important the past, present, and future relationship is with the opponent. We have also
explored questions that you can ask to determine how important
outcome and relationship might be in an upcoming negotiation.
And you've seen us use this two-factor model to prescribe which of
the five styles to use: avoid, accommodate, compete, collaborate,
and compromise. You won't go wrong with this simple but powerful two-factor model. Nevertheless, there are times when you might
want to refine it by considering some additional factors as well.
Each strategy has both advantages and disadvantages that can have
an impact on what strategy to adopt.

THE SITUATION

Study the specific negotiation situation, and try to figure out
which strategy might be best in those circumstances. Do I care a
lot about the outcomes in this situation? If I do, am I willing to
sacrifice my relationship with the other person? Or, conversely,
who is this other party, and what is my relationship with her? Is
the relationship so important that I am unwilling to endanger it
by pursuing the outcome?

PERSONAL PREFERENCES

Analyze your personal preferences for the various strategies. You will probably be more successful using a strategy that feels comfortable. Research has shown that people in conflict have distinct preferences for employing these strategies in conflict situations. Over time, consistently employing some strategies and not employing others leads us to use these preferences as a first response in almost any conflict or negotiation situation. These preferences lead us to develop distinct styles with which we approach many situations.[2] Based on experience and history, we might develop strong biases toward being competitive or collaborative or compromising or accommodating or avoiding in conflict situations—and other biases that may lead us to not use these approaches, even when the situation would dictate that they are the most appropriate.

The stronger your preference is for a particular conflict management strategy (style), the more often you will choose it as a negotiation approach. And the more biased you become in seeing it as an advantageous strategy, the more likely you will be to see that strategy (style) as appropriate in situations where an objective analysis would say it was less appropriate. Thus, if you normally respond to conflict (and negotiation) situations in a competitive manner, you are more likely to see the competitive strategy as widely appropriate—even when it may not be. Similarly, the less likely you are to avoid conflict, the more likely it is that you will not choose the avoiding strategy—even when it may be the most appropriate thing to do.

Your preferences for a particular strategy are also influenced by your commitment to certain basic values and principles. These may be harder in some ways to define than your goals or priorities. Your willingness to use (or not use) certain strategies might be influenced by things like the following:

- How much you value truth, integrity, manners, and courtesy
- Whether respect is an important issue to you
- How important fair play is to you, and, for that matter, how you define "fair"
- How much of your ego (your reputation or image) is involved in this negotiation and how concerned you are about how you

will see yourself—or others will see you—if you get what you want—or don't get what you want

MATCHING OR MISMATCHING THE OTHER'S STYLE

Think about your own style as it interacts with the other party's style, and consider the possible consequences. What will be the effect of such a combination? For example, two competitive parties might have more conflict in their negotiation than a competitive party negotiating with a party that usually yields. While it would be too complex to explore all the possible interactions between each of your five possible styles and the styles of the other in detail, we have summarized the possible combinations in Table 2.1. (Some of the cells on the left side are blank because the information is contained in the matching cell on the right side.) Note that based on your diagnosis of the other person's style, you can intentionally choose to either match this person's style or mismatch in a way that helps you accomplish your primary objectives.

Chances are that your understanding of the other person's style is based on your own experience with that person and how you want that relationship to evolve. How you feel about the other party and what you want to have happen in that relationship in the future will drive your strategy. How well do you like each other? How much do you communicate? How much do you need to work with the other in the future because you are dependent on what he can do for you? How much do you trust him? Your level of trust with the other party will be based on your experience with him and the history and results of other negotiations he has conducted with you or with other parties in the past.

CAN YOU MAKE A "NO STRATEGY" CHOICE?

Some people we have taught in negotiation seminars have argued that it is possible to adopt no strategy: you refuse to make an explicit strategic choice, and let the chips fall to determine what you will do next. This allows you maximum flexibility to adjust your approach based on what your opponent does first, or as the proceedings change.

Table 2.1. Likely Interactions Between Negotiators of Different Styles

	Avoiding	Accommodating	Competing	Collaborating	Compromising
Avoiding	Both parties avoid pursuing their goals on the issues and do not take any action to endanger the relationship.	Accommodator shows strong concern for the avoider, particularly the relationship; avoider attempts to minimize interaction.	Competitor will dominate, or avoider will escape. Avoider attempts to minimize interaction, while competitor tries to engage.	Collaborator shows strong concern for both issues and the relationship, while avoider tries to escape. Avoider may give up.	Compromiser shows some concern for both issues and relationship; avoider tries to escape. Compromiser may give up, or avoider may engage.
Accommodating	Both parties avoid pursuing their goals on the issues, give in to the others' goals, and try to smooth over the relationship concerns.		Competitor pursues own goals on the issues, while the accommodator tries to make the competitor happy. Competitor usually wins big.	Collaborator shows strong concern for both issues and relationship; accommodator tries to make the collaborator happy. Relationship should be very strong, but the collaborator may achieve better results.	Compromiser shows some concern for both issues and relationship; accommodator tries to make the compromiser happy. Relationship will improve. Compromiser may entice the accommodator to focus on issues.

Competing	Both parties pursue their goals on the issues and ignore any concern for the relationship. Conflict and mistrust are likely.	Collaborator shows strong concern for both issues and relationship, while competitor only pursues issues. Competitor usually wins, and both parties become competitive.	Competitor shows some concern for both issues and relationship, while compromiser only pursues issues. Competitor usually wins, and both parties become competitive.
Collaborating		Both parties pursue their goals on the issues; they show strong concern for the others' goals and sustaining trust and a good relationship.	Compromiser shows some concern, while collaborator shows strong concern on both substance and relationship. Good compromise likely at a minimum.
Compromising			Both parties pursue their goals on the issues in a limited way and attempt to do no harm to the relationship.

Source: From R. J. Lewicki, A. Hiam, and K. Olander, *Think Before You Speak: A Complete Guide to Strategic Negotiation* (Hoboken, N.J.: Wiley, 1996). Copyright 1996, Alexander Hiam and Roy Lewicki. Reproduced by permission.

The no-strategy approach has some distinct advantages. You get a chance to find out how your opponent wants to negotiate first, which may tell you a lot about your opponent. It also keeps you from making a commitment to a strategy that may not work or get completed, for example, to be accommodative while the other is being competitive. However, a no-strategy choice is often the lazy negotiator's way of avoiding a key part of the planning and preparation process. We do not think this is a good choice. Although it may give you some negotiating leeway, it could also put you in a precarious position if you have not planned well. The result will be that the opposition gains an advantage over you before you realize what is going on.

If you know that you care about the relationship, or the outcome, or both (or neither), select a strategy and begin to plan around it. If you are proactive about strategy choice, you are much more likely to get what you want than if you wait for the other to initiate action. As we have pointed out, you can always adapt your strategy later as necessary.

Once you decide which strategy is best for you, it is time to take all the information you have gathered and proceed to implement that strategy. In the following chapters, we discuss in depth the implementation of the five most important negotiation games that we set out in this chapter.

SUMMARY

In Lewis Carroll's famous children's book, *Alice in Wonderland*, the Red Queen is a petty tyrant who fails to flex her style to the circumstances. "The Queen had only one way of settling all difficulties, great or small. 'Off with his head!' she said without even looking around."

As this chapter emphasizes, there are multiple styles or strategies, and the master business negotiator assesses the situation before choosing which one to use. Of course, some people are more comfortable with one style than another (if you haven't taken a negotiating style assessment to find out which your most natural style is, we recommend it; a number of options should pop up when you type "conflict style assessment" into any search engine, or go to http://conflict911.com/resources/Conflict_Management_

Styles_And_Preferences/. Because we all have our preferred styles, it's easy to be like Lewis Carroll's caricature of a queen and always use the same approach. Our advice can be summed up in one simple phrase: assess to choose the best approach before you start negotiating.

Notes:
1. G. T. Savage, J. D. Blair, and R. L. Sorenson, "Consider Both Relationships and Substance When Negotiating Strategically," *Academy of Management Executives,* 1989, *3*(1), 37–48.
2. K. Thomas and R. Killman, *The Conflict Mode Inventory* (Tuxedo Park, N.Y.: XICOM, 1974).

CHAPTER THREE

GETTING READY TO NEGOTIATE

Negotiation is not a random process; rather, it has a predictable sequence of steps or stages. We will argue several things in this chapter. First, negotiation can be viewed as a game: it has a relatively predictable set of rules and processes, which lead to relatively predictable outcomes. Second, negotiation has some predictable stages, and important activities need to take place in each of these stages. Third, negotiation can take place with one or more parties, and it becomes increasingly complex as additional parties are added. Fourth, it is critical for negotiators to determine their goals and priorities before entering a negotiation, and we discuss this process in depth. Finally, it is important to learn as much as possible about the other party's goals and priorities.

NEGOTIATION IS A GAME

In Chapter One, we observed that it can be helpful to think of negotiation as a game. We want to explore that analogy. As in any game, your negotiating games have both written and unwritten rules. The written rules include clear do's and don'ts for what can be done in negotiation. In some negotiations, many of these rules are clear, written down, and explicit. For example, if you are negotiating with a government agency, government rules and regulations are likely to constrain what can and cannot be negotiated. In contrast, if you are negotiating for a rug in a Middle Eastern bazaar, you can be sure than almost anything goes. Laws and regulations provide an explicit set of foundational rules to negotiate by. For example, you may be somewhat circumspect in what information you choose to share, but you cannot openly lie and engage in clear deception and fraud, for this crosses the legal line. Nor can you, for example, talk about how to fix prices with your competitors, because there is a law against price fixing. These are clear boundaries. But in the rug bazaar, you can probably be pretty sure that a fair amount of deception occurs in both subtle and not-so-subtle ways. In this book, we will identify some of the more important informal rules—the do's and don'ts—that will help you plan your game strategy.

For example, there is almost always a trust dynamic at work in negotiations. If you can come across as trustworthy and straightforward, as opposed to devious and untrustworthy, people will give you the benefit of the doubt more of the time. They will be less likely to doubt your word or suspect your facts. They will close deals with you more readily. But to be viewed as a principled negotiator, one who is reasonably trustworthy, you need to avoid unexpected and apparently unreasonable changes in your position. You also need to be very careful about revisiting earlier concessions. In general, there is an unwritten rule against taking back an earlier concession, and you should consider it only if the other party has broken some unwritten rules first. These examples of unwritten rules highlight the subtle nature of the negotiation game.

Negotiation Stages and Phases

There are a number of ways to represent the different stages or phases of a negotiation.[1] In this chapter, we propose a simple five-stage model of negotiation (Figure 3.1).

Preparation Stage

The preparation stage, the first stage of negotiation, is the time to gather information and do planning and goal setting.

Gather Information
The first step of negotiation is the process of gathering information. You need to decide what kind of information you need, but it should be of two forms:

FIGURE 3.1. FUNDAMENTAL STAGES OF NEGOTIATION

Preparation Stage → Opening Stage → Bargaining Stage → Closing Stage → Implementation Stage

- Information that will help you define your own objectives and argue for what you want to achieve in the negotiation
- Information about those on the other side, their goals and objectives, how they are likely to view you, and what they may want to achieve in the negotiation

The type of information you need will vary from negotiation to negotiation, but might involve knowing specific things about the issues to be discussed, gathering financial information, examining the history of this issue between the parties, understanding market conditions, understanding the structure and politics of the organizations in which the negotiation is taking place, and understanding the culture in which the negotiation is taking place. Later in this chapter, we focus on how you can gather this information.

There are two essential skills to great information gathering: the ability to ask probing questions and the ability to listen intently. Asking informative, probing questions usually requires being able to ask open questions.[2] An open question is one that gets the other to talk extensively and uses phrases such as, "Why?" "How?" Tell me about . . . ," or "Explain to me . . . " Great listening skills require us to be able to understand what the others are saying, read the emotion in their voice as well as the words, and understand their underlying interests.[3]

Do Planning and Goal Setting

Planning and goal setting are also a key part of the preparation stage. We need to try to map out the way we want the negotiation to proceed, and we need to spend time determining what we want to achieve.

Important parts of planning and goal setting include:

- Defining what you want to achieve

- Defining your limits, or how far you will go before walking away or not settling
- Deciding on your opening, or what you will initially offer or request
- Determining what alternatives you have if you cannot successfully negotiate this deal
- Assembling the information you gathered to understand how the other party will approach the negotiation
- Assembling the information you gathered to decide how to present it in order to achieve your objectives
- Developing a proposed discussion agenda

As we note throughout this book, planning is probably the most important stage of negotiations, yet it is also the stage that many negotiators neglect because they want to "get into the action." *Great planning is the key to successful negotiations.* In this chapter, we look at the planning process and the critical steps to take in this phase, such as identifying interests and planning the agenda for the upcoming discussions. We have more to say about negotiation planning in the next chapter.

You should plan to cycle back from planning and goal setting to information gathering. As you get to know those on the other side better and get more information about what they want, what you want, and the situation you are in, this will give you the opportunity to continually update your plan.

OPENING STAGE

The opening stage is for laying out arguments. You use the information you have gathered to construct the most persuasive argument you can for what you want, why you want it, and why the other side should give it to you. Here is where it is important to be clear about your goals, to be able to argue well for what you want, and to be able to listen to what the other wants so that you can present counterarguments.

You also listen to the other side's presentation. You take notes on what they say and listen clearly for what you think is most important to them. This is also a critical time to ask questions and learn as much as you can about what they want.

Bargaining Stage

In this stage, you play the classic negotiation game of give-and-take. Parties in negotiation normally expect that opening demands are exaggerated and that one or both parties will have to make concessions to reach some agreement. The bidding process is the process of moving from your opening bid toward your target and getting the other side to do the same. Depending on whether the game is more competitive or more cooperative, you will want them to do more of the moving than you, or you will want to move at approximately the same distance and pace. We will have more to say about the information use and bidding process in Chapters Four through Eight, where we lay out the basic game plan for each of the five major approaches to negotiation.

The Bargaining Stage: Formula and Detail

A great way to think about what happens in the bargaining and closing process is called *formula-detail*. When using formula-detail, negotiators should first start with the diagnosis and preparation process. Then both parties should try to create a common statement of what the problem is (the formula stage), such that both sides have a common view of the problem, what caused it, why it exists, and what will be necessary to resolve it. The parties should then move to the detail phase, in which they use the common formula to work out details that will be beneficial to each side. Parties cycle back between formula and detail until they achieve an agreement that is satisfactory to both sides. This method has been around for a long time and has proven useful in a wide range of negotiations, but surprisingly, few negotiators seem to know about it or use it.

Source: W. Zartman and M. Berman, *The Practical Negotiator* (New Haven, Conn.: Yale University Press, 1982).

Closing Stage

This stage is for wrapping up the final agreement. You review what you have agreed to, may write out a contract or written agreement, clarify anything that was left ambiguous or incomplete in the previous discussion, and shake hands. You may exchange money or resources as specified in the deal. Finally, you may celebrate your accomplishment with a meal or drink. Closing rituals are important in negotiations. Even in very short or very competitive negotiations, it is important to use the closing stage to formalize what you have agreed to, write it down in a memorandum of understanding, and work to smooth over any anger or animosity that may have been built up in the bargaining stage.

IMPLEMENTATION STAGE

Implementation may also be a critical stage of the negotiation. Once you have formulated an agreement, you may also be one of the people involved in putting it into action. At this point, parties often discover that the agreement was incomplete or flawed. New issues come up, problems arise that no one anticipated, and those on the other side didn't do things they said they would do. Therefore, this is a critical phase for being able to go back to the other party and fix the agreement you arrived at earlier. Every good agreement should create the opportunity for the parties to reopen discussions if there are problems in implementation.

LENGTH OF THE STAGES

Almost every negotiation goes through all of these stages. The amount of time spent in each stage may vary, depending on several factors:

- Who the other party is and how well you know or want to know this person (the less you want or need to know him or her, the shorter the stage is)
- How well prepared you are already versus how much information you need from the other side to formulate your own interests and goals
- The culture you are negotiating in. In the United States, negotiators are known for spending very little time in relationship building, even in situations when having a strong relationship would enhance that negotiation. In contrast, Japanese and

Chinese negotiators spend a very long time in relationship building and information gathering and a much shorter time in the bidding and closing process.

THE PLAYERS IN THE GAME

Knowing the players in the game is critical to understanding the negotiation. Knowing who they are, what they want, how they are likely to behave, what kind of a reputation they have, and what kind of a role they will take is essential to understanding and playing the game.

Let's take a look at the roles of different players and the consequences when we add additional negotiators to the game.

NEGOTIATING WITH YOURSELF

Most of what is written about negotiations assumes it is a process involving at least two parties.[4] But in fact, we negotiate with ourselves all the time. Self-negotiation is usually a conversation between our more rational self and our impulsive, subconscious self. Our consciousness tells us what we want to do, what we need, what we should do. Our subconscious is telling us what we should do, ought to do, really need to do. These are the "should I or shouldn't I" discussions in our heads, the "on the one hand" versus "on the other hand" debates, and the "I really don't want to . . . " versus "I really ought to . . . " dialogues that we carry on constantly.

A way to represent negotiating with yourself is to think of it as two ways of processing information and making decisions. One way is largely based on facts, figures, and information that lead to a rational conclusion; the other tends to be more emotional and intuitive and based on personal values. Each person tends toward one end or the other of this range, making decisions either more rationally or emotionally. In other words, our personality will lead us to favor one or the other in the way we process information and make decisions.

The most important thing to understand in negotiating with yourself is to continue to pay attention to both sides of your brain. The little voice of your intuition will often try to talk to you when something doesn't feel right, doesn't add up, or doesn't make sense. Particularly those of us whose preferences tend to lean toward the left side of the brain may tend to let the rational side drive out the emotional. Learning to listen to your inner voice—your intuition or your gut—may be the best thing you can do to avoid a negotiation disaster.[5]

NEGOTIATING WITH A SINGLE OPPONENT

Since this entire book is primarily directed toward negotiating with a single opponent, we will say very little about it here. But there are some important aspects of that other person that we need to remember:

- How well do you know the other person? The better you know the other party, the more information you have about her. You know what she is like, how she speaks, what she is likely to ask for, how she plays the game. Players in all types of games study their opponent carefully. The more often they have interacted, the more they know about the other.
- What kinds of a relationship have you had together in the past and do you want to have with the other in the future? If you have a good relationship and want to maintain it, you are probably going to negotiate very differently than if you have had a bad relationship and don't care to improve it. The more you care about the relationship with the other, the more cooperative you want to be.
- Does the other have a reputation that should cause you to be cautious? In negotiations, you often have to deal with people who don't negotiate well or behave dangerously and unpredictably. If possible, you should try to find out how the other party has behaved in negotiations in the past. It is clear that a negotiator who has a bad or unethical reputation is likely to motivate you to protect yourself a lot more than with a good or honest and trustworthy negotiator.[6]

NEGOTIATING THROUGH AGENTS

An agent is someone who negotiates on your behalf. In the most common cases, an agent is someone who is paid to represent your interests in a negotiation. We hire a real estate agent to help us sell a piece of property and an attorney to represent us in a legal conflict, for example. We hire other agents to help us find a job or land new business opportunities.

Agents or representatives are often used in certain kinds of negotiations. You may employ an agent to negotiate on your behalf for several reasons:

• The agent may have some expertise in the subject matter that you do not possess. You contract with a real estate agent to negotiate selling a house because the agent has more expertise in the house selling process (and a better network of contacts) than you do. You hire an attorney to negotiate in a bankruptcy because the attorney knows the law better than you do and can protect your rights better than you can on your own.

• The agent has more negotiating expertise. For example, in many cities you can now find a professional buyer who will buy an automobile for you; companies often hire such experts to conduct major financial transactions.

• You are too emotionally involved in the issue to negotiate effectively. Agents can be helpful as somewhat detached, impartial representatives of a party.

Because agents can represent you in a dispassionate way, they may help to get you a better agreement than if you tried on your own. It is particularly useful to have agents do the bargaining if the principal parties are adversarial.[7] Finally, agents are commonly used when there is a group of people on a side in a negotiation. Because negotiation can get chaotic when many people are trying to speak at once, agents can focus the discussion and keep order in the process.

There are also disadvantages to using an agent:

• When you add agents to the negotiation equation, you are adding more people. The more people there are, the more complex the mix is because there are more conversations going on.

• Agents may not do exactly what you want them to. Although the parties often give their agents clear instructions (what to do, what can be agreed to, and so forth), agents often decide that they cannot follow these instructions directly, or they may not be able to check back with you at every critical juncture. So while you may gain something by using an agent, it is possible that the agent may not come back with the deal you really wanted.

• Agents seldom perform their services for free; therefore, adding an agent increases the costs of negotiation and may mean that you need to get a better deal than if you negotiated yourself.

• Communication can be more complicated as agents are added because the information passes through an additional filter increasing the potential for distorted messages. A prime example of this is a divorce case, where the two parties may have to have some sort of relationship after the divorce is over (for example, with joint custody of children) but have relied on their attorneys to do the negotiating. While the attorneys may have negotiated a good deal in principle, the details of day-to-day coordination are probably best worked out by the parents themselves.

• Agents can sometimes make the deal more difficult. They may get adversarial with each other and lose their ability to represent their constituents well. The agents of two or more parties may form an alliance that affects the outcome. In this situation, the agents may collude to work out a deal that is good for them but not necessarily for their clients.

• The client and the agent may have different aims. For example, the agent might be inclined to behave in a collaborative or compromising manner, while the client prefers a competitive approach. There may also be differences in their ethical values or their definitions of appropriate behavior.

Here are some key points to keep in mind if you are going to be negotiating through an agent or are hiring an agent to negotiate for you:

• If you have the option of picking an agent, find a person you feel comfortable with. Since you are asking this individual to negotiate on your behalf, you need to feel trust and a sense of compatibility with him or her.

• Make sure the agent knows your objectives. You need to spend enough time to help the agent understand what you are trying to achieve, your goals, and other matters that are important to you. You may need the agent's expertise to help you set these points. If the person is a professional, he or she will interview you about these issues anyway.

• Discuss whether you wish to be present for some or all of the negotiations, or whether the agent will conduct all the negotiations independently. If you are to be present, be clear about the conditions under which you will be able to speak and participate, as opposed to letting the agent do all the talking. Make sure you and the agent talk about whether you can conduct any separate and independent discussions with the other party without agents present. Negotiations can get very confused if agents are discussing matters at one level while the parties are dealing with each other directly without the agents' being aware of it.

• Be very clear about how much authority the agent has to make a deal on your behalf. Does the agent need to approve the deal with you before settlement? Can the agent make a tentative settlement? Does he or she understand the limits of a possible settlement?

• Make sure you have discussed a schedule for receiving progress reports.

• Make sure you and the agent understand the terms of the agent's compensation for time and services. Agents usually raise this issue and explain their fee structure—whether a percentage of the sale, by the hour, or some other scale. Remember that these rates are also negotiable, particularly if many agents are available. You should do this if the agent is providing limited services but trying to charge you the standard rate.

NEGOTIATING IN GROUPS AND TEAMS

Team negotiation occurs in one of two ways: within a team, with three or more parties trying to make a decision or agree on a course of action, or between teams, as when teams from two companies sit down to negotiate a long-term supplier contract. In both cases, as the group size expands, the process tends to become more complex and somewhat less manageable. Team members may include the spokesperson or agent, experts who serve as resources, advocates for smaller groups within the group, legal or financial counselors, a recorder, an observer, a statistical analyst, and others.

Between-team negotiation is most common in labor-management negotiations, diplomatic situations, and business deals. In such cases, though there are a number of people in the party, there may be only one spokesperson or agent who represents the group. Most of the formal communication between the parties occurs through the spokesperson, and this cuts down on any inadvertent revealing of information. Spokespersons usually insist on strict discipline within the team, particularly when they are at the table with the other team, so that individuals do not speak out of turn, give away confidential information, or make unauthorized agreements.[8] These are special kinds of negotiations, and we will not address them any further in this book.

WHAT YOU WANT:
YOUR GOALS AND INTERESTS

To start planning for a negotiation, the negotiator must ask two critical questions: "What do I want out of this negotiation?" and "Why is it important to me?" The first is a question about your goals; the second is a question about your interests. To find the answers to these questions, you need to conduct a careful investigation. We cannot emphasize enough how important it is to plan so that you know where you are going, no matter what negotiation strategy you ultimately select.

GOALS

Goal setting is a critical aspect of analyzing and planning your position. Think about what you want to attain in the deal. List your goals in concrete, measurable terms, and try to quantify them into dollar amounts or percentages. A well-framed goal is, "I will spend no more than five thousand dollars for a car." If a counteroffer puts a car's price at six thousand dollars, it will be clear that you have not yet achieved your goal.

A dollar amount is a tangible goal; so is a benefit in salary negotiations or a particular interest rate when you are negotiating a loan. But many negotiation situations also contain intangible goals, such as "making a successful transaction," "keeping everyone in the family happy," "looking like a good negotiator to my friends," or "being viewed as a fair and honorable person." Intangibles are likely to be more difficult to quantify, and you may not be able to tell whether you have accomplished them until long after the negotiation has been completed. For example, if a goal is to "increase the respect that people in my work group have for me," it may take you a long time to know whether they really respect you more. Nevertheless, it is important to be aware of intangible goals and to name them whenever possible.

At the end of every negotiation, you will look back and judge the outcome by evaluating how things have changed. You can evaluate whether you made progress on those tangible goals, while your emotions will be shaped by progress on the intangible goals. Your rational mind focuses on the tangibles, and you need to engage your IQ to anticipate and list these tangible goals up front. But your emotional mind focuses on the intangibles, so you need to engage your emotional intelligence too in order to list intangible goals.[9]

One way to sort out goals is to prioritize them. Ordering them in terms of their importance, assigning each one a dollar value, or using some other procedure to define value will assist you in comparing goals and deciding which are most crucial. This process may also help you eliminate goals that are unrelated to the situation.

Later in the negotiations, when you want to make trade-offs or concessions with the other party, you will see the value of setting priorities. At that point, you will usually be ready to give up a less important goal to gain a more important one. If you know the relative value of each of your goals, you will be able to evaluate the various trade-offs. For example, you might not insist on having four new tires put on a used car if the seller is willing to come down in price by five hundred dollars instead.

Assessing priorities allows you to establish packages of goals for various alternative offerings during negotiation. For example, a car CD player with satellite radio and a subwoofer, plus a manual transmission for better handling off-road, may be more important to you than a roof rack and GIS system. Or intangibles like "a sporty car I really like the look of" may be your top priority when you think it through.

YOUR UNDERLYING INTERESTS?

Beneath your defined goals and objectives, you may have deeper underlying needs, interests, concerns, or fears.[10] An example will illustrate the importance of such underlying interests.

In our example, which is based on an event that occurred at a successful U.S. software company, a talented young software programmer is at odds with her boss, who wants her to put less time into a creative new idea she is pursuing and do more work on the routine upgrade of her company's most popular product. The two have locked heads on it frequently, and when her boss caught her working on the new program again instead of on the assigned project, he threatened to write her up and begin termination proceedings if she worked on it anymore. She then went to human resources (HR) and filed a harassment complaint against him, alleging that he is singling her out for excessive discipline because she is the only female in the department.

The HR director wishes to mediate a dispute in which the manager says the employee is disobedient and behind in her work, and the employee says the manager is harassing her. Is there any middle ground? Not in their demands and claims, but perhaps in their underlying interests. In discussing the situation with each of them separately, the HR director learns that the manager is concerned that his department has not performed very well in the past couple of years and wants to make sure they make a good impression with the executive office this year. He would like to introduce some innovative new product ideas, but he is afraid to put staff time into new ideas unless he is fairly sure they will work out. He doesn't know what this new employee's ideas are, but he assumes they are too undeveloped and risky to be of much use right now.

When the HR director talks to the disgruntled employee, he hears a similar goal. She too wants to be recognized for excellent programming and is eager to make a contribution to the company that will bring recognition to her and her department. And her ideas sound fairly well developed to the HR director, who asks her for a demo and then shows it to the manager. Eventually the manager comes to agree that the new program is promising, and he agrees to let her spend half her time developing it as long as she promises to have a more polished demo ready by the end of the quarter to show headquarters.

The dust settles on this dispute with a collaborative success: the two make up and continue to work together; the new program gets corporate funding, and more staff are put on it; eventually it is launched and proves a successful product, and both the programmer and her boss are promoted and have successful careers in the company.

This case involves differences in position that could best be resolved by exploring underlying interests. Similarly, a supervisor whose goal is to motivate an employee to perform at a higher level may not be happy with a solution involving tighter supervision of the employee. The reason is that most supervisors have a long-term interest in seeing their employees become more self-sufficient. They want to be able to delegate work to competent, committed employees, since they don't have the time to direct everyone's performance closely. If the employee promised to work harder in exchange for more supervision and support, the manager might reject the offer—not because it fails to accomplish the goal but because it accomplishes the goal in a way that is inappropriate to the manager's underlying interests. If the manager hadn't thought through her underlying interests, she might accept the employee's proposal and regret it later.

You get the idea: clarify your underlying interests along with your immediate goals. Just like goals, interests can be concrete (tangible), such as money or interest rates, or more abstract (intangible), such as a friendly interchange with the other or preservation of your image.

Often we have the protection of our relationship with the other party as an underlying interest. Yet it's easy to overlook this relationship interest and employ cutthroat bargaining tactics that win the battle but lose the war. In fact, in our experience as trainers and consultants in the field, we find that this is one of the most common negotiating errors. Most negotiators find out the hard way how important the relationship with the other party was: they spoil it in the negotiation.

You may also be concerned about principles, such as what is fair or right.[11] You may be attentive to the ethics of the situation or what has happened in the past. Many negotiators are as concerned that they be treated fairly and not lied to as they are to get a good deal on the tangibles. We trust that you can recognize underlying legal and ethical issues that matter to you or the other party. Trust your instincts: they'll tell you about any underlying legal and ethical concerns as long as you remember to listen to them. Here is a set of questions to help you surface any issues that may underlie a negotiation:

- Am I worried about any unfairness—to me or the other party?
- Are there things I might find myself doing in this situation that I wouldn't want published in my home town newspaper?
- Are there things I might find myself doing in this situation that might be illegal, such as hurting someone through an obvious deception?

Getting at Interests: Ask the "Why" Question

One way to get at underlying interests is to ask yourself the "why" question: Why do you want a particular goal? Your son comes to you and says, "Dad, I need a car!" You respond, "Why do you need a car? To get to work? To show off to your friends? So you don't have to ask your mom and me for transportation all the time?"

Are you looking for a house in a particular section of town because it is a better neighborhood, or do you need a larger house because your family is expanding? And why do you want to live in a particular section of town?

To use this surfacing tactic for exploring your underlying interests, write as many sentences as possible that begin, "Why do I want to . . ." Then answer them—possibly with another question in the same form. Eventually you'll hit bedrock, and then you'll truly understand your underlying interests—foundational needs that are motivating you to seek a particular solution or obtain a particular result.

The sidebar describes a method for surfacing your underlying interests using "Why do I want . . . ?" questions.

Another good way to look at underlying needs is to ask what will happen if you accomplish the goal. Then ask yourself what will happen if you do not achieve your goal. Sometimes the outcome is worse than you realize and sometimes better because of the relationship of the goal to underlying interests.

Determining your underlying interests will enable you to share them with the other party and thus find common interests. Although the two parties in a negotiation may appear to have conflicting goals, the underlying needs of each party may be similar. The result could be a collaborative solution that will meet both parties' goals and needs. Determining your underlying interests will also help you decide whether numerous possible offers from the other side may not meet your opening demands but clearly would satisfy your needs.

For example, two co-workers who are arguing over whether a window should be open or closed are unable to find a solution.[12] A third person asks each one to explain the problem. The first coworker wants the window open to get fresh air. The other person wants the window closed to avoid a draft. The third person suggests opening a window in the next room, which will provide fresh air and at the same time avoid a draft. This solution meets both coworkers' underlying interests, even though it violates one of their stated goals.

Determining What the Other Party Wants

While it can be difficult to diagnose your own needs and position, understanding someone else's position and interests is far harder. Many negotiators assume it is too difficult to figure out what the other players want and do not even bother. Their strategy is simply to take care of their own needs and let the other players take care of theirs. This is a mistake. It may be appealing at first glance, but in practice, it is likely to produce undesirable results ranging from suboptimal outcomes to failure to agree or, worse, conflict escalation. A look at a real-world negotiation situation helps clarify the importance of understanding the needs and positions of other parties to the negotiation.

Tom Stoner started Highland Energy Group to help organizations convert to energy-efficient technology. But the work required large investments in technology and staff, and Stoner had to raise venture capital to get the business off the ground. That meant negotiating with any potential investors who would give him an audience.

In any negotiation, and especially in negotiations over future plans, the other party's position can offer the key to a successful strategy. Stoner's experience reflects this principle. He recognized that the systems he wanted the firm to bring to market were untested. Large-scale conversions from old to newer, more energy-efficient technologies were not in the mainstream. Most investors knew little about the technology, and his firm had no track record to convince investors that the technology would work. He knew his own position and needs; that was the easy part. But the fundraising task required him to understand the motivations of investors.

Stoner recalls the result of his analysis of potential investors: "I needed to create the belief [in the investor] that these systems would work." But most investors were too busy and skeptical to take the time needed to learn about the technologies, so Stoner targeted HFG Expansion Fund, a venture capital firm founded by Tim Joukowsky, an old friend from college who was willing to learn about the idea. Stoner recalls, "Tim and I went for nice long walks. You can learn a lot about another party's position by going for a long walk with him—and he can learn a lot about your company's technology and plans." (Recall the famous walk in the woods that President Jimmy Carter took with President Anwar Sadat of Egypt and Menachem Begin of Israel, resulting in the Camp David accords.) [13]

The plans made sense to Joukowsky, but he still had reservations about Stoner's ability to carry them out because of their highly technical nature. Knowing this, Stoner agreed to bring in a technically oriented business partner, and finally HFG was ready to invest. After more than $1 million in venture capital, followed by a private offering for second-round financing, the company won its first major bid. It became one of the major contractors to utilities in its industry. [14] This success story would not have been possible without Stoner's commitment to understanding the needs of the other party in his early planning negotiations, because—as Stoner realized—the *other party* is the key to success.

MAKE OPPORTUNITIES TO STUDY THE OTHER PLAYERS

During negotiations, you will have many opportunities to learn about the other party, and you should seek out and use these opportunities. Face time with the other party is particularly important. So is the opportunity to debrief someone who has negotiated with this person before or the chance to do some background research to find out more about his or her position and needs.

If you can manage to take a long walk with the other party, so much the better. But you do not have to be friends to learn what you need to know about the other's position. You should be able to find plenty of ways to disclose your perspective to the key players and research their backgrounds before you negotiate.

Imagine you are preparing for a tough tennis match with someone you've never played before. Rather than simply walk onto the court, you'd want to find out how she has played in the past, who she has beaten, and who has beaten her. You'd also seek opportunities to watch her play and even to warm up or practice with her. And you would certainly treasure any tips or insights others could give you, like "stay away from her backhand." The same is true for negotiation.

How to Understand the Opponent

Knowledge of the other party's concerns and issues will come both from what is said and what is not said. If you are a good reader of body language, for instance, you may learn a lot by just watching the other party. Anxiety is easily betrayed by defensive postures, for example. Crossing legs or arms, turning to sit diagonally to you, putting distance or furniture between you, and avoiding direct eye contact are signs that a player is anxious in the situation.

How you use this insight depends on your goals, but you certainly should use it. If you are competing hard, you might want to push hard now in the hope that this anxiety will lead to a mistake. If you are trying to build cooperation, you would instead devote efforts to making this player feel more secure. But however you choose to use your insight, it will prove key to your success.

Your skill at reading nonverbal cues is remarkably important during negotiations, and you should take every opportunity to practice it. An easy way is to work on your empathy (your emotional understanding of others' feelings) in your daily relationships.

Here is a simple way to practice reading nonverbal cues. Try asking a spouse, friend, child, or associate if you understand his or her feelings at a particular moment when you think you've picked up a good nonverbal cue. Were you right? See how many times in a day you can determine the feelings of this person. Research indicates that emotional intelligence skills like empathy can be improved at any stage of life, so it is a realistic goal to practice and improve your ability to read others' feelings.

Daniel Goleman on Empathy

Goleman, a psychologist and author of the best-seller *Emotional Intelligence,* provides the following insights of aid to negotiators: "Just as the mode of the rational mind is words, the mode of the emotions is nonverbal. Indeed, when a person's words disagree with what is conveyed via his tone of voice, gesture, or other nonverbal channel, the emotional truth is in *how* he says something rather than in *what* he says." He continues: "Empathy requires enough calm and receptivity so that the subtle signals of feeling from another person can be received and mimicked by one's own emotional brain." Try to apply these insights in your next conflict-oriented interaction and see if you can tune into the emotional message behind the other party's words.

D. Goleman, *Emotional Intelligence: Why It Can Matter More Than IQ* (New York: Bantam, 1995), pp. 97, 104.

PLAN THE OTHER PARTY'S NEGOTIATION

Planning a negotiation based only on your own needs won't work. You need to plan it from the other player's perspective, or else he won't go along with the plan. And although it is essential to find out about the other party as you go along, it is not enough. You need to anticipate his needs and reactions and adopt a strategy based on that anticipation.

To plan a negotiation game the other party will want to play, you need to do some research and thinking about his long-term needs. The more you know about him ahead of time, the better. That doesn't mean you can learn everything the first time through because planning is an ongoing activity. As you learn things about the other party—his interests, preferences, primary concerns, areas where he is committed or flexible, and so on—you will want to revise your plans accordingly.

SPY VERSUS SPY?

Remember that while you are researching the other party, he may be checking up on you. Giving and obtaining information can be a somewhat delicate matter, especially if you feel that you need to guard some details, such as weaknesses, for fear that he might use them against you. This behavior is typical in the competitive negotiation process, which we discuss in depth in Chapters Four and Five. In contrast, in the more open communications that characterize collaborative negotiations, both parties share information openly and extensively: the objective is to find a common ground and a solution that will satisfy both parties. The collaborative strategy is the subject of Chapter Six.

Do Some Research and Planning Now

Although it may seem much harder to get information on the other party than it was to figure out your own position, it is at least equally important. The better idea you have of what to expect, the better prepared you will be and the more successful you can be. As we stressed earlier, you need to know not just the information but the reasons behind it.

Your research on the other party somewhat parallels your research on your own position. There are some differences, however, which we will note as we go along.

Before you begin your detailed research on the other party, think once again about your relationship with him. How important is it? Your relationship (or lack of one) will direct the process of data collection and influence your choice of negotiating strategy.

Sometimes you cannot find out much about your opponent beforehand. Nevertheless, do not worry. Here are two substitutes for formal research. First, decide whether you can make any reasonable inferences or assumptions about the other side. For example, if you are buying a used computer, you can assume that the seller will start with the price that was advertised or posted on the computer. Second, you can pick up details as you go along. And even if you have good information on the other party to begin with, you will probably see changes and adjustments as negotiations progress. This is the result of interaction between two parties and the growth of a relationship, whether positive or negative.

What to Research

You will need to conduct research about other players in the following areas:

- Objectives
- Interests and needs
- Alternatives
- Reputation, negotiation style, and behavior
- Authority to make an agreement
- Likely strategy and tactics

Let's look at each of these separately in the following discussion

Objectives

Questions to Ask Yourself

- What does the other player want to get out of this negotiation?
- Are there definite outcomes the other player must achieve?
- Are their definite relationship goals the other player wants to achieve?

It is easy to make assumptions about the other party's objectives. Although they may be true, be careful not to jump to conclusions. For example, if you are considering buying a used guitar, you may believe that the seller is trying to get as high a price as possible. That may be true, but aim to learn specific information rather than relying on guesswork. Perhaps the seller has to sell it, but would rather do business with someone who will take good care of the guitar. Perhaps the seller is in a hurry and just wants to sell it fast.

If you discuss the negotiation with the other party, you may discover her objectives in what she says, or emphasizes, or does not say. Or perhaps the other party may not have carefully formulated objectives at this early stage. And if she reveals several objectives, you may not know which ones are more important. Once negotiations begin and progress, you will be able to formulate a general idea of the other party's objectives, and you may be able to infer by the type and size of her concessions what appears to be more (or less) important to her.

Some commodities are so widely exchanged that you will be able to find informative books and articles about them. For example, numerous books on purchasing an automobile present negotiation advice as well as a great deal of information about dealer costs, the price of options, and so on. Similar information is available about houses, antiques, and artwork. If you want a basic idea of what to expect before starting your negotiations, read about commonly accepted ranges in similar transactions. You can consult with experts in this area or ask other negotiators about their experiences. Bear in mind that each negotiation is different because of the different people involved and the different array of goals and concerns.

Indirect methods of obtaining information include observing the other party, looking through documents and publications, and asking sources who know the other party. The direct method is to ask the other party, but you may not receive an accurate response because she may wish to keep you in the dark. She may limit what she says, so you will not know whether you have a full picture of the situation.

Interests and Needs

Questions to Ask Yourself

- Why does the player care about his or her outcome and relationship goals?
- What underlying interests does this player have?

We considered your underlying interests earlier in this chapter. The other party's interests and needs are no less important. In fact, if you expect to find a common ground with the other party and create a collaborative solution, then you must know the underlying factors of the other party's position. Without knowing his needs, you might assess the situation as competitive when in fact there may be some common ground that can serve as a basis for finding a good collaborative solution, for example.

If you can, ask the other party the "why" question: "Why are these objectives important to you?" And ask related questions too: "How did you come to this position?" "What if you cannot accomplish your goals?" "Have your needs changed since our previous discussion?"

Ask lots of other questions as well. Ask value-free, informational questions to find out what the other party's underlying needs are. Avoid judgmental styles of questioning even if your first instinct is to use them. How you word these questions will help or hinder you in obtaining responses. For example, if you say, "How did you ever think you could get *that* objective?" you will put the other party on the defensive. But if you say, "I'm not sure I understand why that objective is so important to you. Can you explain your concerns?" you are far more likely to obtain useful information about the other party's underlying concerns. And remember two things:

- Keep your mind free of antagonism and judgment since your tone of voice and body language will leak any negative feelings and contaminate even the most politely worded question.
- After you ask a question, listen carefully to the answer. For one thing, you will be gaining information. For another, you will be indicating to the other party that you are truly interested in hearing what he has to say. This will certainly open him up to your future questions, and it may encourage him to listen to your needs.

Alternatives

Questions to Ask Yourself

- What alternatives does the other party have? What will she or he do if the deal is not completed?
- How appealing is the best of her alternatives compared to working with you?

You need to know whether the other party has any alternatives and if so, how strong or weak they are. Someone with a strong alternative does not have to continue bargaining with you. But if the only alternative is weak, you may be in a better bargaining position. If the other party is unwilling to share information, it may be difficult to find out such details before you begin negotiations. But don't be afraid to ask. Again, you may learn something from how she answers, even if she doesn't tell you exactly what you want. And continue to explore their alternatives during negotiations. You will probably learn more over time.

The Other Party's Reputation, Negotiation Style, and Behavior

Questions to Ask Yourself

- What does the rumor mill say about this player?
- What style does this person usually take in conflict situations?

- Is there anything unusual or distinctive about his or her interpersonal behavior?
- How trustworthy is this person?

Knowing about the other party's business and background will assist you in gauging what to expect in negotiation. You can make telephone calls or site visits, assuming that it is not a hostile relationship. You may want to investigate any past negotiations by the other party and how others see her. For example, if she has a reputation as a hard bargainer, then you may expect difficult competitive negotiation.

As we have noted, beliefs and expectations affect how anyone goes into negotiation. Thus, if you believe that there can be only one winner, you will behave accordingly during negotiation. And if the other party holds a particular belief about how negotiation should work, then this will affect both her behavior and the outcome.

Perhaps the most important assessment of the other party is her trustworthiness. Can you trust her? How much can you trust her? Is she competent to conduct the negotiation? Will she treat you well? Is she likely to follow through and keep the commitments she makes in the negotiation?[15] Should you even negotiate with her in the first place? Our answer is, "Not unless you can count on at least a minimum level of trustworthiness."

If I trust you to be open and honest and you are, we have one sort of communication. If I trust you and you are not open and honest, then I will adjust how I respond to you, and our communication will change. Open, trusting relationships cannot be built with players who are suspicious and tricky in their attitudes and behavior. Trust is a necessary foundation for cooperative negotiations. In fact, a certain level of trustworthiness is necessary even to compete because you trust the other party to play by the rules (for example, by not going back on concessions). So make sure you have a realistic view of the level of trustworthiness of the other party.

Authority to Make an Agreement

Questions to Ask Yourself

- Am I negotiating with the right decision maker?

- Are there other players who will be part of this negotiation game at some point?
- Are there other parties who have strong underlying interests in the outcome of this negotiation? If so, to what extent can they constrain this player's negotiations?

You need to know whether the other party will be working alone or with others and whether a constituency will influence this person's agreement-making capability. Furthermore, does he have the authority to make agreements, or is he limited by other parties or by company rules and regulations?

An opponent with limited decision-making authority can often turn this against you. For example, he might use limited authority to advantage by saying, "It is out of my hands" (when it may or may not be). So it's best to clarify who makes the ultimate decision and get that party involved from the start so you do not waste time on a senseless negotiation.

Sometimes it seems that you are working with the right person, until he becomes stuck on a concession point he lacks the authority to concede. Then you must give up on that desired concession, or else backtrack and try to involve other parties. For instance, if you are negotiating with an entrepreneur who values his wife's opinions highly, you may suddenly find the negotiations have ground to a halt because the wife disapproves of the direction they are taking. If you failed to recognize that she had a strong influence on her husband's final decision, you would not have considered her bottom-line requirements, and therefore the deal would be bound to fail.

Likely Strategy and Tactics

Questions to Ask Yourself

- What is the dominant strategy the other party is likely to choose?
- What are his or her favorite negotiating tactics?

A variety of strategies and tactics can be used in negotiation. You will want to anticipate the other party's likely stance. Try to estimate and characterize in general how the negotiations will go.

The other party may be conciliatory and open to accommodations and flexible solutions, suggesting a preference to collaborate. Or the other party may be hard-nosed and appear ready to fight you tooth and nail, suggesting that a competitive style is most likely. And there are a number of other possibilities between these two extremes. Some parties prefer the simplistic rules of a compromise, others are so averse to conflict they generally try to withdraw during the process, and so on. As you do your research, you will develop a good picture of how the other party is likely to operate. This will not only help you select an appropriate negotiating style, it will also prepare you to deal with their style.

A Cautionary Tale About Losing Your Cool

If you don't anticipate and prepare for an angry opponent, you can easily be drawn into playing his game instead of your own. Read this exchange between Vice President Richard Nixon and Premier Nikita Khrushchev of the Soviet Union in 1959. Nixon initiates it by trying to explain that the United States and the Soviet Union shouldn't get engaged in angry threats and ultimatums. But Khrushchev's immediate angry response throws Nixon off balance, and soon they have exchanged threats—precisely what Nixon meant to avoid.

> *Nixon:* The moment we place either one of these powerful nations, through an ultimatum, in a position where it has no choice but to accept dictation or fight, then you are playing with the most destructive force in the world.
>
> *Khrushchev* (flushed, wagging a finger near Nixon's face): We too are giants. If you want to threaten, we will answer threat with threat.
>
> *Nixon:* We never engage in threats.
>
> *Khrushchev:* You wanted indirectly to threaten me. But we have means at our disposal that can have very bad consequences.
>
> *Nixon:* We have too.

Time, Aug. 3, 1959.

TRYING ON THE OTHER PARTY'S SHOES

Given all the time you have spent gaining information about the other, you may be truly able to try on his or her shoes for a while. This process, *role reversal*, involves taking the side of the other person and arguing for that side. Although you can do this mentally and informally, it is more effective to try it with a friend or colleague when you are preparing for a communication. The method is to develop your own point, then look at the possible counterarguments and develop responses to them—somewhat like walking in the other person's shoes for a while.[16]

Role reversal is a great skill to have when you must focus on someone else's problem. Thus, a customer service representative would see what it is like to be a customer frustrated with a product, or a laborer could get a sense of the kinds of decisions management must make. Patients often criticize doctors for having a bad bedside manner, meaning that the physician fails to listen and really understand how the patient is feeling by trying to put herself in the patient role.

You can also use role reversal to "psych out" an opponent by role-playing negotiation with them in which you pretend to be that other person. You can also play yourself, but it can be fun to enlist a friend or associate to play you. Actively arguing the other person's position as though you really believed it can be very helpful in the following ways:

- It can help you understand the other party's position.
- It can help you see similarities between the two positions.
- It can improve outcomes if the two points of view are basically compatible. However, it is usually less successful when the points of view are fundamentally incompatible.
- It may reduce distortions in communication.

Role-playing exercises based on role reversal are a great active research technique for preparing to negotiate. And if you've done your homework on the other players, it should be easy to step into their shoes.

SUMMARY

In this chapter, we have reviewed a number of important planning and preparation tools. These tools are most useful if used in a careful and systematic planning process. Sometimes negotiators skip over the planning stages quickly, because they think that what happens face to face in the negotiation is more important. But in fact, good negotiators often achieve mastery of the situation through the preparation and planning work they do, so give this process your attention. It may make the difference between a mediocre and a great outcome for you.

It can be helpful to put the information gained by the analysis so far into a structured analytical framework. We recommend the following method for complex or high-impact negotiations. Allow plenty of time for this process.

As you go through the analysis steps, be sure you thoroughly understand your strengths and weaknesses at each stage. This will help you make convincing arguments for yourself or against the other party:

- Step 1: Define the issues. Analyze the conflict situation from your own point of view. Look at the issues and decide which are major issues for you and which are minor. Experience can be helpful. Take into consideration the research you have done, including your history in negotiation. Based on the issues, make a list of experts in the field who may be able to contribute advice, information, or expertise.
- Step 2: Assemble the issues, and define the agenda. List all issues in the order of their importance. This should be relatively easy because of the work you did on prioritizing goals. You may find that some of the issues are interconnected and therefore have to be kept together.
- Step 3: Analyze the other party. Although it may be difficult to obtain information on the other party, researching the other side is vital to planning a good strategy. At this stage in your analysis, you should start to think about your relationship with the other party, for this will affect all your ensuing moves as you design your negotiating plan. In particular, your history with the other party

and the degree of interdependence between the parties will affect your interactions. All the research you have done thus far will influence how you work with (or against) the other party.

• Step 4: Define the underlying interests. To define the interests and needs that underlie the issues you specified, remember the question "Why?" Why do you want this item or goal? Why is it important to you? When you investigate the other party's goals in the next chapter, you will again use the *why* questions to get at the underlying reasons for the other party's preferences. This will help you understand where they are coming from and will enable you to find common interests and differences.

• Step 5: Consult with others. Unless this is a simple negotiation, other people will probably be involved. For example, if you are negotiating a bank loan, the loan officer probably has to clear it with higher-ups. Or perhaps you are buying a car to use primarily to drive to work. If your spouse will be driving it occasionally, you will probably need his or her thoughts on the choice of car.

You will also consult with the other party, perhaps on issues or even on how you will negotiate. Talks with other parties can be amicable or hostile, depending on the situation. Nevertheless, any parties to the negotiation should be brought into the proceedings as early in your analysis and planning as possible so you can begin to see the whole picture.

• Step 6: Set goals for the process and outcome. Be sure you have a clear picture of your preferred schedule, site (location), time frame, who will be involved, and what will happen if negotiations fail. You will need to take into account the other parties' preferences that surface in your consulting with them. Be sure you know which items are important enough to fight for and which to be flexible about. Such prenegotiation talks will tend to set the tone for the bargaining session itself.

• Step 7: Identify your own limits. It is very important to know these. These will arise from having a clear picture of your goals and their priorities, your bargaining range points, and your alternatives or BATNA (best alternative to a negotiated agreement). If you know your limits, you will be able to adjust your plan as necessary. For example, if the other side rejects an item during bargaining, you will be more readily able to reevaluate it and decide what your next move should be. If you have a good BATNA, you may decide to walk, but if you do not, you may adjust your expectations and continue to negotiate.

Be sure your limits are realistic. It is fine to have an absolute minimum or maximum acceptable point, but consider having a range for flexibility. The priority ratings you gave to your issues when you were defining them will also help you set limits. You want to do better with the more important issues and be more flexible on the less important ones. You will be in an even better position for negotiating if you have anticipated possible packages that might be offered by the other party, and assigned them values on a scale similar to the rating scale you used for your own packages. They will help you make comparisons.

• Step 8: Develop supporting arguments. Once you know your goals and preferences, think about how best to provide supporting arguments for those goals. You need facts to validate your arguments. You will have accumulated many of these during your research. Methods for presenting facts include visuals such as charts and graphs; people such as experts; and records or files, especially from respected sources. Other similar negotiations can provide clues for how to proceed.

Use the analysis steps regularly to help your negotiation planning. For your convenience, we have summarized these in Exhibit 3.1.

Notes

1. For example, see S. Kozicki, *Creative Negotiating* (Holbrook, Mass.: Adams Media, 1998), and A. Schoonmaker, *Negotiating to Win* (Upper Saddle River, N.J.: Prentice Hall, 1989).
2. G. Nierenberg, *The Complete Negotiator* (New York: Nierenberg & Zeif Publishers, 1976).
3. C. R. Rogers, *Active Listening* (Chicago: University of Chicago Press, 1957).
4. R. J. Lewicki, D. M. Saunders, and B. Barry, *Negotiation,* 5th ed. (Burr Ridge, Ill.: McGraw-Hill/Irwin, 2006).
5. M. C. Donaldson, M. Donaldson, and D. Frohnmayer, *Negotiating for Dummies* (Foster City, Calif.: IDG Books, 1996).
6. Lewicki, Saunders, and Barry, *Negotiation.*
7. Lewicki, Saunders, and Barry, *Negotiation.*

EXHIBIT 3.1. A NEGOTIATION PLANNING GUIDE

Step 1: Define the issues.

Step 2: Assemble the issues and define the agenda.

Step 3: Analyze the other party.

Step 4: Define underlying interests.

Step 5: Consult with others.

Step 6: Set goals for the process and outcome.

Step 7: Identify your own limits.

Step 8: Develop supporting arguments.

---

8. If you are responsible for developing or training a negotiation team, there are numerous resources you can consult on this process. We suggest J. R. Katzenbach and D. K. Smith, *The Wisdom of Teams* (Boston: Harvard Business School Press, 1993), and F. LaFasto and C. Larson, *When Teams Work Best* (Thousand Oaks, Calif.: Sage, 2001).

9. R. Cooper and A. Sawaf, *Executive EQ: Emotional Intelligence in Leadership and Organizations* (New York: Grosset, 1996).

10. R. Fisher, W. Ury, and B. Patton, *Getting to Yes*, 2nd ed. (New York: Penguin Books, 1991).

11. D. Lax and J. Sebenius, *The Manager as Negotiator* (New York: Free Press, 1986).

12. Lax and Sebenius, *The Manager as Negotiator.*

13. L. Blessing, *A Walk in the Woods* (New York: New American Library, 1988).

14. M. Kaeter, "Buddy, Can You Spare a Million?" *Business Ethics*, May–June 1994, pp. 27, 28.

15. R. C. Mayer, J. H. Davis, and F. D. Schoorman, "An Integrative Model of Organizational Trust," *Academy of Management Review*, 1995, *20*(3), 709–734.

16. D. Johnson and R. Dustin, "The Initiation of Cooperation Through Role Reversal," *Journal of Social Psychology*, 1980, *82*, 193–203.

CHAPTER FOUR

THE ART OF THE MASTER COMPETITOR

It's a blistering hot day outside, but in the conference room, the air-conditioning is on high and so is the chill in relations between your team and the representatives of the other company in these joint venture contract talks. In spite of the chill, you can feel a trickle of sweat under your shirt as you watch the other side's reaction to the new cost-sharing proposal from your side.

"It seems to me," their senior negotiator says slowly, laying the paper down and eyeing each of you in turn, "that this represents a *serious* shift in your position." He pauses so long you almost jump in with an explanation, but then at the last possible moment, he continues, as if you weren't even in the room, "A violation of our previous verbal understandings." Another pause, but he clearly has the floor and nobody interrupts. "I'm not sure where this leaves us." Then he sits back, as if withdrawing from the discussions, and the room falls silent.

You take a breath and tell yourself not to get rattled and make any unplanned concessions. Then you catch your boss's eye and try to communicate nonverbally that he shouldn't say anything rash either.

But it's too late. Leaning forward anxiously, your boss begins a lengthy explanation, his hands gesturing more and more wildly as he talks, as if they could somehow compel the other party to understand. "It's really, *really*, not intended as a deal breaker," he says. (You wince at the term; the other party hadn't actually threatened to break the deal yet. He is overreacting. He always overreacts.) "We thought it was, honestly, a very minor thing, and that you'd understand since our situation has changed since we last talked, right?"

Oh no! you think, trying not to roll your eyes in front of the other side. Now he's asking rhetorical questions, which of course they won't answer, leaving him fumbling for an awkward way to continue.

"Well, um, anyway, as I was saying," he stumbles ahead, "our cost structure has changed significantly since then, what with the rising fuel prices, and to tell you the truth, we're having a little trouble with our efforts to roll our labor contract over without having to renegotiate the benefits package. Now don't get upset about that or anything; I'm sure it will all be settled by the time we close our deal, but it does change our view of the cost structure somewhat. I mean, it just makes sense for us to be cautious, and if we index the cost contributions, like, like in the written plan we, um, proposed today, we, um, we won't be quite as exposed to long-term uncertainty, which is a good thing."

He finally sits back, exhausted, and wipes his brow. You make a mental note to sit nearer him at the next meeting (if there is one) so you can reach out and grab him before he starts up again.

Their senior negotiator is still sitting quietly, looking at the lot of you as if you were insects that needed stepping on. He doesn't blink or make any movement. Clearly he has no intention of answering. After a long pause in which your boss shuffles papers nervously, one of their more junior people clears her throat and says icily, "So, let's just get this clear. In addition to going back on your initial proposal about cost sharing, you are also telling us that you have a labor dispute *and* that your energy costs are out of control?" She sits back again, glancing briefly at her boss and asking with her eyes, "Why are we even dealing with these bozos?"

You look at your boss again and realize that this situation is about to erupt like tossing a lit match into a fireworks stand. He's beginning to smoke already, and the only thing keeping him from jumping in with an even more unguarded response is that he doesn't seem to know which part of her statement to tackle first. Something has to be done, now, to get this negotiation back under control.

You glance at your handheld e-mail receiver (it's off, but the other side doesn't know that), push back your chair, stand, and walk around to your boss's chair. Leaning over to whisper in his ear, you say, "Sorry to interrupt, but something very important has just come up that requires your urgent attention. You'll have to ask for a fifteen-minute break. *Now.*"

As you hustle your boss out of the room, you marvel at the skills of the other side. They read your boss beautifully: a guy who runs his business well but negotiates very badly because he thinks his view—and only his view—is the legitimate one. So he gets flustered if everyone isn't pleased with his proposals and remarks. They jumped on a minor issue—probably not the one they intend to negotiate hardest today—and used it to soften your side up and put you on the defensive early in the talks. And they clearly have the emotional control to make the most of the situation. The way their senior guy used pauses and managed to drop his bomb in a few short sentences and then sit back and watch the chaos unfold without saying anything further: *that's* mastery of competitive negotiating! His assistant is no slouch either. She knew just when to step in and twist the knife. If you hadn't pulled your boss out of the meeting, he would have either started yelling and driven them out of the room or uttered some major concession that nobody would have been able to take off the table.

THE COMPETITIVE GAME

Competition is the strategy most of us associate with negotiation and deal making. It is the classic bargaining or haggling style used in open-air markets throughout much of the world, and it also rules in many boardroom negotiations, such as the one that opened this chapter. Competition is also the style used most often to negotiate the price of a vehicle, lease, or salary package. And within companies, rivalries over access to resources, power, and promotions often follow the rules of competitive negotiating (whether they should or not).

In our corporate training work, however, we find that many employees prefer a collaborative style instead of a competitive one. Perhaps this is true of you too. But regardless, you still need to master the competitive game. The competitive game is played frequently, so it is important to understand how it works, even if you do not plan to use it yourself. First, if the other party is negotiating competitively, you need to understand what he or she is doing so you can appropriately defend yourself against it. As we noted in

Chapter Two, competition may be preferred in some situations (when the outcome is important but the relationship is not). It may be preferred when the outcome resources are limited and finite. So you will use it on some occasions since others will often try to draw you into it. And often it is your best choice.

Don't Try This at Home!

Here's an amusing (if not totally honest) anecdote from a comedian who found a creative way to cope with a landlord's expectation for a bribe. His competitive style didn't do much for the relationship, but it got him what he wanted at a bargain price:

> They got some new apartments down on Riverside Drive, so I went down to get me an apartment. I said, "I'd like to have five rooms," and the man said, "Sorry, Mr. White, but we've got to put you on the waiting list. It'll be about two years before we can get you in this apartment house."
>
> I said, "Two years? Okay, get me in as soon as you can." I ran my hand in my pocket, dropped a thousand dollars in the trash-can. I said, "If you find anything, let me know. Here's my phone number."
>
> I go home. About a half hour later the phone rang. "Mr. White, we do have one apartment left." So I go back down and sign a five-year lease. About four days later I get a phone call from the same guy. He said, "Mr. White, that money in the trash can—it was counterfeit. It was no good."
>
> I said, "I know, that's why I threw it away!"

Source: Slappy White, quoted in R. L. Smith, *The Comedy Quote Dictionary* (New York: Bantam Doubleday Dell, 1992), p. 120.

THE IMPACT OF COMPETITION ON RELATIONSHIPS

It's natural to use competitive negotiating if the relationship with the other party does not matter a great deal, or you simply don't need to worry about the other party because you know this person can take care of himself or herself—for example:

- This may be a one-time negotiation with no future relationship (you are buying a coffee table at a garage sale, for example).
- The future relationship may not be important.
- The relationship exists but was poor to begin with.
- The other party likes to negotiate hard and views it as a challenging game.
- The other party has a reputation for hard bargaining or dishonesty, and you need to compete just to make sure you don't get taken advantage of.

This strategy is undertaken with the assumption that the specific outcome is important and worth competing over, and also that the other party is not likely to be on your side but instead will compete for his or her own interests.

Does competition spoil a relationship? Not necessarily. If you play the game properly and avoid improper or unethical behavior or overly emotional outbursts, you may well find it strengthens your relationship. Many businesses and individuals negotiate competitively time and again, and some of them develop efficient norms for doing so. For example, a talent agent representing an actor, model, or athlete frequently negotiates with the same producers, studios, sports teams, and so forth. Both sides get to know each other, and if they are both good negotiators, they come to view each other with respect. At the same time, in order for them to continually be hired by their clients, they have to get the best deal possible. A similar respect for each other's mastery also develops in labor-management negotiations if both sides are good negotiators and neither does anything underhanded.

So don't think of competitive negotiating as necessarily a relationship killer. It shouldn't be if it is done well. When we say that it focuses on the outcome instead of the relationship, we mean that your strategies and actions should be motivated by the desire to win for yourself or your side; you are not to worry about the other side's score, only your own. That's how competitive games work, and that's how competitive negotiating works. If you're going to play the game, you better be clear on the rules. Assume the other party is already clear on the competitive game's rules, unless you see clear evidence to the contrary.

On the other hand, some relationships are hurt by competitive negotiation. Hurt feelings and resentment are things to watch out for and try to prevent. The root of the problem is that competition tends to emphasize the differences between the parties, promoting a we versus they attitude. Competitive negotiations can damage trust and even create additional conflict.

A way to counter the possible damage to an important business negotiation is to talk about the rules before negotiating. For example, if you feel strongly that those in the other party should not lie and should not renege on an earlier concession or commitment, then you might want to ask them if they agree about these rules of conduct. Expectations about conduct can and should be negotiated, but they often are not. In fact, this is the most common cause of resentment in employee-manager negotiations. The manager often forgets having said something or just doesn't take it very seriously and responds, "Things have changed; I can't keep that commitment." Since the boss is in a position of power and the employee is not, the employee has to live with rescinded concessions—but he or she doesn't have to live with them happily. Lowered morale and slower or worse work will result. It would have been far better if the boss had been clearer and more honest up front. If you are the boss and are making a conditional offer or concession, then state the conditions clearly so the employee understands. If you are the employee, ask the boss if the commitment is ironclad or if it's conditional on what happens in the future.[1]

TAKE AS MUCH AS YOU CAN

The goal in competition is to get the other party to give in and thus to satisfy the competitor's needs now. It is based on the "I win, you lose" concept. The competitor will do anything to accomplish the objectives and obtain as much as possible. This can include a variety of behaviors, including hardball tactics, such as the use of a straw man issue that you put forth as if it's key and then concede on in exchange for a deep concession on an issue that *is* important to you.

The straw man strategy is illustrated in the opening example we gave of a tough contract negotiation. Those in the other party to a joint venture grasped an apparently minor request to change a cost-sharing formula and are blowing it up into a major, potentially deal-killing, issue. They will probably concede on it later in the day or at a future meeting, making it appear as if this is a major concession that they deeply resent—and are expecting to be reciprocated in kind. Their real concerns are not yet clear. They are keeping their cards close to their chest, and the other party can't be sure what they really think about the deal.

Is it ethical to pretend you're very upset about a minor concession, and then use the emotional capital you've built up to force the other party to concede on something else? In competitive negotiations, it is considered acceptable to do so, and it's realistic to expect others to do this to you. If you used the straw man strategy in an argument with your spouse, the ethics would be quite different because more personal relationships usually have higher expectations for honesty. But in a competitive business negotiation, you can, and should, be prepared for this sort of deception. (Note that when in doubt, it is always prudent to run a strategy by your attorney before using it. Occasionally people go too far and get in trouble for overly deceptive and deceitful negotiating.)

HOW TO PREPARE FOR A COMPETITIVE NEGOTIATION

To effectively prepare for a competitive negotiation, you must identify four key points. We will define these key points in terms of a buyer-seller exchange, which is usually referred to as the classic competitive negotiation, but they apply to all competitive negotiations equally well:

1. What you consider to be an acceptable deal. This is your *target point*. A target point is the settlement you would like to achieve when the negotiation is finished.
2. Where you will start. Since most people expect that a negotiation involves the process of give-and-take, or making concessions, you probably will have to ask for more than you really expect to get (if you are the seller) or have to offer less than

you will ultimately have to pay (if you are the buyer). This is your *opening offer.*

3. The limits you set in terms of the most you will pay (as the buyer) or the least you will take (as the seller). This is your *walkaway.*

4. What you will do if you cannot strike a deal with this other party. This is your *alternative.*

We'll start the first three points, which we will call the *bargaining range.* (We'll come back to the fourth point later in the chapter.) For the seller, the upper point of the bargaining range is the opening bid, and the lower point is the walkaway; for the buyer, the reverse is true. This is represented in Figure 4.1. Maybe this seems obvious, but take the time to think it through carefully. We find that the majority of negotiators have not given these elementary points enough thought in advance and run into trouble as a result.

You need a well-defined bargaining range, and you need to prepare this bargaining range in advance as best you can. In competition, each side has a bargaining range (whether they have defined it formally or not). Bargaining occurs because the bargaining range for each party is different. During bargaining, you attempt to determine if there is overlap between your bargaining range and the other person's range. If there is overlap, then every point within the area of overlap is a point of possible settlement. Representations of overlapping and nonoverlapping bargaining ranges are shown in Figure 4.2.

Let's look at an example. You're about to start a new job that requires more travel and decide it is time to replace your old car with a newer one. Your brother is also selling his car, which is a lot newer and has fewer miles, and you strike a great deal with him. Now you have to sell your old car. You scan the newspaper ads for

FIGURE 4.1. SELLER'S BARGAINING RANGE

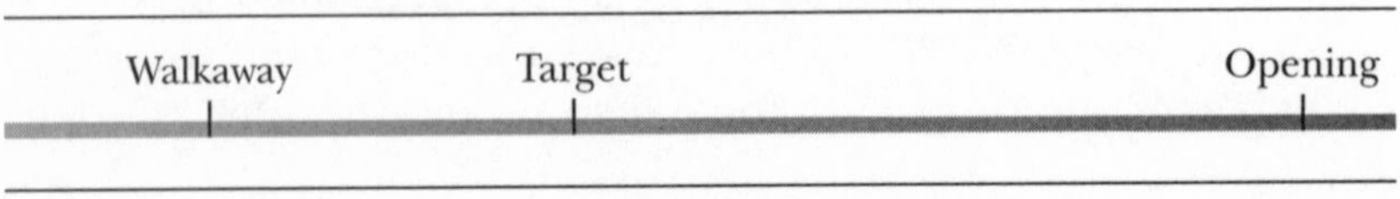

Walkaway	Target		Opening

FIGURE 4.2. BUYER'S AND SELLER'S BARGAINING RANGES

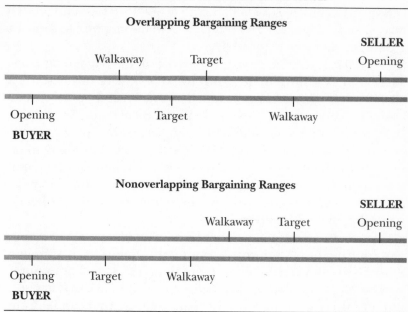

the make and model, and determine that the car is worth about $4,000 (you can also get this information from the Web). So $4,000 is now your target. In order to make sure you get $4,000, you decide to ask $5,000. And you decide that the absolute lowest you will take for the car is $3,500. We have represented this bargaining range in Figure 4.3.

You post a "for sale" sign in the car with your phone number. The next day, you get a call from someone in your neighborhood who says he is interested. He shows up at your house an hour later.

FIGURE 4.3. CAR SELLER'S BARGAINING RANGE

Walkaway	Target	Opening
$3,500	$4,000	$5,000

He wants an older car for in-town use. Privately, he has decided he can spend as much as $4,000, but he would love to spend less. He takes a look at your car and offers $3,000, hoping he can settle for around $3,800 (see Figure 4.4).

As you can see, there is $1,000 overlap in the bargaining range. The seller is willing to go down to $3,500. The buyer starts at $3,000 but is willing to pay as much as $4,500, and hopes to settle around $3,800. Any settlement between $3,500 and $4,500 is an acceptable settlement—although each party would prefer a settlement close to his target point. If the seller were not willing to pay more than $3,499.99 for a car, then there would be no overlap in the bargaining range. The parties might negotiate for a long time and walk away frustrated because they could not find a settlement point that met their expectations.

If you are having a one-dimensional negotiation, say, over price and nothing else, then this bargaining range is fairly simple to think about. But often there is more than one issue. For example, suppose the seller also wants to sell a roof cargo rack that has been fitted to this car or a warranty repair package that can be transferred to the new owner. Or suppose the buyer would like to make several payments over time rather than pay in cash. While each issue might have its own bargaining range (opening, target, and walkway), they often get packaged together as the parties negotiate the deal. We will call this the *bargaining mix* and come back to discuss it in more detail.

Figure 4.4. Car Buyer's and Seller's Overlapping Bargaining Ranges

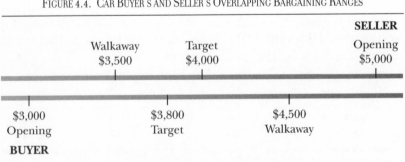

We also do not want to make the idea of a bargaining range overly simple. Although it looks very simple when the information is laid out on a straight line, all of this information is not disclosed to the other party. The seller and the buyer usually disclose only their opening bid. They do not usually disclose their target points, or if they do, they may not tell the truth about them. And they almost never disclose their walkaway point, since this would tell the other what their minimally acceptable settlement is. So much of the activity in negotiation is for the negotiator to disguise his own target and walkaway point, while trying to learn the other's target and walkaway points. It is not surprising that there are many similarities between competitive bargaining and the game of poker. Each party is trying to learn the other's cards while not disclosing, or even bluffing about, his own.

In competitive negotiations, negotiators announce their opening bids. They usually then offer some argument or justification about why that opening offer is fair, reasonable, or justifiable. Usually the buyer makes gradual concessions upward, while the seller makes gradual concessions downward, with the expectation that the two will be able to meet somewhere in the middle between their opening bids. In labor negotiations, labor is usually expected to ask high and management to offer low, again with the expectation that concessions on each side will result in finding a meeting ground. This process may take five minutes or five months, depending on how complex the issues are, how often the parties meet, and how quickly they make concessions.

As we noted, both parties also should decide on their walkaway point—the cutoff point beyond which they will not go. The walkaway point of the other party is usually not known, and this person won't tell you what it is. In fact, he or she will actively try to keep you from learning the walkaway point, because if you knew it, you would offer something slightly above it and expect that he or she would agree. If this point is not reached and the parties agree to a resolution, this point may never be known.

There are some ways that negotiators can use to determine whether the other party is close to or at the walkway point:

- The concessions are getting smaller. People usually make smaller concessions as they get closer to their walkaway

point, signaling that they don't have much room left
to move.
- They make fewer concessions. They dig in and become more
inflexible.
- They are more likely to say things like, "I am at my limit" or
"This is as far as I can go."

THE POWER OF ALTERNATIVES

As long as the bargaining range for one party in some way overlaps
with that of the other party (refer back to Figures 4.2 and 4.4), there
is room for bargaining. If the ranges do not overlap (and this may
not be known at the beginning of the negotiations), there may be
no successful negotiation. The parties will need to decide whether
to adjust their bargaining ranges or end negotiations. And when
they do decide to end negotiations, they look at other options. The
seller will probably try to sell it to someone else (perhaps at a different price) or donate it to a charity. The buyer will keep looking
around for other cars. We will call these other courses of action the
buyer's and seller's *alternatives,* defined as *options that can be pursued
if the current negotiation fails.* An alternative is an outcome outside the
scope of the negotiation with this other party and can be pursued if
it appears more attractive than any potential outcome from this
negotiation. We represent these alternatives in Figure 4.5.

We described the car alternatives as what the buyer and seller
would do after deciding that the negotiation had failed. But alternatives are far more powerful when we know them while we are
negotiating with the other party. Alternatives are good to have
because the current deal can be weighed against the value of any
particular alternative. Knowing the alternative gives us power in
three ways:

- We know that we don't have to be forced into doing the current deal if it doesn't seem satisfactory.
- We know that we are making good choices about what we are
going to do.
- We can tell the other party about our alternative and ask for a
response: "I have this alternative that is equally good and costs
less. Can you improve on your offer to me so that I don't go
off and pursue my alternative?"

FIGURE 4.5. CAR BUYER'S AND SELLER'S OVERLAPPING
BARGAINING RANGES WITH ALTERNATIVES

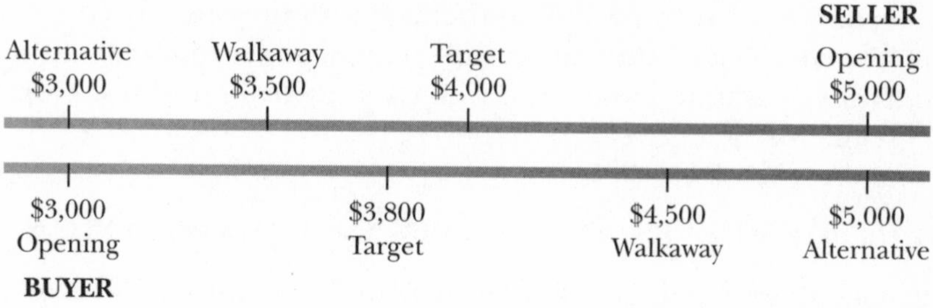

				SELLER
Alternative	Walkaway	Target		Opening
$3,000	$3,500	$4,000		$5,000

$3,000		$3,800	$4,500	$5,000
Opening		Target	Walkaway	Alternative
BUYER				

In the car deal, the buyer ought to have several used cars in mind, or know that there are lots of used cars he can explore if the price on this one isn't right. And the seller ought to think about how to attract other buyers to the car, or whether it might be a good idea to donate it to the local charity. But emotions can get in the way, of course. Sometimes the buyer really likes one car and cannot find another with just the right combination of features and color. Rationally, there may be many alternatives, but if the other party is emotionally attached to closing this particular deal, he or she may go right up to the walkaway point, or even beyond. Good competitive negotiators know that bargaining ranges are some- times flexible and will do their best to get you to move further than you meant to.

Good alternatives are especially powerful because an alterna- tive can become your walkaway point. For example, say you cur- rently make $55,000 in your job and you are job hunting. You decide that you want to find a job making at least $60,000. What do you do if you find a job you like but it pays only $58,000? Do you take it? If there are no other such jobs available (no alterna- tives) because your industry is sluggish now, then you might take the $58,000 job. However, before you decide, perhaps you should see if you can generate another job offer above $55,000.

Now suppose you lose your $55,000 job and are offered $54,000 for a similar job. Will you take it? Perhaps under these cir- cumstances, you will be more likely to do so. In any negotiation, it is wise to be well informed of your alternatives and use them to your advantage wherever possible.

In any competitive negotiation, try to formulate at least one alternative: what you will do if the deal with the other party cannot be completed. Alternatives will give you power to say no to the current deal if necessary and to walk away from unsatisfactory agreements.

THE BENEFITS AND COSTS OF COMPETITION

Competitive negotiating is widespread and often the right choice. But when is it beneficial, and when is it a potential problem? Sometimes, as in negotiations within a family or work group, competition can create bad feelings and get in the way of good, open communications. This is an example of a cost of competition. In this section, we review the benefits and costs to help you decide when competition is most likely to be a good fit and when you might want to avoid it.

BENEFITS: THE SITUATIONS WHERE COMPETITION IS EFFECTIVE

Here are the appropriate circumstances for competitive negotiating:

• The goals of the parties may be short term. The purpose or objective of one or both parties is simply to do the deal and move on.
• The parties have no interest in establishing a deeper or more personal relationship with the other. They care only about getting the best deal on the economic issues that they can. We call these economic issues the tangibles; they are more quantifiable, objective benefits like price, interest rate, number of items, delivery terms, and wording of a contract. The price or economic terms are usually the most common tangible benefit in competitive negotiations. But intangibles, or psychological factors such as esteem, principles, precedents, or the overall well-being of both parties (now and in the future), can push the parties into competitive negotiations. Parties who want to maintain a principle or not lose face and look foolish often persist in competitive behavior.

• The parties assume that their goals are incompatible—there is no way both parties can achieve their goals. The issues under discussion are seen as a fixed pie: what one gains, the other loses, and there are a limited number of ways in which it can be divided. Your objective is to maximize your piece of the pie. If there is more for you, there is less for the other party, and vice versa, so the aim is to get as much as you can. (As we will point out later in the book, this is a perception, and our perceptions can often be wrong.)

• You are likely to use competition when you expect the other party to take a competitive stance. From your research, you probably have a good idea of what strategy the other party will employ. If you know that the other party is going to be competitive, then competition may be appropriate. However, if you are only guessing and the other party uses a different strategy, whatever you have planned may not work. And even if the other party is likely to employ competition, you may still find it desirable to try to shift to a collaborative negotiation in order to increase the outcome possibilities for both sides.

• The negotiators represent somebody else in negotiation—a boss, a labor union, an advocacy group—who will evaluate the negotiator well if the negotiator is strong, competitive, doesn't give in, and forces the other side to give in. We'll call this group a constituency. Thus, while the negotiator may not have a strong competitive bias, the constituency can usually be counted on to care only about the economic issues, to have fixed-pie beliefs, and to expect the other to be competitive.

COSTS: THE SITUATIONS WHERE COMPETITION IS INEFFECTIVE

Negotiations that rely on competition can be costly and time-consuming, especially if each party holds out for all its demands. Much time is spent researching, pressuring, and "psyching out" the other party. Further time is consumed making moves and countermoves, trying to figure out what the other party will do. Competitive strategies are often compared with strategies used in chess, military warfare, and other tactical games. Keep in mind that both chess and warfare take a lot of time and energy. The time spent in these activities is very different from alternative uses of that time; for example, in the collaborative model (as we will describe in Chapter Six), this same time could be spent on mutual exploration of issues, sharing of information, problem solving, and other attempts to find mutually acceptable solutions.

Time and goodwill may also be lost if the competitor antici-pates that you will be competitive and prepares to compete too. If you had not intended to be competitive, you may switch strategies when you discover that the other side has decided to be competi-tive, thus escalating emotions and increasing conflict. Not only does such confusion lose time, but it may hurt the relationship and toughen competitors so that they are now willing to give far less than they might have originally. Competition can also destroy trust between the parties; each expects the worst from the other and has a hard time believing the other, even when the other is telling the truth.

A major problem with competition is that it is a strategy fre-quently used by inexperienced or untrained negotiators who believe that competition is the only way to negotiate. These neo-phytes miss opportunities by automatically selecting competition, which is why taking a class or reading a book on negotiation (like this one) is so important. It is important to select a strategy only after thorough investigation of the issues, an understanding of what strategy the other is likely to pursue, and some clear decisions about the relative importance of the outcomes and the relation-ship with the other party.

Here is a further note on naive uses of competition. One of us, Alex, plays a lot of racquet sports, including racquetball and squash (recently rated by *Forbes* as the best workout of all sports, by the way). Both games are played in an enclosed boxlike room in which the competitors vie for space as they exchange hits off the same front wall. It's very competitive. You might think that the better the other player, the more competitive and potentially dangerous the play, but Alex finds that experienced players are relatively easy to share the space with. They know the unwritten rules, and they can anticipate his movements and avoid collision. It is the eager neo-phytes who are dangerous. They are overly competitive, swinging wildly and risking hitting the other player with their racquet. And they tend to go for those ungettable shots in their enthusiasm, falling down and sometimes running into the other player. Also, they may get upset or angry if they are losing and press too hard, taking risks that more experienced players do not. Technique and experience are the keys to fun, safe play in these sports. Beginner's enthusiasm is often a problem.

Another major source of costs is that it is possible to underestimate the other party's determination in a competitive situation. If they too have adopted the mission to win at all costs, then you are likely to be facing a long and costly negotiation. We see this too often in collective bargaining situations, where the bargainer representing a union does not want to lose face with the union and presses so hard that the result is destructive. For instance, bargaining fell apart in negotiations between transport workers and the City of New York in 2005, resulting in a transport strike and millions of dollars of fines against the union.

When using competition, we tend to underestimate the strength, wisdom, planning, and effectiveness of the other party and assume that although they are preparing to be competitive too, we can beat them at their game. If you do not pay close attention to their behavioral and verbal clues, you may set yourself up for manipulation by the other party.

This is a common problem among small business people, and particularly when they are dealing with a much bigger opponent. Many small business owners have fallen into a dispute with a larger business and, angry, have vowed to pursue the conflict at all costs. If you are smaller than the other party, they can afford to spend more time, hire more lawyers, and make more sacrifices than you can. Davids don't usually beat Goliaths in the real world of business. Small businesses are usually wise to build relationships with key people at large businesses and reach out to them when there is a problem to ask for help instead of rushing to write angry letters or hiring a lawyer to write them.

SELF-FULFILLING PROPHECIES

Finally, you need to be aware of the self-fulfilling prophecy: something we believe so strongly that we actually make it come true. It often happens in negotiation when one party expects the other to behave in a particular way and, as a result, actually makes the party behave that way. This tends to happen if the other party is using competition because they think you are, or you are using competition because you think they will be. Anticipating that the other is going to be competitive, we prepare to be competitive ourselves. The cues we give off in this preparation—our language, tone of voice, gestures, and behaviors—let the others believe that we intend to be competitive. So they behave competitively, which confirms to us that our initial assumptions were right. In essence, we can make the other party competitive by behaving competitively. When we adopt this strategy, we need to understand that we may be making the other side more competitive than might otherwise be necessary or appropriate. Sometimes it is wisest to try to act collaboratively instead and see if the other party follows your lead. If they do not, then you can switch to competition, knowing that at least you tried.

SUMMARY

In the next chapter, we'll walk you through the tactics of engaging in the competitive negotiation. Don't forget your preparation: know your bargaining range and continue to seek alternatives so that you don't lose your head during the negotiations. And don't say anything you hadn't meant to. The other side may be good at rattling you or may use a variety of clever tactics to pry concessions or information out of you. From now on, it's time to control your emotions, think before you speak, and avoid giving away too much through tone of voice, expression, or body language.

By the way, are you wondering what happened in the negotiation over the used car? Competitive negotiations, more than any others, tend to catch us up and create dramatic tension that we want to see resolved. They are exciting. In fact, this excitement can be a danger. Many people find it hard to walk away from a competitive negotiation even if it is not going very well. We believe that the vast majority of people who win an eBay auction, for example, have spent more than they initially meant to just because they got caught up in the competition to win. (In fact, the psychology of eBay bidding is worthy of study, and there are already some interesting academic papers emerging.)

In the case of the used car, the parties found common ground. They should have been able to, if they were efficient negotiators, since there was a thousand dollar overlap in their bargaining ranges. But the seller did better than the buyer. That, as you may recall, is "you" in this hypothetical example. You used two techniques to get a better deal. First, you made sure that your reciprocal concessions were a little smaller than the buyer's, so that as the two of you moved together, you met closer to your goal rather than exactly in the middle. Second, to help move the buyer, you were somewhat slower in responding to some of the buyer's messages and tried to give the impression you had other interested bidders simultaneously. In fact, you had other bidders who were not acting very serious, but you still dropped a casual mention of them now and then. You sold the car for $3,950—considerably more than your minimum and very close to the buyer's upper limit. Good work!

Note

1. R. Walton and R. McKersie, *A Behavioral Theory of Labor Negotiation* (New York: McGraw-Hill, 1965). D. Pruitt, *Negotiation Behavior* (Orlando, Fla.: Academic Press, 1981).

CHAPTER FIVE

EXECUTING A COMPETITIVE NEGOTIATION

We hope you were patient enough to have read Chapter Four about the essential elements of preparation for a competitive negotiation before jumping right into the negotiation with us here. As you begin to interact with the other party, recognize that everything you do and every decision you make is part of the negotiation.

FRAMING THE OPENING CONVERSATION

In the opening stages, much of what you do sets a tone. What tone is appropriate? What message does it send to the other negotiator? Will it establish your authority and strength? We will help you make this decision in a moment. But first, we want you to think about one specific aspect of your opening position that sets a tone and also begins the hard part of your negotiation: your opening position.

HOW TOUGH IS YOUR OPENING POSITION?

Do you want to start with a moderate, reasonable-sounding opening position and set a tone that suggests you will be a reasonable negotiator and expect the other side to be as well? Or do you want to go to the other extreme and take a strong opening position that suggests the other party will not be able to take advantage of you? This is an appealing strategy, and many negotiators favor it. We find that many beginning negotiators, in particular, are drawn to an extreme opening position because they want to come into the negotiation with as much strength as they can. Sounding and acting strong can seem like the best way to be strong as you go into the negotiation, although it may not actually maximize your strength in every situation. You need to think through the advantages and disadvantages of a tough opening position before deciding on whether to use this strategy.

Taking an extreme position at the outset has some obvious advantages:

• It sets a firm tone for the negotiations. It suggests that you are a tough, no-nonsense negotiator and that the other party will probably have to make deep concessions in order to win an agreement with you.

• It leaves a lot of room for concessions, which may give you more time to figure out the other party but can also mean lengthier negotiations. It's tempting to set your opening offer high (or low) enough to ensure that you have plenty of room for movement later on.

• It often makes the other side wonder if you really want to do a deal. It suggests you have alternatives and will have a take-it-or-leave-it approach to whatever is offered. For this reason, an extreme opening position often worries those on the other side, raising concern that you won't be easy to close a deal with. If you're lucky, this concern about your walking away will lead them to make a generous counteroffer.

If you are sure the other side needs to close the deal with you, it might be wise to play hard to get by using a tough opening position. But if you think the others might get discouraged and give up, then be careful not to be so extreme that you drive them away.

Be careful to avoid the many disadvantages of an extreme opening position:

• A major disadvantage of an extreme offer is that the offer may be rejected out of hand, thus bringing negotiations to a halt. In many situations, your opponents will simply refuse any further negotiations and will walk away, particularly if they have a good alternative.

• Your extreme offer may generate an extreme offer in return, perhaps one that is even more extreme. Negotiators sometimes react emotionally to extreme opening positions, saying to themselves, "If they're going to play games, we'll show them *we* can play games too!" When this happens, there is so much difference between opening positions that it can take a great deal of effort and skill to find common ground. In fact, we've seen many negotiations fail because the parties couldn't move far enough from their opening positions to find the possible overlap in their bargaining ranges, even though there was overlap and a deal could have been made if they'd been able to find it.

• An extreme opener can be a drawback if you hope to have a good working relationship with the other party in the future. The premise in competition is that the relationship concerns are at best low and short term. But if you destroy the relationship completely with your opening position, then you may reach a deal, but it may be the only deal you do with this party. And often in business negotiations, you will find yourself negotiating competitively with suppliers, customers, employees, or others you think you will not see again but in fact may need to work with them in the future.[1]

GETTING BETTER INFORMATION AND SETTING THE TONE: WHO STARTS?

There are two good ways to determine what the right opening tone should be and how to make an opening offer: deciding who makes the first offer and asking questions.

Who Goes First?

The opening minutes of a negotiation often look like the opening minutes of a boxing match. The bell rings, the players come out of their corners, and each dances around a little bit, perhaps jabbing at the air, trying to decide how to strike the first punch. If I think I am strong, I can throw the first punch and hope to strike the other before he expects anything. However, I may want him to strike the first punch, because once he throws it, he may be a bit off-balance and I can hit back before he recovers.

Negotiation is the same way. The parties often begin with a lot of opening pleasantries. This can be over in thirty seconds or, in some major complex international transactions, extend over several days. Yet at some point, the negotiator must decide whether he is going to make the first offer or let the other side make the first offer. This often can be a dance in itself, as each party encourages the other to lay his cards on the table first.

Making the first move is significant for at least three reasons. First, it gives lots of information to the other side. The other learns whether you intend to be more aggressive or friendly and gets a chance to size up your offer against his own target and walkaway. Right away, he begins to get a sense of whether the two of you are likely to come to an easy agreement or are looking forward to a long, exhausting deliberation.

Second, once the other knows your opening offer, he can adjust his own opening offer to be more or less extreme than planned. Adjustment in private is much easier than adjustment in public. If you have already made a public opening offer and find it is too extreme, you will have to publicly back up and propose a more conservative opening, but you risk confusing or angering the other side. If you have not made an opening offer, nobody will know if you changed it at the last minute.

Finally, when the other party adjusts his opening offer, he is also likely to be adjusting where the parties are most likely to settle. There is a subtle, unspoken but very important negotiation principle at stake here: once opening offers have been made, negotiators tend to believe that a likely settlement is in the middle of their two opening offers. If the buyer quotes $4,000 for the car and the seller counteroffers at $3,400, both parties are likely to look at $3,700 as a reasonable settlement (assuming that number is not too far away from the earlier planned target). Often, many negotiations are no more than a 1–2–3 deal: (1) you make an offer, (2) I make a counteroffer, and (3) one of us says something like, "Let's just split the difference." The negotiation is over.

Thus, deciding who goes first may be a critical part of an opening move. In general, you should let the other side go first if:

- This is unfamiliar negotiating territory. You have never negotiated for this before.
- You don't know much about the expectations of those on the other side or what they will see as a fair opening or settlement.
- You are not sure whether your opening offer will look reasonable or extreme to the other.

- You want to be able to adjust your opening based on what the other side tells you.

In contrast, there may definitely be times when you should go first:

- You have done a lot of negotiating for these items before and know what a fair settlement would be.
- You know your opponent well and how he is likely to respond.
- You want to convey that you are strong, in charge, and know exactly what you want.

Ask Questions

If you are uncertain about the other side, another strategy is to ask lots of questions. Start out by getting to know them: who they are, their background, and their experience. Have an informal meal together. Visit them on their turf, where they are usually more comfortable and at ease. (There are huge cultural differences in this behavior. Americans want to sit down and do the deal early; negotiators from other cultures, particularly Asia, are much more likely to do extensive relationship building before negotiations ever begin.) And once they begin to warm up to you and you get to know each other, you can ask more specific questions about their objectives in the negotiation—what they hope to get, what they think would be a fair and reasonable settlement, and other matters.

THE GOAL: STRENGTH WITH CIVILITY

A civil relationship is necessary in order to proceed, so your opener must not insult the other players. Since the extreme offer can be problematic, you should use it only if you also have a good alternative *and* you feel it is important to signal to an especially tough or problematic competitor that you aren't going to be easy to push around.

So what is the ideal way to set an opening offer? If you lack specific information about what those on the other side are likely to settle for, try to find the strongest opening offer you can make that falls just under the civility line. In other words, it does not quite qualify as extreme, but it is clearly a firm opening position. The reason to use as strong an offer as you can without seeming extreme is that, lacking clear intelligence about the other side's likely closing position, you will need to explore their bargaining range and discover their issues and interests as you negotiate. And that's easier to do when you have plenty of wiggle room in the bargaining range (by *wiggle room*, we are referring to the amount of room you have to move between your opening offer and walkaway).

But if you have good intelligence about the other party's viewpoint and bargaining range, then it may be better to open with a more moderate position. This signals that you will be fairly easy to work with, and it can set the stage for a fairly easy negotiation that moves toward the expected closing point efficiently and without a lot of play acting, delays, or tough tactics. In dealing with a long-term supplier, for example, you probably know roughly what the supplier can and can't afford to offer you for pricing. If you open the negotiation by demanding a 50 percent reduction in prices across the board, the supplier's representatives will think you are crazy and may begin looking hard for another company to sell those products to instead of you. Let's assume it truly is necessary to ask them to give you a price cut. If you start by asking for 7 percent instead of 50 percent, you are more likely to win the 5 percent discount you want and not to sour the relationship too much in the process.

SETTING A TONE TO ESTABLISH BEHAVIOR NORMS

Your opening offer, and the comments you make with it, sets the tone for their negotiations as well as yours. The other party's behavior will frequently mirror yours, so if you set up an adversarial situation at the outset, then the other party may expect to fight on each point of the negotiation. Both sides' behavior may become belligerent. We've even seen parties take back their opening positions and shift to even more extreme positions because the other's opening tone was so unfriendly that they became angry. If the tone is too competitive, it's possible to get caught up in the competition and move further apart instead of closer together.

A civil opening stance can result in the other party's having more reasonable expectations, which may lead to reasonable concessions and compromises. Remember that your goal is to set them up for movement, not send them off to bring back the heavy artillery. Strength and flexibility need to go hand in hand in negotiating. Set a tone that suggests you are strong and firm in representing your needs, but also flexible and reasonable enough to work with the others.

You cannot establish behavior norms for the negotiation if your tone and style are inconsistent at the opening. Consistency is perhaps the most important quality to convey as you seek to set the right tone. For example, if you try to make friendly, warm opening comments yet make an extreme opening offer, the other party will be confused. The same is true if you start out with a reasonable offer and then back up and take a tough stance. It's even more confusing if you make an outrageous offer at first and then quickly try to act compromising and reasonable. In any case, you appear inconsistent and untrustworthy, and the other side doesn't know how to act around you.

In our workshops and classes, people often ask which is more important in the opening stage: toughness or consistency. If you have the choice, we believe you are better off being consistent—whether consistently tough *or* flexible—than being erratic in your messages. Extreme toughness can sometimes produce better outcomes, but consistency in strategy more often helps your credibility with the other party and is a more reliable way to kick off a clean negotiation that actually gets you to the finish line in one piece. If you start off being tough, you probably need to stay tough unless that behavior produced such a negative response in the other that you decide to be more flexible—at the cost of consistency and therefore some of your credibility. Remember that many negotiations fall apart without resolution because the parties failed to build enough trust to negotiate effectively. Don't let your opening position and behavior set you up for failure.

THE CONCESSIONS

For the negotiation to proceed, a series of concessions must follow each side's opening. Concessions are trade-offs that a party is willing to make, usually with the expectation that the other side will respond in kind and in the same magnitude. For example, if you go up by a hundred dollars in your offer for a used car, the dealer may be willing to come down from the asking price by that same amount. But if you go up by only ten dollars, it is unlikely that the seller is going to come down by a hundred dollars.

Concessions are usually built in to the bargaining situation by the distance between your starting and ending points and those of the other party. There has to be enough space between your offer and the other's that each side can make some adjustments to their offer as they move toward their target. Or they may be moving not toward their concessions but toward the middle of the bargaining range set by their opening offers.

Let's return to the used car negotiations such as the one we described in the previous chapter. Assume that a seller has been running an ad for the car for over a month and is desperate to get rid of it. The buyer looks at the car and shows some interest in it. She says, "How much do you want for the car?" The seller, anxious to do anything to get rid of it, says, "How about $4,200?" The buyer now recognizes that while she set a target of $3,800 to buy the car, if she stays with her same planned opening offer of $3,000, the middle is now $3,600. So she might say something like, "Well, I was going to offer you $3,000, because that's all it's worth to me. But why don't we just split the difference at $3,600? Wouldn't that be fair?" (See Figure 5.1.) While the seller had hoped to get $4,000, he might, after a month of inquiring telephone calls and no sale, be willing to change his target and settle for the deal.

FIGURE 5.1. CAR BUYER'S AND SELLER'S OVERLAPPING BARGAINING RANGES

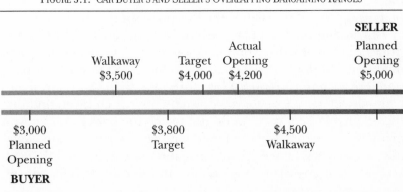

So far, we've stated the obvious about the need for traded concessions. But keep in mind that concessions affect not only the tangible outcomes but also the intangibles such as esteem or reputation. When you make a concession, you are acknowledging that the other party is a worthy opponent. Plan some concessions with these intangibles in mind. You want to make sure you give the other side some wins to go home with, even if you end up winning the overall negotiation. You don't want her to feel embarrassed for giving up too much, or looking weak, or not meeting her target. Even if the other is a weak and incompetent negotiator, never strip her of everything she might give up in the heat of deliberations.

In addition to planning concessions for the sake of the other side's pride and reputation, you may need to plan ways to maintain your own reputation and image. For instance, if you make a concession and the other party either does not make one or makes only a very small concession, you may lose face and thus appear to be the weaker party, particularly to your constituency. The intangibles—your reputation and image—thus figure in the negotiations prominently, particularly when constituencies are present. This means you have to plan some concessions the other side can make for you, as well as vice versa. For example, if you are renegotiating a contract with a large, powerful customer and you know she is going to beat you up for a discount, what can you plan for her to give you in return? Without something to show for the negotiations, your own constituency (your boss, for instance) may not believe you negotiated well. You might want to feel her out in advance to see if she would be open to lending you technical experts to help your company reduce production costs, for example. If so, then you can emerge from the negotiation with this compensating benefit to balance the loss on pricing.

If you don't have much flexibility on your main issue (such as price), then make sure you build something else into your opening offer that does allow her room to move you toward her position. For example, ask for a lot more time than you really need, and then let her negotiate you down on timing. Or if you find that the other side's concessions do not match the ones you offer, you may want to negotiate about how concessions are made. For example, you may say, "I need you to give me some indication that you are willing to negotiate in good faith by indicating where concessions may be possible." Or you can link concessions together: "If you agree to throw in that roof rack for the car, I'd be willing to offer you another two hundred dollars." Another approach is to package concessions: "I will do A and B if you do C and D."

PACKAGING CONCESSIONS

We have been talking about negotiating on a single issue of price, but in many negotiations, there is more than one issue. For example, on the car negotiation, you might also want to buy a custom luggage rack that fits the car, or extra tires, or see that a critical repair is made before you take possession of the car, or even make sure it has a fresh oil change or a full tank of gas.

On each of these issues, you might have your own opening point, target, and walkaway. The opening might be to throw the luggage rack in for free, the target might be to pay an extra hundred dollars for it, and the walkaway might be to simply have the opportunity to buy it at fair used value rather than have to buy a new one. Very competitive negotiators tend to negotiate one issue at a time; they push to get the best deal possible on each issue and then move on to the next issue. More talented and cooperative negotiators seek to package these issues together, because what is most important is the whole deal, not the best deal on each item.

This is even more true because it is common for parties to have different priorities on which issue is more important. Moreover, they often don't discover that they have different priorities because competitive assumptions lead us to believe that we have the same but opposing priorities. Discovering those priorities might be the most important piece of information gathering you can get about the other party. For example, suppose that you are interested in this car specifically because it has the luggage rack. You take long trips in the summer and know that a new rack is expensive. In contrast, suppose that the seller really wants to get a good deal on the car and is willing to throw in the luggage rack just to get it out of the garage. If the parties package their concessions, we have the seeds of a productive negotiation. The seller offers the car. He also asks why you are interested in buying it. You say you need a car with a luggage rack. The seller says he would be happy to throw the rack in as long as he gets a good price on the car. Now you can justify paying a little more than you might for a car without a rack, and the viable bargaining range may actually increase.

Always try to identify all the issues that are important and to package concessions together to get the best deal on everything. We'll say more about this later.

DO YOU SEE A PATTERN TO THEIR CONCESSIONS?

Competitive strategists can learn a lot about the progress of the negotiations by looking at the pattern of concessions. In general, negotiators begin by making large concessions and then making smaller ones as they get closer to their target point and even smaller as they get closer to their walkaway point. So keep a close eye on the other party's pattern and take note when the concessions begin to shrink. This probably signals that you are approaching the target. If concessions then become very small or are difficult to win at all, you can infer the other side is past her target and near her walkaway. You may need to shift and start working on another dimension of the negotiation in order to get much more movement from her. But be careful because she might be bluffing. Some negotiators actually shrink their concessions early just to see if they can fool you into thinking you've reached their limit before you really have. Try to do some outside research about their target and walkaway, so that you can call their bluff if you think they are locking up too soon.

Also, plan your own concessions with the goal of reducing their size each time. Don't start with a small concession and then make a big one, or the other party will be confused and think that you are now a lot more flexible than you were at first. She will want to see significantly more movement in order to be sure she is close to the limit of your range. A better tactic is to walk her toward your limit in an orderly way, with smaller steps each time, so that she is more confident she has negotiated hard and gotten most of what she can from you. Be careful not to run out of room for significant concessions too soon. You want to reduce the size of each concession in a gradual manner, not too quickly. As a general rule, if you can make the first concession to be about 35 to 50 percent of the distance from your opening to your target and then cut that amount in half for each subsequent concession (40 percent, then

20 percent, then 10 percent), you're likely to send a clear message to the other side. But as we describe below, this is not the only thing that determines where you ultimately settle.

When you plan your concessions, remember to leave room for a final concession to use as an incentive to close the deal. Often it takes one more concession (sometimes a small one just to indicate good faith) before the other party feels ready to close. If you've run out of bargaining room before the end, then you won't be able to make this good-faith final concession without imposing unacceptable costs on your side. To avoid this situation, you may find it helpful to save one small concession for the last round. Then you have something to use when you think the other player needs a final incentive to close the deal.

If the other side doesn't need the extra incentive of your final concession, then keep it in your pocket. It's a little extra profit you didn't need but are happy to walk away with. Otherwise, go ahead and spend that final concession to close your deal. As the old saying goes, "For want of a nail, the shoe was lost, for want of a shoe, the horse was lost." Don't lose the battle and the war by forgetting to save a little something for your final concession.

Dealing with Irregular Concessions

If the size of the other party's concessions varies—first large, then small, then large again—it may be hard to discern what is happening. Watch for behavioral clues from the other party. Maybe he is an inexperienced negotiator, struggling to gain enough confidence to close a deal. Or maybe he is getting pressure from a constituent—some boss or authority away from the table—who wants him to be tougher than he wants to be. If you can sleuth out the reason behind his inconsistent concessions, you may gain insight into what it will take to close this deal. And if you can't figure out why the other party is making irregular concessions, you can try asking him what he is doing. There's no harm in saying, "I'm confused by your behavior. I can't see any consistency to your pattern of offers. Can you help me out here? What's going on?" If he didn't mean to act in a confusing manner, he will probably be willing to answer your question fairly honestly, and his pattern may become more consistent in the future. If he was trying to confuse you or throw you off-balance, he will duck the question or simply deny it. There may be times when you want to confuse your opponent, and this is certainly one way to do it. We'll say more about these tactics later in this chapter.

When might opponents want to confuse you by making irregular concessions? If they think that they may be able to develop a good alternative and want to delay the negotiation, confusing you is sometimes an effective way to buy time. Could this be their motive? You may be able to find out by trying to push up the agenda. If they resist strongly, you can guess they are playing for time. You may not be able to do anything about it, but you can try to wrestle a concession from them in exchange for giving them more time. Or you can simply give them a time-sensitive ultimatum and try to close the deal before they have the time to develop their alternative.

Sometimes opponents act inconsistently in order to create confusion and internal argument on your side. They may think that by appearing confused, they will generate confusion and internal disagreement on your side that may lead you or your constituents to likely give in, release information, or let your guard down. Years ago, the actor Peter Falk played a well-known television detective, "Columbo," who appeared to be a disheveled, bumbling, and disorganized investigator. Columbo was able to gain a great deal of information from people because they let their defenses down, thinking he was disorganized and incompetent. Some skilled negotiators play Columbo pretty well. Don't assume that because they look disorganized or behave erratically, it is an accident. It might be a carefully planned strategy.

There is generally a point of no return beyond which the other party has nothing left to concede (get enough concessions, and you reach this person's BATNA). However, the other party may try to convince you that she can't make any more concessions, when she really can. You have to decide whether this message is true or just an effort to have you, not her, make the concessions. Take time to think each concession through rather than reacting quickly or emotionally. If you contemplate her behavior, you can usually figure out when she is bluffing or being dishonest. Give yourself time to think it through objectively before reacting.

Rules of Thumb for Your Competitive Negotiation

Once you get past the opening offers or demands of each side and into a pattern of concessions, any number of things can happen. So from this point, it is a bit more difficult to state exactly what will happen next. If you follow these rules of thumb, you should be able to plot a successful course through the dangerous middle ground of a competitive negotiation:

- *Stick to your planned target and walkaway points.* Try not to be manipulated by the other party. Watch out for the tendency to find a midpoint between the other party's asking price and your first offer and to settle there too quickly. Once both sides have stated their opening, there is a tendency to jump to the middle of those two points and offer a settlement. Don't agree to split the difference unless it is really close to your target (or better). Stick to your planned goals. Remember that you can usually make a better deal if you make more concession moves but smaller in magnitude.

- *Do not reveal your target until you are close.* Provide minimal information to the other party about your real target point. If you let your target point be known, you will be open to manipulation, particularly if you think you can do better than your target point. So reveal your target point only if you can't possibly do better.

- *Never reveal your walkaway point.* Never let opponents know your limits. If you do, they will immediately try to settle as close to your walkaway point as possible. Even worse, they may assume that this was a bluff and try to get you to take a deal less than your walkaway point. Tell them as little as possible about your walkaway even if they keep asking you questions about how far you are willing to go. It's perfectly acceptable to ignore a question like this and refuse to answer, or to respond with a question of your own. Never reveal your walkaway point. Don't even allow yourself to get drawn into any form of discussion about it. And if they are actually at or below your walkway point, don't be afraid to get up and leave the room.

- *Get the other party to make big concessions.* If you believe that the pie is limited in size, then you want to get as much of it as you can while allowing the other side to get as little of it as possible. Keep trying to persuade him that it is up to him to make big moves in his position. Once the range has been set by opening offers, convince him that your target is close and he will have to come to you. Master negotiators are adept at making a smaller concession of their own appear to balance a bigger concession from the other side. Act as if your small concession costs you dearly. Act as if the other side's first concession is so minor you're not sure if this person is serious about negotiating. Always work to make an imbalance in concessions seem balanced to the other party. Or you can package your concession with a token offer on another issue to make the overall package look better.

• *Keep your concessions few, slow, and small.* When you have to give in, do so in small increments, one item at a time. Be patient, and remember that time is on your side. Most negotiators dislike the ambiguity and uncertainty of the middle part of a negotiation and rush their concessions to try to get through to the firmer ground of the end stage. Be patient and wait them out; they may make extra concessions just to make themselves feel better about the pace of the negotiation. (One master negotiator we know likes to give the other party the impression that the negotiation is stalled. The other party constantly struggles to restart the negotiation, not realizing that his impatience is being used against him.)

• *Investigate the other party's level of concern for the outcome, other issues, and his or her costs of ending negotiation.* You may learn this through direct information—for example, if a company claims it cannot withstand a strike. And you may learn it through observing the behavior of those on the other side—for example, if they push to settle quickly. Try to find out whether there are other issues that are important to them. To learn about their concerns while masking your own, ask them questions, but try to deflect their questions to you. Their information can be extremely useful in planning your tactics; we'll offer more on your tactics later in this chapter. For now, keep asking questions, and answer many of the questions posed to you with your own questions.

In the middle part of the negotiation, you want to acquire more information about those on the other side than they do about you. Keep them talking. Sometimes we divide our workshop participants into negotiators and observers and ask the observers to note which side in a role play talks more. Invariably, this more talkative side loses more ground because they have given away too much information, or they fill in silences by talking more rather than listening. Be the strong, silent negotiator who gets the other side talking. Don't be the talkative party who fills the silence just to try to make things more comfortable for you. Learn to like silence, not fear it.

COMMITMENT

How do you know if the other party is committed to closing the deal? How does he or she know if you are committed? This is one of the greatest areas of uncertainty, so give it close attention.

COMMITMENT SIGNALS

One of us (Alex) recently negotiated a very good deal on a contract with a Web service provider. He did it by accident. It happened like this. He came across a Web company that he thought might be a good marketing partner for his business and e-mailed them to find out about their interest in working together. They were interested but wanted a fairly high price. Alex at first said he'd probably be willing to work with them, then got distracted and forgot about it for a couple of weeks. Meanwhile, they assumed he was stalling to get a better deal and made him a time-contingent offer: a 15 percent lower price if he signed by the end of the week. But Alex had just left on a demanding business trip and didn't have time to think about their offer, so the deadline came and went. When he finally recontacted them, they were worried he was not committed and made an even better offer, which he accepted. He might have been willing to work with them at a higher price, in fact. His delays had been due to his busy schedule more than any definite unhappiness with their offers. But they didn't know that and in essence negotiated against themselves. They were filling the silence, to Alex's benefit.

In competitive negotiations, you cannot always be certain about the other player's level of commitment. Sometimes people will just shrug and walk away from a negotiation because they don't like it or feel it is becoming too costly or emotionally stressful. Or they may simply be too busy worrying about another matter to focus on the negotiation now.

Sometimes negotiators send messages about their commitment level in order to signal a lack of commitment so the other party feels obliged to make big concessions in order to make the deal more attractive. You might want to try this ploy, but be careful not to act so disinterested that the other side gives up on you.

Someone who says, "If you do this, then I will do that," is actually giving you a message about commitment level. She is committed to the reciprocation of concessions she described. Now you know what she will do in response to your move. This information is helpful; it allows you to anticipate what you'll get from her.

If you think she is unclear about your commitment level, you might want to give some signals to help clarify your level of commitment. Or you might want to use commitment signals to keep her from knowing how committed you are; if she senses you are determined to close a deal, she may ask for larger concessions than if she feels your commitment is more moderate.

Two Kinds of Commitments

There are two kinds of commitment statements: threats and promises. A threat specifically states what will happen if the other does not do what you want—for example, "If you do not do this, I will do that." This sort of statement puts the other party on the defensive while clearly establishing your commitment. Your own esteem and need to maintain credibility (that you do what you say you will do), coupled with public pressure, can be strong motivators to make good on such a statement. In contrast, a promise is, "If you do this, I will do that." Since you are usually offering to do something good for the other, promises are more likely to help the other party open up and make him or her less defensive.

Like threats, however, promises can cause problems, particularly with credibility. Just as with a threat, you may get stuck with a promise and actually have to deliver on the terms, which may put you in a difficult position. If you promise your team that you will take them on a trip if they complete the project ahead of schedule, you will have to follow through on your promise should they succeed—or risk losing your credibility when you try to make any further promises.

Both types of commitments—promises and threats—decrease your flexibility but enhance the likelihood that the other party will give you what you want. If you decide that a commitment statement would help your position, make it. To have it carry more weight, make it public. State it in front of several people or a group to make it public. To add support to your statement, find allies who will back you on it. But before you decide what commitment statement to make, be sure that you can carry it out.

All commitment statements should be carefully planned in advance. Never make one off the cuff in a negotiation. And make sure you tell any associates this rule too. You don't want someone else committing your side to an unplanned promise or threat.

Avoiding Commitment Gridlock

If you make a bold promise or threat, the other party may retaliate with a similar commitment. Or you may be tempted to respond to your competitor's threat with one of your own: "If you do A, I'll do B." "Oh yeah? Well if you do B or C, I'll do D."

The trouble with this type of exchange is that it quickly escalates and locks the players into corners. In these situations, both sides are usually declaring that they are committed to following through on their statements and unwilling to change their intentions. And if both sides become entrenched in their commitments, neither may feel able to back down. In this situation, the negotiation is likely to stall or fail. So be careful with commitment statements, whether threats or promises. It's best not to say too much about what you plan to do, since you may want to change your mind later.

A Word of Caution About "Final" Offers

A final offer is a form of commitment. It is a declaration that one party has made all the concessions it is going to make, and it is up to the other side to make the rest of the movement to close the gap. The problem, of course, is that once you've said an offer is your final one, you can't very well make another offer without weakening your side significantly. So be cautious about declaring something your final offer. Often it is best to wait for the other party to make this commitment instead of doing it yourself.

It is usually pretty obvious when the other party has made a final offer. Often this is stated explicitly: "This is our final offer." They may include with the final offer a concession of fair size, because it is a common practice to save one concession until the end. Your decision now is whether to give in and move to that point, or make a final offer of your own and hope that they will decide to make more concessions.

It is not uncommon for two negotiators to make concessions that cover 95 percent of the distance between their opening moves, only to deadlock with final offers that leave the remaining 5 percent on the table. Yet 5 percent is usually not a deal killer; in fact, in the majority of negotiations, there is enough left on the table for each party to move 2 or 3 percent without suffering any great harm. So why do deals fall apart when the parties are this close? Their commitment signals have locked them into the final positions, and they don't feel they can close the remaining distance without losing face (to their constituents), losing credibility (they said their offer was final, and now it is not), or looking or feeling like the loser. Don't get trapped by your commitments if the deal is that close to done. There are always graceful ways to get out of a prior commitment.

HOW TO GET OUT OF A COMMITMENT

Since commitments decrease your flexibility, you may need some sort of escape hatch or alternate plan to get out of such a commitment. Having committed yourself, what do you do if you need to get out of it? Here are several ways:

- Say that the situation has changed or you have new information. Today is not the same situation as yesterday; something has changed that makes the commitment no longer relevant.
- Let the commitment die quietly by never mentioning it again.
- Modify your commitment, for instance, by changing the statement to more general terms. You might be able to say, "What you heard me say is that I would never take that offer. What I

meant is that I would never take that offer packaged with all those other conditions; if we can change the conditions, the offer might be acceptable."

To plan ahead, always phrase commitments with a back door so that you can modify them later. Choose the language of your commitments carefully so that there are escape clauses in your words—for example, "Under these conditions, this has to be our final offer." Conditions can change.

How to Help the Other Party Save Face

If those on the other side made a commitment that they now need to abandon, it is usually an astute move on your part to help them save face. This is where you will need to be less competitive than you might expect. If you keep the pressure on them, they are likely to either lock in to their unreasonable position and refuse to budge, or they will feel so embarrassed that they may plot to get even with you later.

Instead, we recommend that you help them save face. You might allow them to change their offer, find a way for them to be flexible without looking foolish, say that this is being done "for the greater good," or make some other generous and supportive statement. If constituencies are involved, you might actively compliment them so that their constituency can overhear.

The simplest thing to do is to act as if there was no prior commitment on their part. Don't mention it again. If they are smart, they'll take your lead and let it fade away.

How to Play Hardball

Playing the tough guy, starting out with an extreme offer, refusing to make concessions, making tough demands, and making final offers are examples of hardball tactics. They are calculated to put pressure on the other party. And they work especially well against anyone who is poorly prepared.

If the negotiation isn't going your way and you are close to walking away, what can you lose by playing hardball? Maybe the other party will back down and you'll salvage the deal. But other parties also can be moved to revenge by your aggressive play. Then the negotiations become a series of hardball moves and counter-moves, all of which may be unproductive or time-consuming. And there are other risks associated with hardball tactics too: loss of a good reputation, negative publicity, loss of the deal, wasting a lot of time, becoming the brunt of the other party's anger about what has happened, and souring the likelihood of any future deals.

With that warning, we want to take a look at some of the classic hardball tactics. You should learn these even if you don't plan to use them, since you may well have to defend against them in a future negotiation. And there will certainly be times when you feel it's worth the risk to initiate a hardball tactic.

Hardball tactics fall into two categories: deceptive and not deceptive.

Tactics That Are Not Deceptive

The following three tactics help win a competitive negotiation without deceit. Although they are focused on the outcome, they don't do any damage to the relationship or hurt the trust between the parties, which means they are useful in long-term business relationships with employers, associates, suppliers, and customers.

Helping the Other Party

Here's a useful tactic from sales expert Kathy Aaronson:

> Say you start a job in which you are promised a salary review and the opportunity to make another $1,000 a month after six months on the job. You go into your manager's office and say, "Well, it's my six-month anniversary. Could we please discuss my salary review?"
>
> He says, "I just don't have time now, but I'll get back to you shortly."
>
> A week goes by, and he says, "Give me ten days—I'm going out of town." Now you're over the moon with frustration, because you've been delayed.
>
> When people delay, they frequently need more information to get them unstuck: with all the necessary information before them, it will be more difficult to justify a delay.

> My suggestion [is] . . . to go back into the manager's office and
> say, "I have a feeling you've been delaying because you need more
> information from me."

Aaronson recommends preparing an analysis and presenting
it in table or grid form in order to give your boss the information
needed to justify your raise. If you can show that you've brought in
a high volume of business and that the company is profiting from
your work, then it is far easier for your boss and the company to
justify that raise. But why should your boss do that analysis? You're
the one who cares the most, so you should do the work. Then
Aaronson recommends giving the information to your boss: "Give
your supervisor a copy of this material and say, 'I know you have to
go through channels, so you could just attach a memorandum to
this if you like.' You have empowered him with information."[2]

It's a good strategy not just for this situation but for any other
situation in which you think you can build a good, rational argument for your cause using objective information.

Shutting Up to Get What You Want

You can't give anything away if you don't talk. In fact, how much
you give away is generally proportional to how much you talk. That
means that all other things being equal, the one who talks the most
loses. (All other things never are equal, but we hope you get the
point.)

So why is it so hard to shut up and listen in a negotiation?

It isn't hard for everybody. Many Japanese negotiators are comfortable with long periods of silence, a cultural difference that gives
them a natural edge over more talkative Americans. (Stop reading
here for a minute and just listen to the silence around you.) But
most people are tempted to fill the void. Remember the boss in
the opening story to Chapter Four who was so uncomfortable with
the silence that he started babbling during a key contract negotiation? You could eat a negotiator like him for breakfast by using
the silent treatment.

Leave a thoughtful gap in the conversation, and many negotiators will fill it with their thoughts. You might get an extra concession. You will probably hear some useful information they
shouldn't have shared with you. Whatever you hear, it is likely to

help you understand the other party and design your next move. And even if you hear nothing of value, you can still have the satisfaction of knowing that by being quiet, you gave away nothing of value.

Asking Questions and Then Shutting Up

Here's a variant on the previous tactic that works well when you need more information. Use silence to bracket a question, focusing the attention of the other party on a topic of your choice. All you need to do is to be quiet for a moment, then ask a question, and then wait silently for an answer or (often) a string of answers as the other player fills the silence.

TACTICS THAT ARE DECEPTIVE

Many people think you have to be deceptive to win a competitive negotiation. In fact, that is usually untrue, and we do not recommend a deceptive approach, by and large. But sometimes negotiators will use deceptive tactics on you, so even if you do not use them yourself, you need to bone up on them and know them when you see them.

Good Cop–Bad Cop Tactic

Sometimes negotiators use the "good cop–bad cop" tactic effectively in negotiations.[3] This is a clever way to use the consistency/inconsistency process we discussed earlier. We have all seen this tactic in cop or lawyer movies, where two investigators are questioning a suspect. First, the "bad cop" leans heavily on the suspect, acting belligerent and aggressive, pushing him or her to the limits. When the "bad cop" gets exasperated and storms out of the room, the "good cop" takes over, trying to persuade the suspect to confess before the bad cop comes back.

In negotiation, the job of the good guy is to try to cut a deal with the suspect, threatening to bring the bad guy back if no deal can be had. A variation on this theme is for the bad guy to talk only when the negotiations are faltering—to "soften the other up"—and the good guy to take over when things are progressing smoothly. The disadvantages of this tactic are that (1) it is sometimes obvious to the knowledgeable observer, (2) the bad guy alienates the other party, and (3) energy is spent on the tactic rather than on the negotiations. Nonetheless, it can be quite effective, especially if there really is a plausible bad guy on your side. We've seen it used to great effect by tough company owners who put a more friendly, junior manager in front of them to negotiate a deal, then storm in and act the tough guy role periodically to give the junior negotiator some tactical support. If you are, or have, an executive who sometimes acts the prima donna role, put him or her to good use by using this tactic in a hardball negotiation. People do accommodate the behavior of senior executives to a surprising degree.

The Highball-Lowball Tactic

The point of this tactic is to make a ridiculous first offer, either very low or very high, depending on the situation. The intent is to get the other party to reassess the opening offer or target, making them think there is no way they can reach their goal or to assume that if they are going to do business with you, they are going to have to improve their offer significantly. It also might work if the other party has been trying to do a deal for a long time or has no alternative deals available. For example, a company that thinks it is a very desirable place to work may make a lowball salary offer to a potential new recruit who is fresh out of college and desperate to start paying off student loans. If the student has no other job offers, she might take the offer rather than go unemployed any longer.

If someone is selling a used computer and the buyer counteroffers at one-third of what the seller has asked, the seller who hasn't done his homework may very well think that either he didn't set his price very well or that this is a fair offer and he needs to accept it. Or the seller may simply end the negotiations, thinking that there is no possible overlap. A skilled competitor may be able to turn the situation around and get the negotiations moving again, but there can be residual bad feelings that will be hard to counteract. So be careful with this tactic. Use it to exploit uncertainty, but avoid it if the other party is likely to see through it or will use it as a way to get even in the future.

The Straw Man

In this tactic, you pretend that an issue is important when it really is not, then trade it off later in the negotiations for something that really is important. (Some negotiators call it a bogey issue.)

To use the straw man, or bogey, you need to know the priorities of the other party. For example, if price is the most important element in a sale and a good warranty is a second concern, you may make some outrageous demands on the warranty (which you know you will not get) and then offer big concessions on the price instead.

In addition, you have to pretend that something is very important when it is not, and this can be difficult and confusing—and dishonest, because it is not really true. If the other side is employing the same tactic, it may be impossible to sort out what is being negotiated or who really wants what.

The Nibble

In this ploy, you wait until the end of the proceedings when everything is almost decided and then ask for something new. Just before the deal is ready to be signed, you try to press for one more concession: "Oh, gosh, I forgot to mention. Can you have this ready for me to pick up in three hours?" The other party is now faced with the thought of aborting the entire deal over one more small concession; as a result, it often gives in to the nibble rather than lose the entire deal.

Sometimes forgetfulness is sufficient excuse; other times you need to get more creative and invent a boss or other constituent who has just e-mailed you with a new request or some other ploy. Plan your nibbles as carefully as your opening position; they are risky and need to be pursued with care.

The art of the nibble is to make it seem innocent. If those on the other side think you are trying to close the deal but just ran into a small problem at your end that they need to help you with, you're golden. If they think you held out and are now trying to take advantage of them, you're in trouble. The nibble usually works unless those on the other side feel they are being nibbled on purpose, in which case they will resent it and may try to go back on some of their earlier concessions.

Playing Chicken

Chicken is a familiar negotiating game. It is similar to the driving game in which two teenaged drivers race directly at each other, each driver waiting for the other to chicken out and turn away. Needless to say, any negotiating strategy modeled on a dangerous adolescent driving game is going to have some risks to it, although countries have often been known to play the game with nuclear missiles.

Chicken is used in competitive negotiation by bluffing and threatening in order to get what you want. The objective is to hold your ground and intimidate the other party into giving way so you can win, or create some action that will ensure mutual destruction. For example, you might make an extreme promise or threat and then wait out the other party, hoping your competitor will chicken out and cave in with a huge concession.

The problems with this strategy are that it has very high stakes, and you must be willing to follow through on your threat. Escalation of war between countries is often the direct result of a game of chicken. But you don't have an army or the power to raise taxes in order to fund one, so you need to be careful with this tactic. Many union negotiators have backed the union into a costly strike by playing chicken and then having their bluff called. And many employers have pushed a union into going out on strike by playing chicken when a more cautious negotiating strategy would have been more prudent. Think about the potential downside of a failed negotiation before you decide whether to play chicken. If the downside could be costly, avoid this high-risk strategy.

HARNESSING THE POWER OF INTIMIDATION AND COERCION

Some negotiators behave aggressively in an effort to intimidate or otherwise coerce the other players. This is an option for you too, but it's a difficult one to pull off. Let's take a close look at ways to use coercion in a competitive negotiation.

Many intimidation ploys can be used to force an agreement in competitive negotiation. One is anger—real or feigned. Another is the use of formal documents such as contracts that force certain responses or postures. Yet another is to press someone to do something by appealing to his or her sense of guilt. Aggressive behaviors such as being pushy, attacking the other person's view, or asking for explanations of positions can also be used to coerce the other party.

Coercive tactics add up to a style of negotiating that the other players will probably find offensive. If intimidated, they may be caught off guard and give up more than they meant to. Or they may become angry and respond with unreasonable demands. Or they may decide they dislike your style so much that they withdraw from the negotiation, preventing you from achieving any outcome. We don't recommend casual use of these tactics because they backfire so often. But we have to admit that some negotiators are masters of using them. We know some contract lawyers who use intimidation to tip the balance in their client's favor, for example. They are expert at coercive tactics and present such an intimidating demeanor that they are genuinely intimidating to just about everyone who comes in contact with them.

One of the safer coercive tactics is to act upset with the other party. It's relatively safe because if it is done appropriately, the other party usually blames themselves rather than you for your behavior. Use this tactic when there is reasonable ground for being upset, such as when the other party has taken back a concession or acted inconsistently or impolitely. You may actually be somewhat upset. Exaggerate those feelings to give the impression you are upset enough you might walk away. Then withdraw (avoid communicating for a little while) and see what response you get. Often the other party will signal continued commitment by reaching out with a concession or even an apology. As this person works to rebuild the negotiating relationship, you can probably gain a small additional advantage by tipping the balance of concessions more in your direction. It's manipulative, it's coercive, and you didn't hear it from us. But sometimes it works.

TACTICAL USES OF TIME

One of the things we emphasize in our workshops is to always think about tactical uses of time. Negotiations take place over time, and you should always be mindful of how time can work to your advantage—or to that of the other side.

Negotiations tend to occur within a fixed time period. In fact, many people claim that deadlines are critical to negotiation because the looming deadline forces people to make concessions, fearing that time may run out before an agreement is reached. Thus, knowing what the deadline is, and who has a greater need to meet the deadline, can become an extremely useful tool in a competitive negotiation.

There are many ways to use deadlines, scheduling, and delays in competitive negotiations. In general, the principle is to create time pressures on the other party. The ways to do this are limited only by your imagination—for example:

• Scheduling can affect the outcome of negotiations, from the day of the week (Monday as opposed to Friday), to the hour of the day (early morning, late afternoon), to the final hour of a schedule. Play with scheduling, and try to be in control of it at all times. One way to do this is to always be assertive about the schedule, even when you don't really care. If you set the precedent that you are particular about scheduling, you may be able to take early and lasting control over this tactical element. So always take the initiative to define the schedule. And whenever you have the opportunity, put other negotiators on the defensive by requiring them to adjust their schedule.

• If a party has to travel some distance to the site of the negotiation, factors such as jet lag may affect how well the negotiations proceed. If a final negotiating session is scheduled for the hour before a party's plane departs, this may have a strong effect on the outcome. If you are the traveling party, be careful when you are setting up your flights and schedules to give yourself lots of flexibility. Don't be pressured into a deal just because you have to leave for the airport.

• In labor negotiations, there may be a pressing time schedule because labor is due to go out on strike at a particular hour or a plant is scheduled to close. The same holds for job offers or end-of-budget-cycle sales. You can take advantage of all these situations by manipulating the scheduling to affect the course and outcome of negotiations.

Delays can be a good ploy to force a concession or resolution, particularly if time is not essential for your side but is a strong concern for the other. Stalling and slowing the process gives you a

Some Thoughts on the Importance of Timing

After all, tomorrow is another day.—Scarlett O'Hara in *Gone with the Wind*

I have noticed that the people who are late are often so much jollier than the people who have to wait for them.—E. V. Lucas

Sources: These are Scarlett O'Hara's last words in the movie, *Gone with the Wind* (1939). E. V. Lucas, quoted in L. E. Boone, *Quotable Business* (New York: Random House, 1992), p. 22.

means for manipulating the other party. Not showing up on time, asking for a rehash of the proceedings, postponing a meeting, talking endlessly about issues, and other such maneuvers can be used to advantage as long as they do not result in the breakdown of negotiation.

Negotiating for time with your own side is a good idea if you are under pressure to close a deal soon. Explain to your boss or whoever else is concerned that you have to have time to close a favorable deal. And if you have to find a new office space, replace an old piece of equipment, or find a new accounting firm, start these projects early enough that you aren't under the gun when negotiating the price. Don't go into a negotiation with a feeling of urgency, or you'll emerge feeling like a loser.

MANAGE THE OTHER SIDE'S IMPRESSION OF YOUR CONCERNS

What does the other party think is your greatest concern? You know this person is wondering. But is it wise to let him or her know? If you reveal this information, he or she will no doubt push hardest for concessions in this area, sensing it's a point of weakness for you.

A good rule for competitive negotiations is to conceal your greatest concerns and divert attention to lesser concerns as you negotiate. For example, let's say you are negotiating for a new office space and you want to sign a short-term lease because your firm may move out of the downtown area in the next year or two. But you know that landlords usually favor tenants who are willing to sign a lease for several years or longer, and you worry that the this landlord will walk away if you bring up your desire for a shorter-term deal in the early stages of the negotiation. When he asks about it, you might say something like, "I agree we need to resolve the length of the lease before we can ink a deal, but it's not very important compared to the cost per square foot and what leasehold improvements are allowed, so I suggest we stay focused on those issues for now. Also, we're very concerned about the restrictions on signage. Can you tell me more about that?"

Magicians call this technique *misdirection*. They use it to distract their audience and to keep us from noticing the trick they are doing. Negotiators use misdirection to conceal their key issue while they gain concessions on other points and draw the other party further into a commitment to complete the deal. In the example of the negotiator who hopes to land a one-year lease from a landlord who usually requires three-year leases, the strategy might work if the landlord:

- Gets increasingly excited about the prospective new tenant and feels this business would be an ideal addition to the building
- Focuses on trying to close this lease and doesn't actively develop a better alternative tenant
- Wins concessions on pricing and other points that make the tenant seem desirable

As the deal begins to seem more attractive and the landlord is increasingly committed to closing it, the issue of length of lease may become more negotiable in the landlord's thinking. And the tenant can frame the request carefully when it is finally laid on the table to give the impression that there is a relatively low risk of nonrenewal at the end of the year. It's hard to get a landlord to agree to a short-term business lease, but this negotiator just might succeed with careful use of negotiating tactics. The trick no doubt will be to avoid giving the impression that this is the key issue. A landlord who knew that would quickly seek an alternative tenant who was more willing to make a long-term commitment.

You can manage the other player's view of where you stand and what you want out of the negotiation if you:

• Use body language or be emotional to convey your attitude, real or feigned. Make the other party think you are angry when you are not. Act concerned, nervous, or worried about a minor issue when he or she brings it up. Be casually dismissive or disinterested in your key issue if he or she tries to discuss it before you want to.

• Give the impression that you do not have the authority to make a decision. Use someone else as a team spokesperson, or use a lawyer or agent, or say that the boss has to approve everything. The other person may think the outcome is of less importance than it is.

• Bring up lots of items for negotiation, many of which are unimportant. Increase the "fog index" and confusion in the negotiation. Do not let the other side know which issues are important. This is often easy to do when negotiations are over technical or complex information or involve experts—accountants, lawyers, engineers—who are not good at explaining technical issues to laypeople.

• Present selectively. Give only the facts necessary to your point of view. This allows you to lead the other party to a particular conclusion.

• Misrepresent your information. In some cases, exaggeration and argument lead to outright distortions of facts and misrepresentation of issues. In the extreme, this is outright deception and lying. We are not advocating lying, but in competitive negotiations, there is a gray area in which you will be taken advantage of by others if you don't take advantage of it yourself.

• Make the costs of the negotiation seem higher. Manipulate facts and behavior to make the other party think the proceedings are more costly to you than they are.

• Manipulate the actual costs of delay or ending negotiation. This can be done by prolonging the negotiations, introducing other issues, or asking for other parties to be brought in.

• Conceal information. Omitting information pertinent to the negotiation can manipulate the outcome but may have dire results.

If you conceal important information, you may be engaging in fraudulent business behavior (which is illegal). Even if it doesn't rise to the level of illegality, your behavior may be sufficiently underhanded to ruin the business relationship and create animosity and distrust. Concealing information is therefore not a good strategy to use. But it's an important strategy to keep your eye out for. Many negotiators try to conceal information. If you catch them, act upset and leverage their improper behavior for all it's worth. You can probably win additional concessions from them.

• Use emotional tactics. Negotiators often try to manipulate the other party's emotions to distract them and get them to behave in a less rational manner. Get them angry or upset, flattered, or amused; then try to get concessions while they are not paying attention. Highly emotional ploys such as threatening to end the negotiations sometimes achieve your purposes. Another tactic is to appear angry when you are not to get them feeling contrite or guilty. Disruptive actions may have the desired effect but may escalate the emotional climate and thus block your efforts. Refusal to concede sets a tone for the proceedings. So does silence. Our point is that you need to be cautious in your use of emotional tactics. Don't do anything rash: it's all too easy to get burned by the backfire.

• Ally with outsiders. Political action groups, protest groups, the Better Business Bureau, and other supportive groups may be able to assist you in putting pressure on the other party for a resolution. Simply threatening to talk with such groups may prod the other party to action. But don't make hollow threats. Most business managers know that the Better Business Bureau of their area, if there even is one, doesn't have any teeth to regulate their behavior. Find an outsider who has some weight to throw around, and make sure you have a good reason for this person to take an interest in helping you before you approach him or her. It takes time, care, and good planning to develop allies useful in a negotiation.

COPING WITH TOUGH TACTICS

The best way to cope with competitive tactics is to be prepared. Know the various tactics, why they are used, and how they are used. Have a firm understanding of the other party's position, and keep in mind your own alternative. Also, don't get rattled into any thoughtless responses. Whatever the other party does, take time to consider it and develop your response.

Here are a number of specific ways to handle the other party's tactical moves:[4]

- Ignore them. Pretend you did not hear what was said; change the subject; call a break in the proceedings and when you come back, change topics. This is our favorite way to handle any tactic we don't like or think is overly coercive or tricky. It's amazing how often it works.
- Confront the issue. Discuss what is going on and what you see. Say something like, "I don't use the nibble tactic, and I don't want you to either. If you forgot about something while we were negotiating and you can't live without it, we'll just have to start all over again." (Negotiate about how you will negotiate. Suggest changes. This is easy if you remember to keep the people separate from the problem.)
- Retaliate. Respond in kind. This might escalate the emotions and result in hard feelings. However, it is often useful if you are being tested by the other party. For example, we tend to respond to an attempt to nibble by simply suggesting a couple of bigger nibbles of our own. In an innocent tone of voice, we say something like, "Oh, that reminds me: I promised so-and-so I'd ask you about [name your nibbles]. As long as we're revisiting things, you don't mind if we throw those in too, do you?" But you know full well they *do* mind, and so they may back down on their nibble rather than open the deal up to more concessions.
- Sidetrack it before it happens. For example, start the negotiations with a discussion of how the negotiations will be conducted. Offer to behave in a specific way, and ask the others to comply with your request. You can specifically rule out tactics you don't like. For example, you might say to a prospective employee, "I am going to answer all your questions about the company and the job offer as accurately and honestly as I can. I expect you to answer my questions about your qualifications and past work experiences accurately too, and not to leave out any relevant information that I ought to know about." Now the candidate can't as easily hide the fact he was fired from his last job.

Negotiate Slow, Close Fast

We've urged you to go slow in the middle part of the competitive negotiation and play for control of time to as great an extent as possible. Time is on your side if you are feeling more patient than they are, and time pressure is a great ally as you try to win concessions from them.

But if you move them to your targets and there is a good deal sitting on the table, don't be afraid to close it and move on. Many negotiators get pretty close to the deal they wanted, but start questioning the terms and wondering if they could win more concessions. So they leave the deal sitting there on the table for too long, and the other party loses patience or finds an alternative and walks.

The point is not to negotiate so hard that you win a permanent place in the negotiation hall of fame. The point is to see if you can negotiate a reasonable deal that you or your business can live with and profit from in the future. The deal is not the end in and of itself; it's a means to some business end. Close the deal, and get back to work. Nobody but the lawyers make money from negotiating. Wrap up the deal and go back to doing whatever you do to make money. At some point, you have to let go and stop negotiating, even if the deal is not perfect.

That's our "let's get on with it!" lecture. But we do need to introduce a note of caution too. If the deal is at all complicated or technical, get someone with the relevant technical skills to review the contract before you sign it. Often this means getting a legal opinion. If you haven't already run drafts by your lawyer, do so now. You want to make sure there isn't some mistake or hidden problem you hadn't noticed. But don't let your experts reopen the negotiation. Confine them to a safety check role and avoid needless rewriting. You don't want to create ill will by nibbling over minor things instead of inking the deal.

The exception is that if those on the other side suddenly say their lawyers are revising the contract, expect them to go another round. Bring your own lawyers in, and be prepared for some final-round game of hardball. Often in business, the managers "close" the deal and then let their lawyers negotiate it all over again. If this happens, there's nothing you can do to stop them. But you can hold them to the main points of the earlier agreement and refuse to make any major new concessions.

The other things we like to check before finalizing a contract or sale are ambiguity and omissions. Is there anything unclear or overlooked in the agreement? It's amazing how often conflicts arise later over something the negotiators forgot to discuss. For example, many business partners create detailed contracts describing how they will work together, but fail to include anything about how they will divide the assets and liabilities in the event that they decide to split up. So check for omissions and make sure everybody is clear on all the details and is interpreting the language the same way.

After these basic checks, go ahead and ink the deal. Your advance planning and clarity about your bargaining range should give you the confidence to know when the deal is a good one. By planning your bargaining range in advance, you have the ability to accept the terms without worrying about what might have been.

Notes

1. L. Putnam and T. S. Jones, "Reciprocity in Negotiations: An Analysis of Bargaining Interaction," *Communication Monographs*, 1982, *49*, 171–191, and G. Yukl, "Effects of the Opponent's Initial Offer, Concession Magnitude, and Concession Frequency on Bargaining Behavior," *Journal of Personality and Social Psychology*, 1974, *30*, 323–335.
2. K. Aaronson, *Selling on the Fast Track* (New York: Putnam, 1990).
3. Many of the tactics reviewed in this section are described more fully in G. Fuller, *The Negotiator's Handbook* (Upper Saddle River, N.J.: Prentice Hall, 1991), and other trade books on competitive negotiations. See also R. J. Lewicki, D. M. Saunders, and B. Barry, *Negotiation*, 5th ed. (Burr Ridge, Ill.: McGraw-Hill/Irwin, 2006).
4. R. Fisher, W. Ury, and B. Patton, *Getting to Yes: Negotiating Agreement Without Giving In*, 2nd ed. (New York: Penguin Books, 1991), and W. Ury, *Getting Past No: Negotiating with Difficult People* (New York: Bantam Books, 1991).

CHAPTER SIX

MASTERING THE ART OF COLLABORATION

Every now and then as we lead workshops, some grizzled veteran from the back row raises his hand and says, "I don't like the word *collaborate*. That's what they called the people who sold out during the war: collaborators." Well, you can't please everyone! Of course, those who remember serving in the last world war are not likely to be a party to your next business negotiation, since time does march on. But they have a point. Sometimes the word has a negative connotation. Real negotiators aren't supposed to collaborate; they are supposed to fight to the bitter end for what they want.[1]

We collaborate, and often. We're quite open and clear about it. Writing this book is a collaboration. Doing anything in business these days is a collaboration—between associates, department, divisions, companies, even nations. And collaborating is often the best way to handle differences and conflicts too. Here's why.

Collaboration, as it has evolved in the field of negotiation and conflict handling, brings problem solving into the conflict equation. It treats the conflict itself as a puzzle or problem and harnesses all the combined abilities of everyone involved to find a good way to solve the problem or crack the puzzle. As a result of this problem-solving orientation, collaboration often creates breakthrough solutions that make all parties happier than if they had competed, compromised, or walked away.

In addition, the problem solving of a good collaboration advances the business interests of the organizations touched by the conflict. Businesses grow through innovation, not stagnation or entrenchment. When the people working in an organization use a collaborative approach to problems, they come up with improvements and innovations more often and are held back by roadblocks less often. They do better, more innovative work, and create progress that translates into profits and other bottom-line benefits.[2]

ADVANCING YOUR INTERESTS BY THINKING ABOUT THE OTHER PARTY

A collaborative negotiation is one in which both parties consider the relationship and the outcome to be important and so work together to maximize both. To achieve the goal of collaborative problem solving, you need to put yourself in the other party's shoes and think about their problems as well as your own. This is quite a change from the competitive negotiation, where you try to exploit rather than solve the other side's problems.

The collaboration style is also referred to as cooperative or win-win because it permits both sides to achieve winning positions. By collaborating, you can put your energy into creative problem solving instead of into competitive tactics. And by so doing, you often find new ways to think about the conflict—ways that make it possible to replace trade-offs with mutually desirable outcomes.

CAN YOU ALIGN YOUR GOALS?

> Any kid will run an errand for you, if you ask at bedtime.—Red Skelton

In collaboration, the parties to the negotiation either begin with compatible goals or are willing to search for ways to align their goals so that both can gain (often by aligning underlying interests). This is in sharp contrast with competition, where the parties believe their goals are mutually exclusive, so that only one side can win.

Which view is right? Are conflicts either-or, or is it possible to reframe them so that everyone wins? Remember that in negotiations, you have the opportunity to decide what game you want to play. If you want a win-lose game, you'll get it. But if you want to seek win-win opportunities, you'll find them instead. Most conflicts of interest can be viewed from either perspective. But the collaborative perspective is often harder to see and so tends to go over-looked much of the time.

Negotiators usually assume that conflicts are more competitive than they really are. This is a strong, widespread bias. It's just some-thing that we human beings do. When we are in an interdepen-dent situation where conflict is possible, we tend to focus on the trade-offs[3] and the who-gets-what of the situation, to the exclusion of the collaborative win-win possibilities. Watch out for this bias. Don't let it blind you to the potential for productive and profitable collaboration.

How do you identify opportunities for profitable collaboration? First, you take a moment to ask yourself if there might be a bene-fit to collaborating. Perhaps there is some common ground, some grist for the collaborative problem-solving mill. Next, look for the more common sources of collaborative benefit. Here are some of the sources of value creation—things that can be turned into value for each side of the conflict if they collaborate instead of compete:

- If you have different interests from the other party, even slightly different, there may be ways to meet both sets of interests without a direct trade-off between what you get and what they get. For example, if you are negotiating a salary package with a new employee, you may view medical insurance and retirement bene-fits as the most costly to your company. But the new employee may view these as secondary and focus more on monthly take-home pay. This difference in how each side values different elements of the compensation package can lead to a win-win where each feels he or she has gotten a good deal. But this will happen only if both sides get to the point where they are talking openly about what they value, so they can explore the different possibilities together.
- There may be alternative ways to work together if you take the time to find out about each other's business interests. This too can be a source of ideas for win-win outcomes. For example, your business may be planning to get out of the warehousing and ship-ping sides of its business and outsource those. When you negoti-ate with your landlord to get out of your seven-year lease on warehouse space, the landlord is naturally disinclined to be help-ful. But what if you share your company's strategy and explain that you will be adding more office workers and a new, bigger

showroom? Perhaps the landlord has a building with retail show-room space plus offices and would be willing to let you out of the warehouse lease in exchange for signing a new lease. Your future needs affect the relative value of these two kinds of spaces. The landlord just wants to generate rent. It may not matter to him which kind of space he rents you, so long as he doesn't lose your rent.

• Another kind of win-win agreement comes from difference in judgments about the future. For example, a real estate developer is usually looking for long-term investment value in a property. A business is often looking for short-term usability when seeking space. They could have two different perspectives on the same property. Sometimes a business can negotiate a low rent on retail or office space if it is willing to put up with things that reduce the short-term value. Is the building in need of remodeling? Is the neighborhood up and coming—but not quite there yet? If these problems don't affect your business and you want a good deal, then you can probably come to terms with a long-term investor who just wants to hold that property and cover costs until the day she is ready to redevelop it.

• Differences in risk tolerance can be a source of collaborative win-win solutions. Your business may be conservative and risk intolerant. Perhaps it's just the culture to avoid risk. Or maybe the business is having cash flow issues and has to be careful now. But another business might be flush with cash from a successful public stock offering and eager to invest in some risky ventures with the potential for future growth. If you combine your company's ideas, systems, or technology with the other firm's capital, perhaps you can negotiate a joint venture that will allow you to develop some exciting new products that your company would never fund in-house.

• Time frames can differ, creating opportunities for win-win agreements. A management team bought out an old manufacturing firm with bank financing that included a balloon payment—a large sum they have to pay back in two years. Their goal is to turn the company around within that time frame. If you are one of its suppliers, you might find it irritating that the company is now fighting over every penny and pressuring you to cut your prices. In this situation, consider if you can profit from its time pressure. You know it needs rapid growth. Do you have any additional products it might be able to sell? You could provide some ideas and suggest that if the company increases its purchasing from you, you'll offer the discount it needs. Since you don't have the same two-year time horizon, you may be able to focus on building your volume for a few years, while it sweats over generating enough profits for the payout. If you are this company's biggest supplier two years from now, you should be able to profit from the relationship in subsequent years.

Collaboration takes advantage of differences in time frame, risk tolerance, interests, and business objectives and strategies. It uses these differences to create value by finding creative ways to approach the problem of how to work together. Later in this chapter and in the next chapter, we will help you master this art of creating value instead of just fighting over it.

The other aspect of collaboration you want to think about is its impact on relationships. Collaboration is a good way to invest in relationships. It can help you strengthen your business network, build teamwork, develop a junior employee, or cement your relationship with a customer or supplier.

Do You Want to Build the Relationship?

In successful collaborations, the relationship between the parties is often an ongoing one, with some established history of give-and-take, so that the parties trust each other and know that they can work together. In addition, collaborative strategies are often initiated when the parties know that they want to establish long-term goals for particular outcomes and for the relationship.

To make collaboration work, both parties to the negotiation must be willing to collaborate; if one side employs it and the other uses a different strategy, the chances are that both parties cannot achieve good outcomes. In fact, one-sided collaboration is usually a relationship-damaging experience.

We often encounter people in our workshops and classes who are natural collaborators; they like to get along with others, are open and trusting, and dislike the gamesmanship and deviousness of competitive negotiations. They do well when interacting with other collaborators, but they pick up a lot of scars when they encounter more competitive people in business and in the rest of life. They often ask us for advice about how to handle a problematic negotiation in which they are having trouble because the other side isn't being trustworthy and helpful. Our short answer is, "Stop being a sucker!" Hugging steam rollers is a good way to get flattened. If the other party is persistently competitive, you are not going to benefit from collaborating with them. They may benefit, but it will be at your expense. So, yes, use collaboration to build stronger business and personal relationships. But don't expect to convert the die-hard competitor. Some people never collaborate, and you'll only get hurt if you think you can get them to play by different rules.

What about the team member or associate who won't collaborate? It's difficult when you work with someone daily who continues to behave competitively. In fact, this is one of the biggest sources of stress in many workplaces. People are hard to collaborate with if they do any of the following in your workplace:

- Keep information to themselves and try to use it to increase their power
- Hoard resources for their own use instead of sharing
- Quickly accept any help from you but fail to reciprocate when you need help
- Fail to keep confidences and tell stories or spread rumors that hurt your standing
- Go above you or behind your back to get what they want if they think you won't give it to them

Office politics often generates this kind of behavior. It is highly distributive, breaks down cooperation, and damages the organization's performance. And it makes collaborating very difficult, if not impossible. So how can you build good collaborative relationships if office politics is in the way?

The first thing to do is to state what behaviors you find problematic. For example, you might say to a teammate, "I want to collaborate with you to work out a better way to share the workload. But here's my concern: in the past, you have tended to act in a noncollaborative manner." Then describe two or more very specific behaviors in context in an accurate, nonjudgmental way. Don't generalize from them, or you'll never get the other party to accept your feedback. For example, you might say, "The last time we tried to work on a project together, I ended up doing it and you took the day off. I don't usually like to carry other people's weight unless they sometimes reciprocate and do the same for me."

It could be that you haven't ever complained or explained the situation to this person before. Often collaborative people avoid these difficult conversations, and assume that others are as polite and sensitive about matters of conduct as they are. But that's not a fair assumption. If you don't talk about your expectations for conduct, you can't expect others to know what they are. This is especially true when collaborative people interact with more competitive people. Each comes at the interaction with a different mind-set, and the collaborator often has to spell out the rules of collaborative conduct in order to achieve collaboration.

WHEN COLLABORATION IS KEY

Collaboration is particularly appropriate within an organization, when two parties have common ground, and when two parties have the same customers, same clients, same suppliers, or same service personnel. In any of these cases, the parties have or want to establish a working relationship and to keep it working smoothly.

In addition, we strongly recommend collaboration whenever the obvious outcomes of a negotiation are *undesirable* to the players. If you are all fighting over a small pie, the temptation is to compete all the harder. But what's the point of fighting over a small pie? As the old saying goes, it's far better to figure out how to bake a bigger pie or at least lots more little pies. Collaboration switches you from dividing the spoils to searching for more. If you use your collaboration to search for new and better approaches to the conflict—treating it as a puzzle rather than a fight—then you are likely to improve the outcomes for both parties. And so we want you to remember the following principle:

COLLABORATION IS THE BEST RESPONSE TO
CONFLICTS IN WHICH THERE DOESN'T SEEM
TO BE ENOUGH TO GO AROUND.

By collaborating, you can redefine the problem so as to make
more desirable outcomes possible. Why accept limits when you
have a chance to redefine them?

A FOUNDATION OF TRUST AND HONESTY

For a collaboration to work, there must be a high degree of trust,
openness, and cooperation. The parties look for common needs
and goals and engage in mutually supportive behavior to obtain
them. Both parties realize that they are interdependent and that
their cooperative effort can solve the problems and meet the needs
of both sides.

Because trust creates more trust, which is necessary to begin
and sustain cooperation, it is important to make the opening
moves in collaborative negotiation in a way that engenders trust.[4]
Opening conversations may occur even before the formal negotiations begin, when the parties are just becoming acquainted. If one
party finds a reason to mistrust the other party at this time, this may
stifle any future efforts at collaboration.

If the parties are new to each other or have been combative or
competitive in the past, they will have to build trust. Each party will
approach the negotiation with expectations based on the research
they did on each other or on history. Generally we trust others if
they appear to be similar to us, have a positive attitude toward us,
or appear cooperative and trusting. We also tend to trust them if
they are dependent on us. Making concessions also appears to be
a trusting gesture, so we are likely to respond in kind.

In contrast, it is easy to engender mistrust. Suspicion is seeded
with either a competitive, hostile action or an indication that one
player does not trust the other. Once mistrust gets started, it is very
easy to build and escalate and very difficult to change over to collaboration.

Trust escalation and deescalation have often been compared
with the children's game Chutes and Ladders. In this analogy, it is
easy to move down the "chute" of mistrust, rapidly sliding to the

bottom, but much more difficult to climb back up the "ladder" that will restore and sustain good trust between parties.[5]

What Builds Trust?

Research has generally shown that the following actions are effective in building trust in a negotiation:

- Creating and meeting the other party's expectations. Stating what you intend to do and then doing what you said you would do.
- Establishing credibility. Making your statements honest, accurate, and verifiable. Telling the truth, and keeping your word.
- Keeping promises, and following through.
- Developing a good reputation. Building a trusting relationship with other people, and using them as references to your relationship with this other person.
- Developing similar interests, goals, and objectives to the other.
- Stressing the benefits of having the other party act trustworthily. Emphasizing the importance of mutual trust. Stressing the advantages of taking a risk to trust the other rather than the possible costs if that trust is betrayed.

Source: Based on R. Lewicki and C. Wiethoff, "Trust, Trust Development and Trust Repair," in M. Deutsch and P. Coleman, *Handbook of Conflict Resolution*, 2nd ed. (San Francisco: Jossey-Bass, 2006).

Being honest yourself is as critical as requiring the other to act trustworthy. In collaboration, communication between parties is open and accurate. This contrasts greatly with the competitive strategy, in which the negotiators have a high level of distrust and guard information carefully to prevent the other side from obtaining the advantage.

Deceit is often an element in competitive deals, but collaborative deal making requires honest sharing of positions. The kind of information you seek in analyzing your own and the other players' positions should be put on the table for collaboration to work. That way, each player can help the other think about how to meet their goals in creative ways that satisfy other players' goals too.

The players in a collaborative game need support from their constituencies. The constituencies must trust the parties to find common ground and support them in doing so. Doing so may mean not achieving absolutely everything the constituency wanted on the substantive issues, and the constituency has to accept this as valid. In contrast, in competition, the constituencies usually push the negotiator to get everything he or she can, regardless of the future of the relationship.

Collaborating parties respect deadlines and are willing to renegotiate the time frame if necessary to achieve everyone's goals. Contrast this with competition, where time is used as an obstacle or as a power ploy to accomplish one's own ends.

Collaboration is hard work, especially if the game is new to you, but the results can be rewarding. It takes extra time and creativity to build trust and to find win-win solutions, but the outcome and relationship results are usually better for both parties.

KEYS TO SUCCESSFUL COLLABORATION

Collaboration has traditionally been underused because most people do not understand the fine points of the strategy and because collaborations are less familiar than competitive negotiating methods. Many negotiations are based on the competitive model, which is the way most people view negotiation: as a competitive situation where one is better off being suspicious of the other, and the fundamental object is to get all the goodies.

For collaboration to work—to find those creative solutions that give both parties more than they initially expected—both parties need to be committed to:

- Understanding the other party's needs and objectives
- Providing a free flow of information in both ways
- Seeking the best solutions to meet the needs of both sides[6]

Understanding the other party's goals and needs is critical to collaboration. We suggested that this is important in a competitive negotiation as well, but for very different reasons. In competition, you may know or think you know what the other party wants, but your objective in learning this is to facilitate your own strategy development and also to strategize how to beat the other side by doing better than them or denying them what they want to achieve. In collaboration, your objective is to understand their goals and needs so that you can work with them to achieve their goals as well as your own. Good collaboration frequently requires not only understanding the other party's stated objectives, but also their underlying needs—*why* they want what they want. In a collaborative negotiation, both parties must be willing to ask questions and listen carefully to the answers to learn about the other's needs.

To provide a free flow of information, both parties must be willing to volunteer information. The information has to be as accurate and as comprehensive as possible. Both sides need to understand the issues, problems, priorities, and goals of the other. They need to fully understand the important context factors in the negotiation. Compare this with competitive negotiations, in which information is closely guarded or, if shared, often distorted.

Finally, having listened closely to each other, the parties can then work toward achieving mutual goals that will satisfy both. To do this, they will need to minimize their differences and emphasize their similarities. They will need to focus on the issues and work at keeping personalities out of the discussions.

Collaborative goals differ from competitive goals. In competition, the goal is obtaining the largest share of the pie at any cost and without giving away any information or conceding on any issue. In collaboration, each party must be willing to redefine its perspective in the light of the collaboration, knowing that the whole can be greater than the sum of the parts. In this light, having a strong knowledge of the problem area is a definite advantage. While a lack of information can be overcome, starting out with the knowledge is an asset.

To achieve success, each party from the beginning must send signals to the other that will help build trust between and among those negotiating. Be careful not to send mixed messages if you want to collaborate. There is no point in putting half your cards on the table. It precludes collaboration or competition.

OBSTACLES TO COLLABORATION

Both parties to a negotiation must be willing to collaborate if this strategy is to be successful. It will be difficult, if not impossible, to employ collaboration under the following circumstances:

- One party does not see the situation as having the potential for collaboration.
- One party is motivated only to accomplish its own ends.
- One party has historically been competitive; this behavior may be hard to change.
- One party expects the other to be competitive and prepares for negotiation based on this expectation.
- One party wants to be competitive and rationalizes this behavior.
- One party may be accountable to a constituency that prefers the competitive strategy.
- One party is not willing to take the time to search for collaborative items.
- The negotiation or bargaining mix includes both competitive and collaborative issues. Sometimes the two parties can collaborate on collaborative issues and compete on competitive issues. Our experience however, is that competitive processes tend to drive out collaborative processes, making collaboration harder to achieve.

Most of these obstacles reflect a lack of commitment to collaboration on at least one player's side. Again, commitment is the core issue if you want to make collaboration work.

You can still collaborate if there are obstacles such as these, but recognize the obstacles first and work to remove them. We recommend talking to those in the other party about any obstacles. Ask them if they agree collaboration is a good idea. And ask them to help you deal with the obstacle to collaboration. If they are motivated to collaborate, they may be able to help you deal with or remove the obstacle.

For example, a salesman was under strong pressure from his new boss to increase the profitability of his accounts by reducing discounts and minimizing service and support. The sales manager was all fired up about eliminating what she viewed as caving in to the customers. Her get-tough philosophy was causing a lot of trouble, however, because the sales force had built collaborative long-term relationships with their key customers, who were accustomed to good service and competitive discounts. How could the salesman continue to work collaboratively with his key accounts given this new pressure on him?

The purchasing manager at one of these key accounts was about to switch to another supplier but decided to try an appeal to the sales manager first. He asked the new sales manager to come out and meet him, and in the meeting, explained that he would be sorry to give up on a long-term, mutually beneficial relationship—but that was just what would happen if the supplier continued to play hardball. The sales manager was impressed by the honesty and sincerity of the purchasing manager and also by the threat of withdrawing all of the business and giving it to another supplier. She promised to think about it. And later that week, she quietly took the salesman aside and told him it was okay to leave that customer's discount structure in place and to continue to provide the same level of service and support.

This story illustrates the importance of trying to remove barriers to collaboration instead of just assuming that collaboration is impossible. Unless you have already tried to move it, you don't know how permanent a barrier really is.

ARE YOU SERIOUS ABOUT COLLABORATION?

Some negotiators think they are collaborating when in fact all they have done is wrap their competitive strategy in a friendly package. Thus, they put on the image of collaboration, only to move in for a competitive grab near the end of the negotiation. This is not collaboration: it is competitiveness in a collaborative disguise. True collaboration requires the parties to move beyond their initial concerns and positions and go on a joint quest for new, creative ways to maximize their individual and joint outcomes.

As described in Chapter Two, both the relationship and the outcome are important to both parties in collaboration. The two parties usually have long-term goals that they are willing to work for together. Both parties are committed to working toward a mutually acceptable agreement that preserves or strengthens the relationship. Because each party values the relationship, they will attempt to find a mutually satisfying solution for both parties. Working together effectively in a collaborative negotiation process can itself enhance the quality of the relationship. This approach is very different from the competitive strategy, where both sides want to win so badly that they pursue their goal at all costs and ignore all the factors that might allow a collaborative process.

PAY ATTENTION TO THE SOFT STUFF

In the collaborative model, intangibles are important and accounted for. These include such items as each party's reputation, pride, principles, and sense of fairness. Because these concerns are important, the negotiations must stay on a rational, reasonable, and fair level. If the parties get angry at each other, the collaborative atmosphere will degenerate into a competitive one. Allow plenty of venting time if you or the other party begins to get irritated, and be sure to listen to complaints about your behavior with an open mind to avoid conflicts that can derail collaboration. There must be a great deal of trust, cooperation, openness, and communication between the parties to engage in effective problem solving.

ARE YOU READY TO MAKE CONCESSIONS?

To collaborate, the parties must be willing to make concessions to accomplish their goals. These concessions should be repaid with creative win-win solutions, but they represent a risk for each party that the other party must be careful not to abuse. If you aren't willing to run some risks, don't bother with collaboration.

USE TIME AS A RESOURCE, NOT A WEAPON

Collaboration relies on deadlines that are mutually determined and observed. They are not used for manipulation as they are in competitive negotiations. Information flows freely and is not used to control the situation or guarded to maintain power. The objective is to find the best solution for both sides. Similarities between the two parties, not differences, are emphasized.

THE FOUR-STEP COLLABORATIVE PROCESS

There are four major steps in carrying out collaboration: (1) identifying the problem, (2) understanding the problem, (3) generating alternative solutions, and (4) selecting a solution. You need to master each step.

STEP ONE: IDENTIFY THE PROBLEM

Identifying the problem may sound like a simple step, but it's not. In the collaborative model, both sides are involved equally in the process of problem definition, and both need to agree fully on what the problem is.

When you were gathering information, you focused on your point of view, but for collaboration to work, you will need to work closely with the other party to find a common view of the problem. When defining the problem, try to use neutral language and keep it impersonal. For example, you might say, "We are not able to get our work out on time," rather than, "You are preventing us from doing our work and getting it out on time." It is important to define the obstacles to your goals without attacking other people.

Try to define the problem as a common goal. Keep the goal definition as simple as possible. Try not to load the situation with peripheral issues that are not really related to the central concern. Stick with the primary issues.

Each party needs to be assertive but cooperative at the same time. You need to be clear about what you want to achieve, yet not at the expense of dominating the other side. Because the relationship is important, you need to see the problem from the other party's perspective—"to walk a mile in the other person's shoes," as the saying goes. Understanding and empathy help you find the common issues.[7]

Watch out for a tendency to define solutions before you have fully defined the problem. In fact, you should avoid discussing solutions until you have thoroughly defined and understood the problem. The point of collaboration is to treat the outcome as variable, not fixed. So don't fix it up front.

STEP TWO: UNDERSTAND THE PROBLEM

In this step, you try to get behind the issues to the underlying needs and interests.[8] As noted earlier, an interest is a broader perspective that is usually behind a position. You need to learn not only about the needs and interests of each party, but also about their fears and concerns. The reason for getting behind the positions is that they tend to be fixed and rigid; modifying them requires the parties to make concessions either toward or away from the target point.

In contrast to positions, interests define what the parties care about more broadly, and there are often multiple ways to resolve the conflict between these competing interests. In addition, a focus on interests tends to take some of the personal dimension out of the negotiation and shifts it to the underlying concerns.[9] Since there is bound to be a difference in thinking styles, people approach even similar issues in different ways. Positions offer only one way to think about an issue; interests offer multiple ways to think about it. Thus, you can find out where they are coming from more effectively by discussing interests than by stating positions. By using the "why" questions discussed in Chapter Three, you can dig deeper into the reasons for each party's position.

Collaborators stand on shifting ground. Remember that even if you define interests carefully, they can change. Since the negotiation process is an evolving one, you may need to stop from time to time to reconsider interests. If the conversation begins to change in tone or the focus seems to shift, this may be a signal that interests have changed. Collaborative negotiators with changing interests should be encouraged to share their shifts in needs. The other party may be able to help achieve new needs by expanding resources, extending the time frame, or changing the details of the negotiation to accommodate the changed interests.[10]

STEP THREE: GENERATE ALTERNATIVE SOLUTIONS

Once you have defined the issues to the satisfaction of both parties, you can begin to look for solutions. Notice that this is plural: *solutions.* You want to find a group of possible solutions, then select from among them the best solution for both parties. In collaborations, the more potential solutions, the more likely it is that the parties will find one that both can embrace.

There are two major ways to go about finding solutions. One is to redefine the problem so you can find win-win alternatives for what at first may have seemed to be a win-lose problem. The second is to take the problem at hand and generate a long list of options for solving it.

To illustrate the different approaches, we will use an example suggested by Dean Pruitt about a husband and wife who are trying to decide where to spend a two-week vacation.[11] He wants to go to the mountains for hiking, fishing, and some rest; she wants to go to the beach for sun, swimming, and night life. They have decided that spending one week in each place will not be adequate for either person, because too much time is spent in packing, unpacking, and traveling between the two locations. Here are some options:

- *Expand the pie.* If the problem is based on scarce resources, the object would be to find a way to expand or reallocate the resources so that each party could obtain his or her desired end. Knowing the underlying interests can help in this endeavor. For example, the parties could take a two-week vacation and spend one week in each place. While this would require more time and money, each person would get a one-week vacation in the chosen spot.

- *Logroll.* If there are two issues in a negotiation and each party has a different priority for them, then one may be able to be traded off for the other. For example, if problems A and B are common to both parties, but party 1 cares most about problem A and party 2 cares most about problem B, then a solution that solves both problems can provide each party with a happy resolution: "You get this and I get that." If there are multiple issues, it may take some trial and error to find what packages will satisfy each party. In our example, if the husband really wants to stay in an informal rustic mountain cabin and the wife really wants to stay in a fancy hotel, then another resolution is for them to go to the mountains but stay in a fancy hotel (or an informal beach house at the shore).

- *Offer nonspecific compensation.* Another method is for one party to "pay off" the other for giving in on an issue. The "payoff" may not be monetary, and it may not even be related to the negotiation. The party paying off needs to know what it will take to keep the other party so happy that he won't care about the outcome of this negotiation. In a house sale negotiation, for example, the seller might include all window coverings (curtains, drapes, blinds) as part of the deal. The buyer may be so delighted that she decides not to ask for any other price break. In our vacation example, the wife might buy the husband a set of golf clubs, which will make him so happy that he will go anywhere she wants to go (since there are golf courses everywhere).

• *Cut costs.* In this method, one party accomplishes specific objectives, and the other's costs are minimized by going along with the agreement. This differs from nonspecific compensation because in this method, the other party can minimize costs and "suffering," whereas in the other method, the costs and suffering do not go away, but the party is somehow compensated for them. This method requires a clear understanding of the other party's needs and preferences, along with their costs. In the vacation example, the wife says to the husband, "What can I do to make going to the beach as painless as possible for you?" He tells her that he wants to stay in a beach house away from the big hotels, get some rest, and be near a golf course and several places where he can go fishing. They both go down to their favorite travel agent and find a location that offers all these.

• *Find a bridging solution.* In bridging, the parties invent new options that meet each other's needs. Again, both parties must be very familiar with the other party's interests and needs. When two business partners bring in a third partner who can offer resources neither of them wanted to contribute, this is an effective example of bridging. In the vacation example, the husband and wife go to a travel agent and find a place that offers hiking, fishing, beaches, swimming, golf, privacy, and night life. They book a two-week vacation for Hawaii and have a wonderful time.

All of these tactics for generating solutions focus on redefinitions of the original problem. That's a powerful strategy, but not always necessary. The second approach to inventing solutions is to take the problem as defined and try to generate a lengthy list of possible solutions. Sometimes there is a solution nobody had thought of before that works quite well once it is uncovered.

The key to finding answers in this approach is to generate as many solutions as possible without evaluating them. The solutions should be general rather than party specific; that is, they should not favor one party over the other. At a later stage, each solution can then be evaluated to determine whether it adequately meets the needs and interests of both parties.

What is interesting in this process is that both parties engage in trying to solve the other party's problem as much as they do their own.[12] It is a cooperative endeavor. And as you have probably heard many times before, two heads are better than one.

If you get to this stage but the issues still seem murky, you may need to go back to the problem definition and rework that step. It should be easy to generate solutions if the problem is clearly stated in a way that does not bias solutions toward one party or the other. Otherwise, if you are comfortable with the definition of the problem, forge ahead.

Remember that you are only generating solutions in this step, not evaluating them or deciding whether to use them—yet. That will happen in the next step. There are a number of ways to generate ideas for solutions:

- *Brainstorming.* This common method for generating ideas usually works best in several small groups rather than one large one, depending on the number of people involved. Write down as many ideas as possible without judging them. It is best to write or post the ideas on a flip chart, chalkboard, or similar display device so that everyone can see them and keep track of what has been done. The key ground rule is that ideas must not be evaluated as they are suggested. Don't let anyone say, "Oh, that's a dumb idea!" or "That won't work!" Keep ideas flowing and keep focused on the problem and how to solve it, without associating people with the problem or the solutions.

It often happens that people quickly think of a few possibilities and then run out of ideas. At this point, it is easy to think you are done because you have a few solutions. Don't stop here, though; stick to it for a while longer. Otherwise you may miss some good ideas, particularly creative ones that no one has considered before. Ask outsiders for ideas too. Sometimes they bring a fresh approach to the problem.

- *Piggybacking* can be used in conjunction with brainstorming.[13] This technique builds on someone else's idea to produce yet another idea. It's often done by working in a sequence order: one person starts with a brainstormed idea, and then the next person has to "piggyback" until possible variations on the idea are exhausted.

• *Breakout groups.* In this method, each negotiator works with a small group—perhaps his or her own constituency—and makes a list of possible solutions. These are discussed within the breakout group and then considered, one at a time, by the larger group. They can be ranked in terms of preferences or likely effectiveness. The drawback of this method is that anyone not present at the session will miss offering input or helping to shape the solution.

• *Surveys.* Another useful method is to distribute a questionnaire stating the problem and asking respondents to list possible solutions. In this case, each person works alone on the survey, so people miss out on the synergy of working together. However, the advantage is that a number of people who have good ideas but are normally reticent about getting into a group's conversation can offer their thoughts and ideas without being attacked or critiqued. Another advantage is that this draws in the ideas of people who may not be able to attend the negotiation or formally participate in it.

Once you have a list of possible solutions, you can reduce the number of possibilities by rating the ideas, much as we prioritized the issues in previous chapters. In communicating your priorities and preferences to the other party, it's important to maintain an attitude of firm flexibility: be firm about achieving your interests while remaining flexible about how those interests might be achieved. There are a number of tactics to keep the discussion collaborative while being clear and consistent about your preferences:

• Remember that you are only prioritizing the list, not yet deciding on the actual solution.
• Be assertive in defending and establishing your basic interests, but do not demand a particular solution.
• Signal your flexibility and willingness to hear the other party's interests by practicing your listening skills. For instance, use active listening, trying to repeat what they said back to them in order to see if you understood their point.
• Indicate your willingness to modify a position or have your interests met in an alternative way. Perhaps you will be able to

trade one point for another. This will demonstrate your openness to suggestions and willingness to work together.

- Show your ability and willingness to problem solve. Skill in problem solving is valuable here, especially if you get stuck on a particular point and need to find some way to resolve it to everyone's satisfaction. If you can settle this issue, it will help when you get to the next step and are actually deciding on the solution. You will have set the stage for collaboration.

- Keep lines of communication open. If tempers flare, take a break, and talk about the problem if need be. Also talk with the other party about how you can continue to work on the problem without getting angry or losing control. Make sure both parties feel that they are being heard. Steer discussion away from personalities, and concentrate on the issues: "Separate the people from the problem."[14]

- Underscore what is most important to you by saying, "This is what I need to accomplish," or "As long as I can accomplish ..., I'll be very happy." Resist the temptation to give in just to get a resolution. Giving in is an accommodating strategy that will not result in the best outcome for both parties.

- Reevaluate any points on which you disagree. Be sure that both sides agree on the adjusted prioritized list so that you will both feel comfortable as you move to the final step.

- Eliminate competitive tactics by identifying them and either confronting them or renegotiating the process. If the discussion becomes competitive, point out that this is happening. Then try to resolve the problem before the entire negotiation becomes competitive.

STEP FOUR: SELECT A SOLUTION

Using your prioritized list of potential solutions from the previous step, narrow the range of possibilities by focusing on the positive suggestions that people seemed to favor most.[15] One way to prioritize is to logroll by packaging each person's first choice together. If parties have the same first choice but very different preferences for it, try to invent a way for both sides to win on this issue.

Try to change any negative ideas into positive ones,[16] or eliminate them from the list. Stating alternatives as positives keeps the negotiation upbeat and on a positive note. Avoid attributing negative ideas to any particular person or side.

Evaluate the solutions on the basis of quality and acceptability. Consider the opinions of both parties. Do not require people to justify their preferences. People often do not know why they have a preference; they just do. If you foresee any potential problems with the solution selection process, you may want to establish objective criteria for evaluation before you start the selection process.[17] In other words, before you move toward choosing among prioritized options, work against a set of objective facts, figures, data, and criteria that were developed independent of the options.

If a car owner and a garage mechanic are having a dispute about how much it should cost to repair a starter motor, there are books available that indicate the standard cost for parts and labor for this repair. Similarly, if a group of people is trying to pick a job candidate from among those who applied for the job, their work will be considerably facilitated if they spend time developing criteria by which to evaluate the applicants before they actually look at résumés and interview people.

Consider Fairness and Similar Intangibles as a Way to Choose Among Options

Intangibles are often operating in the selection of a solution. For example, gaining recognition or looking strong to a constituency may be important factors in someone's selection decision. Acknowledge the importance of intangibles by building them into the decisions. For example, if those on the other side need to maintain esteem with a constituency, they may be willing to settle on a lesser point that still allows them to appear in a favorable light. In fact, it will help them greatly if you work with them to determine how to make them look strong and capable to the constituency.

How Do You Know It's Fair?

Fairness is usually one of the most important intangibles. In a win-win negotiation, both parties want to achieve a fair outcome. There are a number of ways to decide what is fair, but three common criteria often apply:[18]

- *An outcome that gives each side equal outcomes.* It is not surprising that one of the most common ways to solve negotiation problems—particularly win-lose, competitive ones—is for the parties to agree to "divide it down the middle."

- *An outcome that gives each side more or less based on equity,* that is, what it has earned or deserves based on the time or energy committed. In this case, the side that puts in more should get out more. Equity is usually based on the ratio of outcome to input, so that the person who works harder, suffers more, and so on deserves a proportionately larger share of the results.

- *An outcome that gives each side more or less depending on what it needs.* In this case, if one side can create a legitimate claim that it needs or deserves a better outcome, there may be a good case to be made for dividing up the resources so that those with greater needs actually gain more.

Are Emotions Escalating?

If emotions surface or people get angry, take a break. Give people an opportunity to discuss the reasons for their dissatisfaction. Be sure everyone has cooled off before you start again, and try to keep personalities out of the deliberations. If taking a break does not work, seek out a third party to help you. Anyone with a modicum of interpersonal and problem-solving skills can be of help, provided he or she doesn't have a personal stake in the outcome. And if you wish, you can bring in a trained mediator, facilitator, or problem solver.

Don't Rush

It is very important not to rush the process of selecting solutions, appealing as it may be to do so. If you get to the bottom line too quickly, you may miss some good potential options, and you may fail to ensure that both sides participate equally.[19] Collaborative efforts require the participation of both sides; they may also require time to mull over alternatives and think through all the consequences. Good collaborative negotiation requires time and cannot be rushed.

Nothing Is Settled Until Everything Is Settled

Remember that everything is tentative until the very end. During the solution-generating phase, some people may even object to writing anything down, as this may make them nervous. They may feel they are being railroaded into commitments they have not agreed to. Other than the working documents that you may create as you define the problem and invent options, you may want to begin to record decisions only when the group is close to consensus. That way, nothing is set in stone until the very end. This open, fluid approach makes it possible to share creative ideas and suggestions. The minute one party says, "But you said yesterday you'd be willing to . . . ," the collaboration starts to unravel as participants begin to worry about being held accountable for positions. This difficult and critical rule is violated too often as people revert instinctively to a competitive style without realizing the impact on idea generation and sharing.

Write It Down!

Once the parties have agreed on solutions and prepared a document to outline the agreement, it should be passed around for everyone to read. Some people have suggested that this may even be an excellent way to manage the entire prioritization and decision-making process. Start with a tentative draft of what people agree to. Then continue to pass it around, sharpening language, clarifying words, and writing out agreements so that all agree with it and pledge to live by it.

COLLABORATIVE NEGOTIATION STRATEGIES

Researchers have identified several strategies that help produce successful collaboration.[20] They are useful as a checklist for strategic negotiators in planning and implementing a collaboration. And if you find your collaboration is falling apart, these are also helpful in diagnosing what's gone wrong:

• *Create common goals or objectives.* There may be three ways the goals will be played out: all parties will share in the results equally, the parties will share a common end but receive different benefits, or the parties will have different goals but share in a collective effort to accomplish them. In any of these cases, both parties believe they can benefit by working together as opposed to working separately and that the results will be better than they would be if each party worked separately.

- *Maintain confidence in your ability to solve problems.* This is more or less a matter of, "If you think you can, you can." It helps to have a strong knowledge of the problem area, but lack of knowledge can be overcome if the desire is there. Probably the most important element is to develop skills in negotiating collaboratively, since it is a less common form of negotiation. The more you do it, the better you will become at doing it.

- *Value the other party's opinion.* Valuing the other party's point of view is difficult if you have been accustomed in the past to focusing only on your own position and maintaining it. In collaboration, you value the other party's position equally with your own.[21] You need good listening skills and openness to hear the other party's point of view.

- *Share the motivation and commitment to working together.* In collaboration, you are not only committed to the idea of working together with the other party; you take actions to do so. You pursue both your own needs and those of the other party. This means each party must be explicit about his or her needs.

In collaborative negotiation, the parties strive to identify their similarities to each other and downplay their differences. The differences are not ignored; they are simply recognized and accepted for what they are. The parties are aware that they share a common fate, particularly if they expect to work together after this negotiation has been completed. They know they can gain more if they work jointly than if they work separately. To do this, they focus on outputs and results.[22]

Motivated, committed parties will control their behavior in a number of ways. Individuals will avoid being competitive, combative, evasive, defensive, or stubborn. They will work at being open and trusting, flexible, and willing to share information and not to hoard it for their own use.

TROUBLESHOOTING COLLABORATIVE NEGOTIATIONS

Collaborative negotiation is a lot of work, but the rewards can be great. Sometimes, however, no matter how much you want to succeed, obstacles may prevent you from moving ahead with collaboration. You'll certainly get stuck if one (or both) of the parties do any of the following, so be sure to avoid these mistakes and try to weed them out of your collaborations, even when the other party plants them by mistake.

Problems arise when one or both parties:

- May not be able to do the required work.
- May have a win-lose attitude.
- May not be able to see the potential for collaboration.
- May be motivated to achieve only their own goals.
- May not be capable of establishing or maintaining productive working relationships.
- May see the world as more distorted than it is because of biases.
- May have a constituency that is pressing for competitive behavior or quick outcomes.

Furthermore, the situation may contain elements that require a mix of strategies. Then you need to separate the issues into the component parts and deal with each separately.

Sometimes you may feel that you do not have the time or energy to push forward with collaboration, especially if you encounter one or more of the preceding situations. If this happens, check to see if you can fix the underlying problem. If not, then switch back to a more competitive style.

WHAT IF THERE IS A BREAKDOWN?

If there is a breakdown in the collaboration and an argument seems to be brewing, try to move the discussion to a neutral point and summarize where you are.[23] Summarizing is a helpful tactic because it:

- Slows the pace to give everyone time to cool off
- Reminds the other party of any progress to date, which can help reframe the situation in a more positive way
- Checks everybody's understanding to make sure they agree with your perception of what has been accomplished or agreed so far
- Acts as a way to move toward either resolving ambiguities or moving on to issues yet to be discussed.

Summarizing may reveal an unexpected difference of viewpoints that can then be talked through, allowing the negotiations to resume with some adjustment.

But what if summarizing doesn't work and there is a total breakdown in communication? If you cannot get the negotiation back on track, you may need to resort to conflict resolution strategies or third-party intervention. And also note that at any point, you and the other party can reach a mutual agreement to abandon your collaboration and adopt another negotiating style. For instance, you might try collaborating, decide you don't like working together, and decide that you will agree to disagree and revert to a conventional competitive strategy or toward a more expedient and simple outcome through compromising. Remember, however, that you will give up the relationship benefits, so do not advocate competition unless you decide your initial estimation of relationship importance was too high.

A word of caution is in order. Because you will have shared much information through your collaboration attempt, it can now be used against you in a competitive negotiation. Therefore, the slide from collaboration to competition is not generally a happy or profitable one because some of the actions you undertook under the assumption that you could trust the other and work with him or her may now be used against you as weapons. This is a good reason to try to work out your differences and get the collaboration back on track.

Negotiating a Strategic Alliance

Negotiating a strategic alliance presents a challenge. "A bad negotiation tactic may do lasting damage; good negotiation tactics must be repeated a number of times before the partner accepts this as a pattern."[*] In a strategic alliance, the relationship concerns will be very important.

For example, more than a decade ago, Corning and Ciba-Geigy formed Ciba Corning Diagnostics, an alliance based in the United States, designed to enhance Corning's medical diagnostics business. Ciba-Geigy is a global pharmaceutical and chemical company based in Switzerland. Corning, based in New York, is a world leader in glass and

(Continued)

Negotiating a Strategic Alliance *(Continued)*

ceramics technology. The alliance would combine the strengths of the two partners to develop innovative medical diagnostic tests.

There was synergy in what each partner could offer to the alliance. Negotiation went smoothly, as Ciba was willing to have Corning manage more extensively in the beginning. Corning's managers were willing to concede on points of strong interest to Ciba, and thus they were able to agree on a time line for their work. Each partner appointed its director of research and development to the board of the new alliance, which signaled to the other party a willingness to share technology, while garnering internal support for the alliance as well.

Each side had representatives to build consensus, improve communication, and obtain support for the parent organization. Ciba and Corning actively looked into ways for each partner to gain by opening up possibilities for broadening the product line, marketing, technology, and growth. They were able to negotiate any issues that arose because as mutual trust grew, they were willing to discuss such problems clearly and openly.

A strategic alliance will not succeed if the two potential partners have conflicting underlying motives. If they are both leaders in their field, it may be difficult for them to collaborate. And if they have strongly differing views of which activities should take priority or what the time lines should be, the success of such an alliance would be questionable.

To create a successful alliance, each organization must be willing to support the efforts to create an alliance agreement. This means that political support must be generated within the organizations of the potential partners. Building support may take time. For example, the Japanese and Chinese take a long time to complete this process (at least from the American point of view). Conversely, the Japanese and Chinese see American firms as too pushy.

*S. Gates, *Strategic Alliances: Guidelines for Successful Management* (New York: Conference Board, 1993).

NEGOTIATING COLLABORATIVELY WITH YOUR BOSS

Since everyone has had some sort of experience dealing with a boss, we will look at ways to negotiate collaboratively with a manager.[24] Although performance review, salary, and benefits are usually the major areas for discussion and possible conflict with one's manager, there are others that arise more often. For example, what if your boss asks you to do a project that you realize you cannot possibly complete without working overtime? If you do not mind staying late, go ahead. But if you find yourself doing this frequently and resenting it, maybe you need to consider negotiating about it the next time.

Negotiating with the boss is often viewed as a competitive, win-lose, or fixed-pie situation. It can also be viewed as a lose-win situation, in which it is better to accommodate and let the boss win all the time rather than try to argue for a preferred outcome and have the boss be angry at your "assertiveness." But if you think about it, both parties might be able to gain something from collaborative negotiation.

Consider the steps in collaboration we covered earlier in the chapter. Look at your own needs, as well as those of your boss. Remember that the key to collaborative bargaining is to find a way to solve the other person's problem.

In our hypothetical situation, your boss may have been asked by her boss to drop everything and get this project out at any cost. (Your boss may have some bargaining of her own to do.) At any rate, your boss has to have this project done, and there is no way for you to complete it during normal hours given the other work you have to do and the deadlines for those projects. Your boss could ask someone else to do it, but perhaps she knows you can do the job better and more quickly.

First, clarify the situation. Find out the circumstances from your boss. Be sure you understand the details of the project. Gather information you may need about what you are already working on.

When it is time to discuss the project again, you will be prepared. Be sure your boss knows and understands the situation from your side. List what you are working on now, and make sure she is willing for you to put those things aside to work on this rush project. Or does she prefer to have you give it only part of your attention? We knew one person who, when her boss piled new work on her desk, made a list of all the projects she was currently managing. Then she handed the list to her boss and asked him to number the list in the order that he wanted things done. It made him decide what his priorities were.

You can make a number of suggestions for how to complete the project given the circumstances. (This means you will have brainstormed for ideas before you met with her.) One option might be for the boss (perhaps with your help) to find more resources. Two people could perhaps help with the project, thus halving the time it will take to complete. Another option would be for your boss to get an extension of the time allotted for the project. To do this, she would have to negotiate with her boss. A third option might be to change the specs of the project, perhaps making it less detailed or more streamlined, which would allow you to complete it in less time.

You also could suggest, "If I stay late several nights to do this project, I would like to take compensatory time off," or "If I do this project, then I need help to complete my other projects on time or else an extension." These are compromising strategies, which we take up in the next chapter.

This example illustrates that even an apparently simple negotiation can be more complex than it at first appears. In this case, it involves not just you and your boss but her boss as well (and who knows who else?). In any situation, it helps to break down a problem into its component parts and try to get at the underlying needs.

SUMMARY

When you play the collaborative negotiating game, your objective is to maximize your outcome on the substantive issues and sustain or enhance the quality of the relationship between you and the other side. To do so, you need to meet your outcome needs as well as the needs of the other party in a manner that strengthens the trust, mutuality, and productive problem solving in the relationship.

Good collaboration is a wonderful thing to be able to create and sustain. But it is not an all-purpose panacea, and making it work well often requires a large commitment of time and energy. There are times when the parties might be just as well off to compromise, accommodate, or even avoid negotiations. In the following chapters, we take a look at these alternative negotiating strategies.

Notes

1. J. Camp, *Start with No: The Negotiating Tools That the Pros Don't Want You to Know* (New York: Crown, 2002).
2. L. Bossidy and R. Charan, *Execution: The Discipline of Getting Things Done* (New York: Crown, 2002).
3. G. F. Shea, "Learn How to Treasure Differences," *HR Magazine*, Dec. 1992, pp. 34–37.
4. C. M. Crumbaugh and G. W. Evans, "Presentation Format, Other Persons' Strategies and Cooperative Behavior in the Prisoner's Dilemma," *Psychological Reports*, 1967, *20*, 895–902; R. L. Michelini, "Effects of Prior Interaction, Contact, Strategy, and Expectation of Meeting on Gain Behavior and Sentiment," *Journal of Conflict Resolution*, 1971, *15*, 97–103; S. Oksamp, "Effects of Programmed Initial Strategies in a Prisoner's Dilemma Game," *Psychometrics*, 1970, *19*, 195–196; V. Sermat and R. P. Gregovich, "The Effect of Experimental Manipulation on Cooperative Behavior in a Checkers Game," *Psychometric Science*, 1966, *4*, 435–436.
5. R. J. Lewicki and B. B. Bunker, "Trust in Relationships: A Model of Trust Development and Decline," in J. Z. Rubin and B. B. Bunker (eds.), *Conflict, Cooperation and Justice* (San Francisco: Jossey-Bass, 1995).
6. J. Kotter, *Power and Influence: Beyond Formal Authority* (New York: Free Press, 1985).
7. R. Fisher and W. Ury, *Getting to Yes* (Boston: Houghton Mifflin, 1981); R. Fisher, W. Ury, and B. Patton, *Getting to Yes: Negotiating Agreement Without Giving In,* 2nd ed. (New York: Penguin Books, 1991).
8. Fisher and Ury, *Getting to Yes*; Fisher, Ury, and Patton, *Getting to Yes.*
9. A. Williams, "Managing Employee Conflict," *Hotels,* July 1992, p. 23.
10. D. G. Pruitt, "Strategic Choice in Negotiation," *American Behavioral Scientist,* 1983, *27*, 167–194; Fisher, Ury, and Patton, *Getting to Yes.*
11. D. G. Pruitt, "Achieving Integrative Agreements," in M. Bazerman and R. Lewicki (eds.), *Negotiating in Organizations* (Thousand Oaks, Calif.: Sage, 1983); R. J. Lewicki, J. Litterer, J. Minton, and D. A. Saunders, *Negotiation,* 2nd ed. (Burr Ridge, Ill.: Irwin, 1994).
12. M. B. Grover, "Letting Both Sides Win," *Forbes,* Sept. 30, 1991, p. 178.
13. D. G. Pruitt, "Strategic Choice in Negotiation," *American Behavioral Scientist,* 1983, *27*, 167–194; Fisher, Ury, and Patton, *Getting to Yes.*
14. Fisher and Ury, *Getting to Yes.*
15. A. Filley, *Interpersonal Conflict Resolution* (Glenview, Ill.: Scott, Foresman, 1973); D. G. Pruitt and P.J.D. Carnevale, *Negotiation in Social Conflict* (Pacific Grove, Calif.: Brooks-Cole, 1993); G. F. Shea, *Creative Negotiating* (Boston: CBI Publishing, 1983); R. Walton and R. McKersie,

A Behavioral Theory of Labor Negotiations (New York: McGraw-Hill, 1965).

16. Shea, "Learn How to Treasure Differences."

17. Fisher and Ury, *Getting to Yes.*

18. B. H. Sheppard, R. J. Lewicki, and J. Minton, *Organizational Justice* (New York: Free Press, 1992).

19. R. H. Mouritsen, "Client Involvement Through Negotiation: A Key to Success," *American Salesman,* Aug. 1993, pp. 24–27.

20. Pruitt, "Strategic Choice in Negotiation"; D. G. Pruitt, *Negotiation Behavior* (Orlando, Fla.: Academic Press, 1981); Filley, *Interpersonal Conflict Resolution.*

21. Fisher, Ury, and Patton, *Getting to Yes.*

22. R. J. Lewicki, D. M. Saunders, and B. Barry, *Negotiation,* 5th ed. (Burr Ridge, Ill.: McGraw-Hill/Irwin, 2006).

23. Mouritsen, "Client Involvement Through Negotiation."

24. T. Gosselin, "Negotiating with Your Boss," *Training and Development,* May 1993, pp. 37–41; M. B. Grover, "Letting Both Sides Win," *Forbes,* Sept. 30, 1991, p. 178.

CHAPTER SEVEN

MASTERING THE ART OF COMPROMISE

With its appeal to fairness and equity, compromise is a powerful concept, and we urge you to treat it with respect. Compromise strategies may seem simple and easy to execute at first glance. But there is an art to compromise, and master negotiators are mindful of many factors and tactics as they work on a compromise deal.

Compromises are, at least on the surface, simple, fair ways of settling differences. If you and a coworker each want to take early lunches but one of you needs to stay on duty, it's easy to compromise by alternating days. You get the desired early period every other day.

Perhaps there are more elegant solutions. Maybe you would prefer to take early lunch two days in a row next week when you have a scheduling problem, but other times you'd be willing to skip lunch hour all week if you could leave a little early in exchange. To explore more sophisticated alternatives such as these, you'd need to engage in a more involved negotiation. Competition or (even better) collaboration would do the trick. But to achieve a simple, equitable solution in a hurry, compromising will do.

Compromising may be thought of as an "adequate for most occasions" approach to negotiation. In this strategy, each side will have to modify its priorities for the relationship and for the preferred outcome. In both cases, the parties are making a decision that compromising is preferred because *both* parties gain something (an advantage over accommodation or competition), both parties gain *something* (as opposed to nothing—an advantage over avoiding), and yet compromising does not require all the intentional effort required for collaboration.

While many negotiators usually don't start off planning a compromise (particularly if a competitive or collaborative negotiation is possible), compromising is often seen as an acceptable second choice. You should turn to compromise when more involved negotiations don't seem worth the trouble but you still want to take care of outcome and relationship concerns.

We also feel that the spirit of compromise is an important one in many difficult negotiations. There are times in business, especially in multiparty negotiations, where it's hard to bring all the parties into a like-minded agreement. Durable differences may always exist. For example, when businesses negotiate with environmentalists over plans to expand facilities or develop land, we know that the grounds for common cause are limited and that there will be ongoing disagreements. Collaboration can help in these situations, and it often does. Many times the business will agree to set aside some land for conservation or public use, and the environmentalists and local zoning board will permit some development in exchange. You cannot come up with such plans unless you share some of each side's information and requirements in a collaborative style. But in the end, the solution usually has to take the form of a compromise, with clear accommodations on each side reaching some reasonable middle ground. To gain acceptance for any solution where it is impossible to make anyone completely happy, compromises work well because they bring a sense of fairness and balance that helps the parties live with something short of their ideal.

Before we get into the details of the compromise strategy and how to use it, we want to emphasize the value of this spirit of compromise and recommend that you evoke it whenever you seem to be stuck in a difficult negotiation—even if that negotiation has been based on a different style so far. Compromises can be great problem solvers whenever parties seem stuck at loggerheads and don't know how to move forward or when time or other pressures push you toward a less-than-optimal solution.

WHEN TO COMPROMISE

There are several other major reasons to choose a compromise strategy (particularly as a default alternative to other strategies):[1]

- A true collaboration does not seem to be possible but the relationship is important. Perhaps one or both parties don't believe that a true win-win can be achieved because the situation is too complex or too difficult to find a way to expand the pie. Or the relationship may already be too strained for the parties to work together in a manner that fosters and supports good collaboration.
- A party's position is weaker than that of the other side. Weaker parties may not feel comfortable fully sharing interests or engaging in collaboration because they are afraid that disclosing information will create greater vulnerability. It may also be used by a party who wants to show some degree of concern for the other and sees the other as weaker—but also does not want to give the other everything. It can help avoid prolonged conflict.
- The parties are short of time or other critical resources necessary to get to collaboration. Effective competition and collaboration usually require lots of time to pursue effectively: competitive strategy because it may take a long time to wear the other side down and collaborative strategy because it takes an equally long time to find a good solution and preserve the relationship. In contrast, compromising is usually quick and efficient. While it may be suboptimal on the quality of the outcomes achieved, the trade-off between achieving a great outcome and the time required to do it may lead you to prefer saving time over investing too much in trying to achieve a higher-quality result.
- Your competitors are chasing the deal. The most common source of time pressure for many business negotiators is competitive pressure. Just yesterday, the business of one of us (Alex), which publishes training materials for employers, lost a big sale to a competitor. The competitor undercut Alex's price by one penny. But the purchasing agent, who works for a large government agency, is required to buy at the lowest price and therefore had to switch. How did this happen? Perhaps by trying a bit too hard to negotiate a good price from that customer. In the future, Alex's staff are

determined to close such deals more quickly in order to make it harder for competitors to learn about the deal and submit competing offers. If you have a lot of competitive pressure, it often pays to close deals quickly through an efficient compromise with the customer instead of dragging the negotiations out and leaving the deal vulnerable to competitors. Strike when the iron is hot, as the old saying goes!

• Compromise when the resources are limited and can't be expanded or creatively shared. Rather than engage in a big argument in which both sides try to compete to win the resources or try to collaborate but can't find an inventive way to satisfy either objectives or interests, compromise may be a satisfactory solution.

• Compromise if both parties want to be assured that they gain something, and don't lose anything, on their key issues. In a competitive negotiation, there is always the chance that you'll end up a loser. Compromising ensures some gain on both the outcome and relationship dimensions of the negotiation, even though it may not give you the maximum possible gains.

• If there are good options available on each side, one party might propose a compromise to obtain a concession on one of their more important objectives.[2] This works well, for example, if you know that the other party wants a particular concession badly and you are in a position to trade off for something that you want. When the parties have multiple issues on the table, compromising often employs a quick and expedient logrolling process in which first one side and then the other offer straightforward concessions to achieve a deal with ease.

There are also times when compromise is clearly the wrong strategy. For example, if you are representing an employer in a salary negotiation, you may have some clear boundaries you have to live within. You have probably researched the pay range in the marketplace for this position and don't want to go above it. And you may want to make sure the new employee's compensation fits into the existing pay scale in your organization. It might not be practical to pay this person twice as much as you do others who already hold similar positions on your staff.

If you have constraints such as these, you need to make it clear up front that you aren't negotiating freely but instead have to work within these constraints. Signal that you are not free to compromise. Otherwise the other party may just throw out an extreme offer and then expect you to move halfway between your offer and his or hers.

To see a constrained bargaining system that prevents people from using extreme offers to bias compromise in their favor, visit www.rubylane.com. This Web site represents thousands of antique dealers. The dealers set a price for each item but also can give the shopper the option to make an offer. When you click on the Make an Offer button, you see a screen warning you to make a reasonable offer because the counteroffer will be worse if your offer is too far below the list price. And indeed this is the case. The best way to get a good price on Ruby Lane is to make an offer that is 10 to 15 percent off list. In this case, the system often brings back a split-the-difference compromise. But if you offer 25 or 50 percent off, you will get a counteroffer that has moved down only a percent or two from list. We find this system a good model for compromise. It demonstrates the power of establishing norms for reasonable behavior. Let people know what you think is reasonable and make it clear that you won't "play ball" unless they stay in the reasonable range.

A CLASSIC CASE OF COMPROMISE

There are times when compromise is the only way to move ahead on a business project. The Whitney Museum's struggle to expand is a great illustration of the power of compromise to break a logjam and move forward.

The Whitney Museum of American Art in New York City knew it needed to expand, and so it had gradually acquired a row of six brownstones, traditional brick residences, next to it. And it had hired a famous architect, Renzo Piano, to design a new addition. The design called for the demolition of two brownstones so that the Whitney could expand out to the street with a tall, modern entry hall.

Funds were raised, approval given by the museum's board of directors, and everything seemed ready to go. However, there was one small hitch: the brownstones fell under the regulatory authority of the New York City Landmarks Preservation Commission, whose mission is to save old buildings, not to agree to see them replaced with new ones. In earlier hearings, the members of the Preservation Commission were clearly upset by the architect's plans. They voiced strong opposition and sent the museum back to the drawing board.

Over the previous two decades, the museum had presented expansion plans twice before. And each time, opposition from the Preservation Commission and neighbors had been responsible for the plans having to be abandoned. This time, the Whitney's chairman, Leonard Lauder, was determined to resolve these differences and find a way to reach agreement with the commission. The architect was also eager to negotiate. Nobody wanted to have to shelve the plans for another decade.

That's why the new plan they submitted to the commission called for the demolition of only two of the six brownstones the museum owns. The idea was to build a nine-story tower behind four of the brownstone houses and to replace two of them with a thirty-two-foot-wide entry hall. The remaining four, they told the commission, would be rented out to retail shops and left in their current architectural condition.

Some of the commission members felt that this proposal was a reasonable compromise. In fact, most people following the case thought the Whitney had enough votes on the commission to win approval for its plan if it forced the issue. However, other commission members were unhappy with the plan, and the debate threatened to be a tough one.

The Whitney didn't force a vote. Instead, Piano, the architect, drew a new plan that preserved another brownstone, and narrowed the museum entry from thirty-two feet to only sixteen feet. This goodwill gesture won "effusive praise for the project" from commission members.[3]

There is always controversy about such projects, and at the hearing, protesters showed up and displayed a large sign complaining that the new building would ruin the appearance of the block. But the Whitney's flexible approach won praise from most people and created a positive feeling about the project that the museum's board hopes will benefit it in years to come.

Was the compromise worth it? Piano was quoted in the same *New York Times* story as saying that the new plan "was not a compromise." But, he added later, it was "a limitation" to the design that would take hard work to get around.[4] Call it what they will, it sure looks like a compromise to us.

What do you think? Should the Whitney and its architect have accommodated the Preservation Commission to the degree they did, or should they have forced a vote and tried to win approval for their original design? What would *you* have done? Would you have made the series of compromises that permitted this project to go ahead in a spirit of goodwill, or would you have fought harder for a plan that was more favorable to the museum?

MIXING STYLES TO ACHIEVE COMPROMISE

Compromise is at the center of our negotiating strategies in Figure 2.2. When implemented, the compromise style of negotiating is often a blend of other styles. The approach in compromising is to gain something on the outcome dimension, but not push for completely meeting one's objectives and needs. This often translates into splitting the difference in some way between or among the parties; by not pressing for the maximum, everyone gets something equitable. It is also a way to gain something on the relationship dimension, between working hard to develop the relationship (collaboration or accommodation) and not working hard to develop the relationship.

A compromise does not have to be an exactly even split, but because it is some kind of symmetrical or logical split, it is easier to obtain agreement with the other party than it is through competing or collaboration. Moreover, the outcome is likely to be more beneficial than through avoiding or accommodation.

With compromising, you show some concern for the relationship because you do not insist on a complete win (as in the competitive strategy), and you demonstrate empathy by ensuring that the other party gets something on the outcome dimension as well. You are also showing that you care, to some degree, whether the other party achieves its outcomes in the negotiation, demonstrating empathy for the other's concerns.

By showing that you care enough to seek an equitable compromise, you may well enhance your image with the other as someone who is reasonable, fair, and willing to help both sides gain something quickly or expeditiously—key intangibles that often make a difference to both outcome and relationship.

BALANCING THE COSTS AND BENEFITS OF COMPROMISE

The low negotiating costs of an agreement through compromise are beneficial but are balanced by the higher opportunity costs of the strategy. The compromise may result in satisfying some of each party's objectives, but it does not optimize the situation in the way that collaboration can. In the case of the Whitney Museum addition, the museum's board and architect have to live with a sixteen-foot-wide entry instead of a thirty-two-foot-wide one. But they were able to get started on their construction project instead of being tied up in continued debate.

Basically, compromise often means trading equivalent concessions. Although both sides end up with less than they wanted ("50 percent of something is better than 100 percent of nothing"[5]), they also don't maximize. The objective is for the deal to benefit both parties to some degree, so that both are invested in making the agreement work.[6]

Beginning negotiators sometimes say, "Why aren't all concessions roughly reciprocal?" Indeed, why aren't they? In competitive negotiations, the parties engage in gamesmanship in order to achieve asymmetrical concessions in their own favor. They use clever (even deceitful) tactics, or leverage their position power, or take advantage of time pressure, for just a few examples of ways to get more than you give away during a negotiation. But in a proper compromise, the negotiators are more committed to fair and equitable concessions. For this reason, compromises are fundamentally more ethical and well mannered. They are a civil form of distributive bargaining. If you have qualms about the ethics of tough competitive negotiations, then the compromise strategy may be the best for you. But we think it is important for each negotiator to decide how ethical and fair they want to be, and want others to be, in negotiations. If you find some forms of competitive negotiation to be distasteful and to offend your sense of ethics, that's a good reason for compromising instead of competing. But try to convince the other party to embrace this ethical approach too, or you'll find that your concessions are fair but theirs aren't.

There is a lot of gamesmanship in some negotiators' approach to compromise, so consider yourself to be forewarned. For example, the "after you" tactic can bias the concessions toward the savvier negotiator.

MASTERING THE "AFTER YOU" TACTIC

"Let's compromise." How many times has someone said those famous words as an invitation to strike a quick, simple deal when a conflict bogs things down? By saying, "Let's compromise," you immediately signal your willingness to expedite the resolution of the problem by behaving in a reasonable, flexible manner.

But if you are concerned that the other party may still want to try to "play" you, don't stop there. In the "after you" tactic, you say, "Let's compromise. What do you think is fair?" This invites the *other* party to make the first concession, and it sets the bottom limit on what you'll have to give up. It also gives you the opportunity to simply say no if the offer is clearly more than twice as low as your target. If so, politely say something like, "Maybe compromising isn't such a good idea after all." Postpone the compromise, treating the first round as a trial balloon. Then try to initiate a compromise later with a more favorable opening (using the same "after you" tactic).

But most likely, the other party's opening offer will be reasonable, and you can start bargaining from there. If she wants a compromise too, she will make a reasonable or even generous opening offer. By letting her go first, you often get a more favorable outcome than if you had made the first offer. The party who makes the opening offer is more likely to end up giving slightly more away.

THE TACTICS OF MASTER COMPROMISERS

Following are some suggestions for how to compromise successfully. We consider success in compromises to be a personally satisfying outcome that also leaves the other party reasonably satisfied. Here are the tactics:

- *Do your homework.* Know what you want. Be sure you have clear goals and objectives. You need to know what you want to fight for and what you are willing to give up. You need to be strongly committed to your objectives, or you may be forced into a position of giving away everything, or at least those things that you wanted most.

- *Prioritize your goals.* If you are going to compromise, you need to know what you must have, as opposed to what would be nice to have. The nice-to-haves may be given up for obtaining the must-haves. Remember that you need to be prepared to make significant concessions in order to compromise. Don't begin if you aren't flexible.

- *Know your walkaway and alternatives.* This can give you power in the negotiations, because at some point, you may be better off pursuing your alternative than settling for a suboptimal agreement. Know your walkaway point, so that if you need to, you can abandon the negotiation. This too can give you power.

- *Know which person will make the decision.* If the person you are negotiating with does not have the authority to make an agreement, you may be spending a lot of time waiting while he or she consults with the one who does. It may be better and more efficient for you to present the benefits of your proposal to the decision maker.

- *Show that you want to negotiate.* Say and do what is necessary to overcome the other party's reticence or distrust. Look at the other party's problems, and try to make sure that your proposal effectively resolves some of their key issues. This will give you an image of empathy and fairness, which is necessary for effective compromises.

- *Try not to be the first side to make a major concession.* Since making concessions may be interpreted as a sign of weakness, the other party may take advantage of this and become aggressive, pushing you further than you wish to go. This will escalate the proceedings so that the more you give in, the more the other party will ask for. You will find yourself moved into an accommodating strategy, not a compromising one.

- *Do not wait until the deadline to offer a compromise.* Compromises should be offered from a position of strength, not as a last-ditch gesture, which would suggest to the other party that you are in a weaker position. If the deadline is close and you want to offer a compromise, offer it early enough that the other side can truly consider it. If you wait too long, the other party's deadline may have passed, and either he or she will be very upset or may have lost all possibility of advantage and now may simply want to sabotage the negotiation process.

- *Start with small compromises.* A gradual or staged approach can help you to move toward more compromise. If you work in small steps, each party can move toward a reasonable solution. Moving too fast may escalate the other party's demands.

- *Use your concessions to your advantage.* When you make a concession, be sure that the other party gets the message that you are interested in a positive outcome and want to deal with him or her. Ask for a reciprocal concession in return.

- *Don't make unreciprocated concessions.* If you've made a concession and the other party isn't responding, it can be tempting to make an additional concession. But this just conditions him or her to wait you out. You never want to give the impression that you're negotiating with yourself. Make him or her reciprocate before you move again.

- *Use your offers to communicate where you stand.* As you approach the end of your offers, they should be smaller and fewer to signal the other party that you are near the end. If the other party is alert, he or she will understand that you cannot be pushed to make further offers. The same is true for your side: watch the other party's offers, and be alert for signs of distress. When he or she have reached their limit, you should not push for more concessions. You risk breaking off negotiations entirely.

- *Do not push too hard.* Try to avoid the classic assumption of negotiation that you have to win everything you can. Pushing may result in negotiations coming to an abrupt halt, since it sends the message that you are competing instead of collaborating. Imagine you are interviewing a young manager who seems perfect for the job of leading a project team, a position that normally pays $85,000 per year. If the candidate says she's interested in the position and would be happy to do it for $150,000 per year, you may be put off by her pushy first offer and have second thoughts about continuing to negotiate with her. If another candidate asks for $90,000, you may think he's reasonable and easy to deal with and compromise on a salary of $87,000. Perhaps that was the target of the first candidate too, but her pushy first offer destroyed her chances of landing the job.

- *Remember that the split does not have to be even.* In compromising, it may not be possible, or even desirable, to split it down the middle, although that is the most frequent way it is done. A compromise is often based on where the two parties currently stand, but that does not mean that they made equal concessions to get to that point. If one party has moved $2,000 from the starting point and the other party has moved $5,000 and they are still $4,000 apart, a split down the middle is a compromise, but it yields a deal that means one party had to concede only $4,000 while the other conceded $7,000. It's a good idea to remind the other party about how you got to where you are if you find yourself in danger of getting the short end of the stick in a situation like this. (If it's the other party's problem, then you have to decide whether you want to be strictly fair and ethical, or if you want to suggest that split down the middle and see if you can get away with a compromise that goes slightly in your side's favor. Think your ethics and values through in advance so you are clear on the extent to which you want to keep this compromise strictly symmetrical.)

- *Seek win-win compromises.* Ask the other party about his or her underlying interests and concerns. It may be that while your solution can't meet all his or her needs or interests, what you can do together is an improvement over the existing situation. The compromise looks distinctly better than no agreement.

- *Try not to close too quickly.* Although a scarcity of time is one of the primary motivators of the compromise strategy, it does not mean you have to do it with lightning speed. You may be eager to complete the transaction, but if a deal occurs too quickly, people frequently wonder whether they could have done better. If you are selling, make at least one counteroffer so the buyer will be confident of having obtained the best price. If you are buying, offer low at first and then move up. People like to feel that they have earned what they've won. Resist going for the 1–2–3 deal (offer, counteroffer, and then split it down the middle). It takes at least a few more rounds to be sure you've forged a decent compromise.

- *Promote the long-term benefits.* Point out that there can be an ongoing relationship between the parties (if this is true). One benefit of a successful compromise is that at best, the future is not put in jeopardy, and the possibility of future business together remains viable. In fact, a compromise now might lay the groundwork for future collaboration. Looking at it from another angle, a negotiation that does not go well presents the potential of lost future business.

• *Stay focused on the issues.* The other side may use dirty tactics in trying to push for more concessions. Try to ignore these if possible, and stay with your established bottom line. In other words, be firm, particularly if the other party switches to a competitive style.

• *Be polite.* Avoid the hardball tactics of competition. Compromises should be civilized deals, marked by respect and good manners. As Miss Manners so ably put it, "Everybody wants other people to be polite to them, but they want the freedom of not having to be polite to others."[7]

Avoiding the Dangers of Compromise

While compromise has a number of advantages, there are also a number of pitfalls to avoid. Here are a few to keep in mind.

Avoiding the Compliance Trap

When seeking collaborative resolutions for stalled compromises, you need to take care to avoid falling into compliance.[8] Compliance is agreeing to go along with something that you would really prefer not to do or agreeing to something you really did not want to.

Sometimes people comply with requests when they prefer not to. Why they do this is something that even they may not know. For example, in spite of numerous private and public pledges to the contrary, people buy product offers (books, computer software, investments) or make gifts and contributions to telephone marketers and door-to-door solicitors. They just can't say no, even to someone they don't really care about and for a product that they don't care much for either.

For example, a solicitor for a charity will call and request a gift of fifty dollars. Rather than say no, people often give a gift of twenty-five dollars just to "compromise" and get the solicitor to go away. This is not compromise; it is compliance. You need to be aware of this possibility and take time to evaluate what you really want out of the situation. If you have done the careful thinking and evaluation we recommend, this should not be difficult. But because salespeople and marketers often catch you unaware, you have not had a chance to do any of your planning; hence, you comply with at least part of their request.

AVOIDING THE RECIPROCITY TRAP

Compromises are based on fairness, and so it is easy to be drawn into compromising in the name of fairness when you really didn't want to make a deal at all. Reciprocity is the theme in compromising: give and take, tit for tat, I give you something and you give me something.

People may even offer compliments or favors to get something in return. If the exchange seems fair and appropriate and you want it, accept the offer, providing it does not have unwanted strings attached. But if it is a favor given with the notion of getting something in return, be sure you fully understand what is going to be expected of you.

While writing this chapter, one of us (Alex) was called by a representative of a marketing firm. The firm offered a choice of "free" videos; once the author had selected the free video he wanted, he was then told that it was indeed a free gift but required considering other videos to purchase, one per month, for twelve months. The implication—without ever saying so—was that since the marketing firm had started off doing something for the respondent, it was his "obligation" to reciprocate and do something for them. This is a very popular sales tactic. So what did the author do? Not unsurprisingly, he just said no.

GETTING GOOD AT SAYING NO

Our lives are full of attractive-sounding offers from salespeople, business associates, and friends, but many of these deals turn out to be undesirable. You should feel free to reject even the most attractive-sounding offer if you don't like the smell of it or even if you simply haven't the time and energy to research it at the moment. But if you decide to refuse an offer, be careful how you do it.

A person making a genuine offer with no strings attached may be insulted if you attack or impugn the offer or the person's motives in offering it to you. Also in some cultures, gift giving may be much more acceptable than in others. For example, in the American public sector, gift giving is frowned on, but in Japan, presents are traditionally part of the early relationship-building process.

You can refuse any gift or other offer, of course, but do so politely and with an explanation of why it's impossible for you to accept it. For example, you could say, "My company's policy forbids me to accept gifts" or (to that pesky marketer) "I make a practice of never deciding about deals on the phone. You'll have to write to me if you want me to consider it." If they object that *they* never do deals by mail, then you know something's fishy and you won't mind offending them by hanging up.

One of us (Alex) was recently invited to present to a group of faculty at the U.S. Coast Guard's leadership academy. After the workshop, the lieutenant commander took the floor to thank him and offered him a polo shirt with the academy's logo on it. Caught off guard and wanting to reciprocate, Alex quickly inscribed a thank-you message on the inside cover of a book he had written on leadership—he happened to have a new copy of it in his briefcase. Then he thanked the group and presented the book to the lieutenant commander. In fact, this was an improper thing to do, since nobody in U.S. government employ is permitted to accept gifts from "vendors," which Alex arguably was since he'd been paid for leading the workshop. Fortunately, the lieutenant commander handled the situation with grace. He thanked Alex for the gift and announced to the group that he would place the book in the academy's library. It turns out that it is fine to donate a book to the academy but not to give it to an individual. By handling the gift this way, the commander managed to take care of etiquette and also comply with the Coast Guard's regulations concerning gifts. In essence, he managed to say no without embarrassing Alex by rejecting his gift.

Avoiding the Commitment Trap

If you are heavily committed to obtaining something that looks unbelievably attractive on the surface, you may find yourself the object of a bait-and-switch tactic.

A classic example is a store advertisement for a product such as a better-quality cell phone that looks like a real bargain. When you arrive at the store to buy the cell phone, a salesperson tells you that they are "all out," but that they have another product "of equivalent quality"—but it is not on sale and actually retails for twenty dollars more. If you really want a new cell phone, you may fall for the bait-and-switch tactic. You may end up with a good product but wind up paying twenty dollars more for it than you expected. Or, worse, you may end up paying more for an inferior product, since there is also the possibility that it is inferior to the one advertised.

In a variant of the commitment trap, the other party may conceal secondary commitments or terms until you are already committed to the main deal. For example, maybe that cell phone really is free—but only if you buy a three-year calling plan with a high monthly cost. By the time you learn this, you have been imagining yourself using the cool new features of that cell phone, and you may get pulled into the deal even though it's not a reasonable one. Many negotiators engage in reasonable, even excessive, concessions early in a compromise, as if trying to bait you with an offer that is too good to be true. Then they, like some unscrupulous advertiser, begin to add new wrinkles and make it harder for you to close the deal than you thought. If this happens, explain that you are concerned about the new issues or costs and need time to think about these. Walk away for long enough to regain objectivity and make sure you aren't falling into a commitment trap.

The bait-and-switch tactic often surfaces in negotiation when one party promises to do something and then suddenly switches to a different commitment, saying it is "just the same." But, of course, it probably isn't equivalent. To avoid this problem, write down what has been offered. This may increase and lock in their commitment to the initial offer and prevent switching tactics.

Sometimes we fall into the commitment trap because of concerns about losing face. It can be embarrassing to admit (to others and even to yourself) that you made a mistake and that the deal you thought was good actually isn't. The cure for this is humility. Admit that negotiating is difficult and that you, like all other negotiators, sometimes make mistakes.

The commitment trap takes many forms. One of them is termed *social proof* in the academic world: endorsements and statements of support from others, especially people whom we see as "experts," tend to lead us to commit to something. If a person with some perceived expertise on the subject says it is true (remember the old cigarette advertisement that promised, "Out of 100 doctors, 73 percent prefer x brand cigarettes"?), then we think it must be true. Many negotiators will give the impression, or state as fact, that other businesses accept their terms, so you should too. Social proof is not a good reason to accept their terms. Even if it is true that others do it this way, the deal may not be advantageous to you or your organization.[9]

Do not let yourself be railroaded by what looks like strong "expert" proof. Even among specialists, people do not always agree. Any body of knowledge is open to interpretation. If you are concerned about a source's qualifications or education, ask for substantiation of the person's background and credentials or get a second opinion. Request more time to consider what has been presented. Ask an objective person whom you know, respect, and trust and who will give you good information. A good example of the expert proof variation on the social trap is in the use of an appraisal in real estate deals. Appraisals, in the United States at least, are supposed to be performed by independent, objective, licensed appraisers. But if you obtain more than one appraisal on a piece of property, you will get more than one number. So just because the other party presents an "objective" expert appraisal, don't take the number for granted. Get one or more appraisals of your own, or simply point out that this appraised value is only an estimate and shouldn't be taken as gospel.

Sometimes a clever negotiator will solicit or buy opinions from several different experts, then use only the one that is most favorable to his or her interests. We don't recommend this as a tactic because it means concealing information in a manner that is certainly unethical and may be illegal in some cases as well. But recognize that others may do this. When the other party presents an expert opinion to bolster the claim that his offer is reasonable, ask if he has any other expert opinions or appraisals. He may be hesitant to lie outright by denying it if he does. So if he says yes or acts equivocal or uncertain, then you can request, firmly but politely, to see all of the appraisals or opinions. Now you are in a stronger negotiating position. If he lets you see the others, you can use all of them, not just the one the other party liked the best. If he doesn't, you can discount the one he showed you.

Avoiding the Likability Trap

We also tend to be more easily influenced by someone we like or find personally attractive. Based on that fact, a negotiating team may be selected for its friendliness, congeniality, and warmth. When engaged in a negotiation, ask yourself if the other party is intentionally trying to be as likable as possible, and if this may in fact be an effort to manipulate you instead of a genuine interest in you. It is much easier to do business with people who are friendly and pleasant to be around. But if they ask you to make a concession that is not fair and balanced, be aware that they may be leveraging the relationship unfairly.

In many negotiations, the parties spend some time "getting to know each other" before getting down to business, and in this phase of the process, likability can be critical to "warming the other up." This can also be seen as a variation on the good cop–bad cop technique. To set you up for the tough "bad cop," the other party may first be warming you up to the "good cop."

It is important to be aware of your personal feelings about the other party and to be able to separate personalities from the negotiation. Remember that this is a negotiation, and stay focused on your objectives.

Avoiding the Authority Trap

From the time we begin school, we tend to respect people who have formal authority over us—teachers, principals, police, clergy. Other authorities in our lives include those who make and enforce rules and people with titles (doctor, reverend, vice president, CEO, judge). We are expected to respect these authorities. However, we need to watch out for overbelieving and overrespecting titles and status, particularly when those people also have an agenda to persuade us. It is too easy to find yourself giving larger concessions simply because of the assumed power of the other party's title or position.

Although some parties have authority by virtue of their title, formal position, or expertise, people tend to overgeneralize the scope of their expertise, and those with that authority may tend to overextend its application. For example, in our culture, we tend to view attorneys as smart people who know the law and its applications. Often lawyers are hired to negotiate for us, even though they may have less training in negotiation than you who are reading this book. Don't get pushed into compromises by people who may claim expertise, but who may want to steer you away from what you really want.

AVOIDING THE SCARCITY BIAS

Scarcity of resources affects our attitude toward them. If you want something and you learn that the supply is running short, or that only one item remains, or that the merchandise is an "exclusive," are you more tempted to acquire it? Are you more pleased when you manage to get it? Is your curiosity piqued when you are told that something was censored? Some people are willing to pay a lot for one-of-a-kind or limited-offering items.[10]

To guard against scarcity-based compliance, consider your underlying reasons for wanting an item or option. Be aware of the temptation associated with scarcity.

COMPROMISING WITH YOUR BOSS

Negotiating with the boss is not always easy or pleasant, but most of us have to do it occasionally. Although salary is a common topic for competitive negotiation, that usually occurs only once a year at most. What is more frequently an issue for negotiation is a situation where you are asked to do work above and beyond the call of duty—in other words, more than your job description or time will permit. Such requests often lead to a compromise since it is important to the employee to avoid a negative style of negotiating.

From the employee's perspective, a collaborative style is preferable, because this style is most likely to satisfy the employee's needs. While employees would like to use a collaborative style with their boss, it is not always feasible. More frequently, employees find themselves entertaining accommodating, avoidance, and compromising deals. There are two primary reasons for this. First, employees tend to believe that resources are fixed (that is, they cannot be expanded). Money may already be budgeted, the number of employees is limited by a hiring freeze, the machines can operate only a certain number of hours a day, and so forth. Thus, there must be trade-offs. Second, we do not want to make the boss angry or upset by actively pursuing a competitive or collaborative negotiating style that is high on the outcome dimension (to maximize our own outcomes). Because the boss has great control over us, we want to keep him or her happy, and so we pursue the other three strategies.

Employee-manager negotiations, particularly ones that center around discussions about work and getting a job done, tend to focus on three basic components: specifications, time, and resources.[11] When you are asked to do a project (before you engage in any negotiation with your boss), you should evaluate it with respect to these three factors.

Specifications have to do with the details of a project—in other words, what the actual task is, such as making a product, providing a service, or writing a report. In evaluating a project and whether you can do it, you need to know and understand the exact nature of the project. All your estimates and planning will depend on your specifying the job correctly. If you are not sure, ask for more details.

Time is of major importance in evaluating a task. Your estimate should include not only the time involved in completing the task, but also any administrative time, such as writing a report on completion of a project or overseeing the production or printing of a report. Estimate as accurately as possible how long the project will take. Your estimate should include enough time to do a good job—not a slapdash one. Also be sure you build in a contingency plan or time buffer in case of problems. Remember Murphy's Law: "If something can go wrong, it will." If your time frame is too tight, you may suddenly have to renegotiate the project when you are in the middle of it.

Resources, the third component of a project or task, are the materials that go into the project, such as human labor, physical materials (such as paper for a report), computer time, or raw materials for the production of a product. It is important to take account of all the resources that you may need for the project and whether you can make trade-offs among them. For example, if the schedule suddenly becomes tighter, can you hire a consultant or temporary help to complete the project on schedule? Part of your own strategy should be to ensure that you will have adequate resources to complete the job.

Once you account for these three factors, they may be traded off, one for another, if necessary. Thus, if your boss wants a project done in five days instead of ten, you will need to increase resources to offset the diminished time. You may also need to make clear what jobs are not getting done so that you can devote full attention to this one, and secure additional resources to make sure your other commitments are met. If the specifications change on a project, you may need more time to complete the job according to the new specs or different labor with different skills.

You will need to know if any of the factors are fixed and therefore unchangeable. This will have considerable effect on the project, especially if another factor changes. Think about what substitutions and trade-offs you can and cannot make. Often a careful examination reveals hidden opportunities, in which case you can go back to the boss with a creative compromise that trades off something that is not so limited, thus securing you a better outcome than you at first expected was possible. And explain your position clearly, making the requirements and trade-offs in all three areas clear to your boss. You want to frame the negotiation this way by anchoring it in a discussion of the practical aspects of getting tasks done. Otherwise your boss may make impossible or unreasonable demands.

When your boss asks you to do a nearly impossible task, it is tempting to say no immediately, but this may give the impression that you are lazy, disloyal, or uncooperative.[12] Therefore, it is wise to avoid responding with a no. Instead, buy some time by saying that you would like to think about it (use the avoidance strategy to temporarily withdraw from the boss's invitation to negotiate, since you know that you have no good response to his or her opening position). It is possible that the whole problem will go away, the storm will pass, and you will not have to consider the situation again.

However, the request may well come again, in which case it is a good idea to be prepared. Asking for time gives you an opportunity to look into the situation and evaluate what you want to do. It allows you to try to redefine the problem and initiate collaboration, or—more likely with directive bosses—to keep exploring the situation and discussing the problem until a compromise can be achieved.

When you have evaluated the situation and can no longer avoid responding to your boss, we recommend that you frame the negotiation carefully by spelling out the (perhaps unreasonable) specification and defining the boss's request in terms of the amount of time and other resources needed. Then you should try to initiate a compromise with a response that is carefully worded to prevent accidental competitive negotiation and conflict.

As you discuss the unreasonable demand with your boss, use the phrase "Yes, and" rather than "Yes, but," which sounds more like "no." You can educate your boss about the costs in time and resources just as well by saying "Yes, and . . . " For example, if your boss asks you if you can cut costs by 50 percent in a month, you can say, "*Yes*, we could try to do this, *and* this would probably require us to pull people off all the other project teams, as well as to increase the budget for new equipment and supplies. Do you want me to work up a detailed plan for how much time and cost would be involved, as well as to look into how much cost savings we might be able to find in a short-term project like this?" Your boss would like you to give him a winning lottery ticket too but knows that's not a reasonable request. Your "yes, and . . . " explanation will help sort out the reasonable from the unreasonable aspects of his desire to have you cut costs. He will probably compromise on a more reasonable assignment, such as a six-month project team with the goal of a 10 percent cost cut.

Another good phrase to use if you are going to offer a compromise is "if . . . then . . . "—for example, "*If* I do this, *then* I need to have you do that for me." An even more polite variant is, "If I do this, then can you help me . . . ?" For example, you might say, "If I assemble and run a cost-cutting team, then I'll need to be relieved of at least half of my normal duties for six months. Can you help me figure out how to reassign some of my duties to others?"

"Yes, and . . . " tells the boss you are willing to help with the task. It also adds what you will need—the missing resources—if you are going to be able to do what you are being asked. You are agreeing to do the task but setting limits on what is possible—for example, "Yes, I will do it, and I will need an assistant for five days." Or, "Yes, I can do it, and it will cost a thousand dollars more than previously budgeted." Or, "Yes, and I'll need to clear my desk of other work for the week in order to get it done. Can you reassign my other projects so I can do this for you?"

This approach maximizes the chances that your boss will respond in this same spirit, in which case you will be able to implement a compromise. You and the boss will have to trade one thing for another. And even if the attempt fails and your boss responds rudely that you "better do it or else" without offering supporting resources, you are at least no worse off than when you started.

And remember: with any special request from a boss, be sure you understand exactly what the boss wants, what the time frame is, what resources are available, which aspects are fixed, and which are flexible. The trade-offs you make can result in something close to a win-win situation if you plan carefully.

Compromises are an important form of deal making, and mastering the style is well worth your effort. There are many cases in which its ease of use makes compromising the best approach. And in other situations—as when your boss makes impossible requests—it is a great ploy to turn the situation into an opportunity for compromise. Once you get used to compromising, you will find it an easy style to master.

The appeal to reasonable and fair concessions is at the heart of every compromise. With practice, you can learn to take a creative approach. Think about alternative ways of splitting the difference until you come up with a creative but fair-sounding approach that is a little more in your favor. As with all forms of negotiation, compromises benefit from creativity.

HAGGLING: A COMPETITIVE FORM OF COMPROMISE

We turn now to a strategy that is becoming more popular because of the downturn in the economy: haggling, sometimes called *dickering* or *hardball bargaining*.[13] It is a stylized variant of the compromise strategy, often with some competitive tactics and collaborative tactics thrown in for good measure. This method of settling on the price has been used in a number of other countries for a long time and is now becoming more common in the United States in retail stores that, because of the economy, are ripe for making deals. Although we are most familiar with haggling in the case of new car purchases, it is becoming more frequent in other areas as well.

The willingness to haggle varies across cultures. People from Latino, Asian, and Middle Eastern countries tend to be comfortable with haggling as a method of setting price; it is the usual way of conducting business in many countries, where bargaining is more than just agreeing on the price. There is a social value to it. It involves relationship building. In contrast, in the United States, we don't tend to haggle on most items except those with a high price tag. Thus, a second way that haggling varies is on the relative price of an item. For example, there are international differences in the things we haggle over; in the United States, we tend to simply pay what is asked for low-priced items (such as a fresh chicken for dinner) but haggle on high-price items (cars, houses, boats). In other countries, it is reversed: people pay the sticker price for a high-priced item but will haggle for an hour over the price of a chicken. The size of the store often makes a difference too. Although it is possible to bargain on some items at some department stores, it is more common and usually more successful to haggle with the owner of a small store. Sometimes the owner of a small store will not reduce the price but will throw in a gift or offer a discount to a faithful customer. The goods that are commonly haggled over are sports equipment, antiques, jewelry, suits, and shoes. Another area where haggling occurs is in the price for services: everything from cutting the lawn to washing a car to big events such as catering a wedding. It is also common to bargain about the prices of apartments, rental cars, and mortgages.

To haggle over a price, follow these suggestions:

- It is all right to ask for a price break, but be prepared for the possibility of being told no.
- Haggle only if you reasonably expect to buy the item. Once you begin to haggle with the other party, you usually are creating the expectation that you will consummate the deal if you can agree on the price.

- Be polite but firm. It is poor form to be pushy.
- Sales are good places to haggle. Items are on sale because sellers want to get rid of them. Sometimes they simply want to get them out of inventory so they don't have to pay storage costs—so you may be able to get the price tag down even further.
- Haggling is usually possible when there is no posted price. If you have to ask how much something is, the chances are you may be given a different number than the last buyer was. This is a good time to consider haggling.
- It is easier to haggle in stores where you are a regular customer than in ones where no one knows you.
- It is much easier to haggle in a small store, where you can talk with the owner directly. In larger stores, the clerk probably has no authority to make a decision about whether a price or service can be changed.
- It is often easier to haggle when you are going to pay in cash rather than with a credit card, which costs the owner when you use it. It is easier to haggle for merchandise that is marked down or on closeout sale. You might simply be able to haggle for a cash discount as compared to paying by check or credit card.

SUMMARY

In this chapter, we have reviewed techniques to master the art of compromise. While we have stressed the importance of collaboration, compromise is often a highly desirable result and one that may not be as challenging to achieve. The compromise strategy has a number of advantages and negotiators need to learn in order to master its effective use.

Notes

1. D. G. Pruitt and J. Z. Rubin, *Social Conflict: Escalation, Stalemate and Settlement* (New York: Random House, 1986).
2. R. J. Lewicki, D. M. Saunders, and B. Barry, *Negotiation*, 5th ed. (Burr Ridge, Ill.: McGraw-Hill/Irwin, 2006).
3. R. Pogrebin, "Revised Whitney Plan Wins Panel's Approval," *New York Times*, May 25, 2005.
4. Ibid.

5. J. Calano and J. Salzman, "Tough Deals, Tender Tactics," *Working Woman,* July 1988, p. 74.
6. Calano and Salzman, "Tough Deals, Tender Tactics," pp. 74–97.
7. "Polite Company: Interview with Miss Manners (Judith Martin)," *Psychology Today,* Mar.–Apr. 1998, p. 27.
8. Most of the concepts in this section are fully presented in R. B. Cialdini, *Influence: Science and Practice,* 3rd ed. (New York: HarperCollins, 1993).
9. R. Cialdini, *Influence: Science and Practice,* 4th ed. (Boston: Houghton Mifflin, 2001).
10. Cialdini, *Influence,* 4th ed.
11. S. M. Pollan and M. Levine, "Turning Down an Assignment," *Working Woman,* May 1994, p. 69.
12. Pollan and Levine, "Turning Down an Assignment."
13. "Bargaining Chips," *Los Angeles Times,* Feb. 22, 1991, pp. E1, E5.

CHAPTER EIGHT

MASTERING ACCOMMODATION AND AVOIDANCE STRATEGIES

Sometimes a negotiation is not worth the trouble. When your reaction is, "Why bother?" then perhaps you should not. There are two distinct ways to handle situations where the outcome does not seem worthwhile.

First, you can cave in, allowing the other party to have what he or she wants. Accommodating makes most sense when you care more about the relationship than the outcome—and where losing won't hurt you too badly. It also makes a lot of sense if there is a longer-term picture of reciprocal accommodation—in other words, if you are in a context in which the old saying, "What goes around, comes around," may apply. Many workplaces have a culture of mutual help and support, and you never want to ignore this longer-term perspective when negotiating a specific point or issue.

Second, you can sidestep the conflict and avoid the negotiation entirely. Don't give in, but don't pursue a win either. Avoiding makes most sense when you anticipate negatives. If the negotiation would be unpleasant because the other player is angry, for example, then avoiding makes good sense. And if neither the outcome nor the relationship is too important, then you might want to avoid the negotiation so as to be able to devote your energy to more important issues.

Avoiding is also a good option if you feel your chances of getting a good result are slim in this negotiation, and you have a more attractive alternative to pursue. Rather than spread your energy across two negotiations, avoid the less attractive option while you focus on trying to close the more attractive one. If you push forward, you may be able to find out whether you can close a good deal before your less attractive option evaporates. Leave it for a fallback.

Accommodating and avoiding: neither gets you a big win, but each is nonetheless an extremely important approach—and ones you should master in order to be well prepared for all circumstances. In this chapter we'll teach you the essence of both strategies, starting with accommodation.

ACCOMMODATION

Before we get into the details of tactics—when and how to accommodate—think about your own pattern of accommodation. When do you accommodate others? How often? How does it make you feel? Do you get good results from accommodating?

In our workshops and employee trainings, we've often administered assessments to measure individual negotiating and conflict-handling styles (they actually are one and the same; as we pointed out in the Preface, negotiation is just a specialized set of skills and behaviors for resolving conflict). Whenever we assess a group, we find that many of the people are accommodators—somewhere between 10 and 30 percent in most workplaces, and higher in traditional helping industries like health care and social work.

This means we have a fair number of people in any workshop who prefer to accommodate others. When we ask them how that works for them, they often tell us it does not work very well. The problem, it usually turns out, is that they tend to be knee-jerk accommodators. When someone is assertive, they respond by being cooperative—whether this is a good strategy or not.

What we've learned from talking with accommodators in many workplaces is that people tend to accommodate when they should not—and do not when they should. This means that they are not using accommodation strategically. It's not a difficult strategy to implement, but if you use it in the wrong contexts, no amount of tactical skill will make it a success.

We start our examination of accommodation by exploring the natural appeal of the strategy—why most of us feel the urge to accommodate and how we can retune this urge so that we are selecting the accommodate strategy appropriately, and not setting ourselves up for disappointment.

WHY WE ACCOMMODATE

People who score highest on the accommodate style in a negotiation or conflict assessment are likely to have a high prosocial orientation: they concern themselves with outcomes that benefit the group and feel responsible for helping and caring for others around them. Any healthy, normal person has a prosocial orientation, of course, which is why anyone reading this book can use styles like accommodation and collaboration. However, for some people, this prosocial orientation is stronger than their pro-self orientation. They generally default toward social behavior, as opposed to those whose balance tips a bit more toward self orientation. These pro-self individuals score higher on the compete style in their assessments. Many workplaces have a lot of these individuals, and they tend to be good competitive negotiators and bargainers because they are good at staying focused on the outcomes they wish to achieve.

When we talk about this spectrum of people with relatively stronger prosocial or pro-self orientations, we are referring to something the social scientists term *social value orientation*.[1] This orientation is one of the things that determines how often you feel an urge to accommodate. But recognize that it is a very broad aspect of temperament and does not have much to do with the specific situation and what is most likely to work in it.

The other personality-oriented variable behind accommodation (and avoidance too) is your comfort level with stressful social interactions. Some people are well hardened and aren't bothered by the rough and tumble of conflict. They don't find difficult conversations difficult for themselves. They have no trouble being assertive in social settings. Their colleagues know them as open, honest, outspoken, and perhaps fearless (they are the ones who are sent to talk with the boss, make a tough sales call, or handle an enraged customer). Others of us are more conflict averse. We find it difficult to keep our heads and manage ourselves well when interactions get stressful. In fact, for many people, conflict is so unpleasant that they avoid it in the same way that people with stage fright avoid public speaking. The majority of us don't suffer from conflict fright to a great degree, but most people find conflict at least mildly unpleasant and uncomfortable, and a fair number of us find it extremely uncomfortable.

Now, to answer the question we posed a moment ago: Why do we accommodate? First, there is a natural tendency toward prosocial orientation, that is, wanting to help others, especially in workplaces where we have ongoing relationships with many other people and groups. Second, there is a common aversion to the discomfort of dealing with stressful human interactions. Put those together, and the emotionally easiest path is often to simply accommodate: cave in and say yes, or not say anything, when really we are thinking that the other party is being inconsiderate or thoughtless and ought to have been more accommodating of our interests or ideas.

Daniel Goleman, in his book *Emotional Intelligence,* does a great job of summarizing the research on how we react. In social settings and indeed in general, we react emotionally first.[2] The more primitive parts of our brain are lower, closer to the spine, and more central to our entire nervous system. This primitive emotional reaction occurs so rapidly that we are rarely even aware that it is happening. By the time we think about it—using our cerebral cortex, which is the fancy, intelligent stuff behind our forehead—we have already logged an emotional orientation that, often unconsciously, determines how we are going to think. Yes, *emotional intelligence* is a misnomer. It sells books, but a more accurate term might be *emotional stupidity.* Unless we learn to make ourselves aware of that basic emotional response, we cannot truly bring intelligence to many of our actions, including the decision of when and how to accommodate.

Too often the managers and employees in our workshops report that they are accommodating not for thoughtful, intelligent reasons but just because, well, because they are. They don't even know why. It's that emotional stupidity rearing its primitive head again. And after they've accommodated their boss (even though she doesn't really know how to do this project and is giving them the wrong instructions), accommodated the pushy colleague who keeps dominating the meetings, or given in to the angry customer even though she wasn't right, they finally begin to feel pushed too far.

A surprising number of people in our workshops who report that their top style score (on an assessment) is accommodating also say their second-highest score is competing. If you're accommodating by nature, why would you also be competitive? This becomes a fallback strategy if you accommodate too much and in the wrong situations, until you feel pushed against the wall and finally push back.

Often others don't know you've been accommodating all along; all they see is that suddenly you are reacting strongly and assertively, and so they think you are unpredictable, difficult, and assertive. When this pattern has happened among multiple people in an office, team, or other work group, it can get to the point that almost everyone is unhappy with everyone else, communications are poor, and little cooperation actually goes on. We suspect that this pattern is at work in many workplaces, reducing productivity and making work a lot more stressful than it needs to be. And we also believe that the root of a lot of these productivity and stress problems is a lack of strategic accommodation. It is very important to know when and how to assert, and when and how *not* to assert. If you've ever been to or heard of assertiveness training, this is the core skill it is (or at least ought to be) all about.

Now let's go back to the question of when to use accommodation as a rational strategy rather than an emotional knee-jerk reaction.

When to Accommodate

Accommodation is used when the relationship is more important than the outcome of the negotiation. The person using this strategy prefers to concentrate on building or strengthening the relationship. Since other people are usually happy when we give them what they want, we may simply choose to avoid focusing on the outcome and give in to the other side, thus making this person happy. And since accommodating someone generally pleases him or her, it is often wise to make some accommodations as an investment in goodwill. As John F. Kennedy put it, "The time to repair a roof is when the sun is shining." Accommodation can be a good way to invest in and maintain strong business relationships.

But note that accommodation usually needs to be a visible strategy. You want to be clear about your interests and let the other party know you are forgoing them. Don't suffer in silence, or you aren't accommodating in an emotionally intelligent way; you are instead being walked over. Send a clear signal that you are forgoing your own interests in order to work effectively with the other party.

Another reason to accommodate is that we may want the other party to accommodate us in the future. Since many social relationships are built on informal expectations and rules of exchange,[3] giving something away now may create the expectation that the other person needs to give us what we want later. So we give the other his or her preferences now to obtain a better future outcome. A short-term loss is exchanged for a long-term gain. For example, in a manager-employee relationship, the employee may want to establish a good relationship with the boss now to have a good evaluation, a raise, or a better position in the future.

Tactical Accommodation with Your Boss

Employees often choose an accommodating strategy with their supervisors. For instance, you might decide not to push for a salary increase now, at your three-month review, if you expect that this will put you in a better position for a raise at the six-month review. But if you use this approach, make sure your boss knows it. Many employees assume their supervisor knows they feel they are making accommodations—but the supervisor never reciprocates. Saying something like, "Of course, I'm happy to accommodate you on this, even though it isn't what I expected [or what my job requires, or what you said earlier]. I know you're keeping track and will make it up to me later, right?" If you say things like this with a smile, your boss will probably accept them without rancor. And you've made your point so the boss knows you expect a future benefit.

Accommodation may be used to encourage a more interdependent relationship, increase support and assistance from the other party, or even cool off hostile feelings if there is tension in the relationship. If the relationship is ongoing, then it may be particularly appropriate to back down now to keep communication lines open and not pressure the opponent to give in on something that he or she does not want to discuss. In most cases, this strategy is short term. It is expected that accommodation now will create a better opportunity to achieve outcome goals in the future. For example, a manager might not urge an employee to take on an extra task right now if the employee is overloaded with projects and the manager can find another person to complete the task, especially if the manager knows that a big project is coming next week and everyone is going to have to put in overtime.

In a long-term negotiation or over a series of negotiations, it may happen that one side constantly gives in. This precedent may be noted by the other side and seen as accommodating behavior (which it is). It should not be construed as an invitation to the other party to be competitive. But sometimes it is. If this happens to you, the other party will begin to compete and take advantage of your guard being down. You will need to learn how to do damage control by switching to a competitive style. And you may also need to reconnect by communicating the relationship costs of the other party's constant push for accommodations.

BUYING TIME WITH ACCOMMODATION

Will Rogers once said that "diplomacy is the art of saying 'Nice doggie' until you can find a rock." Sometimes you feel very strongly about the outcome but haven't the strength to press for a satisfactory settlement through a competitive, compromising, or collaborative negotiating style at the moment. Maybe you lack support since you haven't been able to get in touch with your management or some other powerful constituency. Perhaps you are waiting for information, funding, or other resources to arrive. Whatever the problem, your hands are tied behind your back.

In this situation, you can use an accommodating-for-now approach to delay the negotiation. The way to use this tactic is to make it clear that although you don't agree with the other party, you will go along for now—but discuss it again later. Use wording like "for now" and "until I have time to look into it" or "it's okay for now, but I'm not satisfied with it and we will have to go into it later." Such phrasing makes it clear you are using the accommodating-for-now tactic and have reserved the right to negotiate later.

WINNING BY LOSING?

We call accommodation a "lose-to-win" strategy because you sacrifice the outcome for the sake of the relationship. You do so because the primary purpose of the strategy is to keep the other party happy or to build or strengthen the relationship. A lose-to-win strategy is usually a passive one, employed by a party that does not want to dominate.[4]

In general, you should accommodate to build or strengthen personal factors. Use accommodation to:

• Build trust between the parties or not destroy trust by pressing for one's own outcome concerns.

• Enhance a show of respect for the other's skills, contributions, and assets.

• Affect the scope of the relationship—the number of different ways we interact with key people. If we have other negotiations going on in other aspects of our relationship where we strongly care about the outcome, we may want to accommodate in this negotiation.

• Make the other party feel good because we want to please the person, make the person happy, show empathy, or celebrate an accomplishment. If today is the other person's birthday, we might accommodate to requests that we won't accept tomorrow.

• Bank some goodwill. In complex relationships with multiple ongoing negotiations, the parties tend to "keep score." Over the course of time, people generally expect a balance of winning and losing for each side—this time you win and I lose, and the next time it will go the other way. Thus, if we have won in the past or want to win in the future, it may be best to accommodate now.

• Pursue a hidden agenda. Accommodation may be used when a party has a hidden agenda. An example might be an employee who is planning to ask the boss for a raise in six months. In the meantime, the employee does rush jobs or other tasks beyond the call of duty, without making a big issue of them in the expectation that the raise will be able to be negotiated in the future. Accommodation is a good strategy when you want to build up a supply of credits with the other party that you can cash in at some point.

• Keep the peace. If you want to keep conflict to a minimum and keep the other in a good mood, trying to pursue a trivial outcome is not worth the effort and accommodating is a better choice.

Drawbacks of Accommodation

The major drawback to accommodation is that the party using it may appear to be condescending toward the other party, or the other party may feel uncomfortable with an easy win. You may want to consider putting up a symbolic fight before accommodating, just so the other player doesn't feel that something is wrong.

In addition, it is important to be careful about the extent of use of this strategy. It is not generally appropriate to establish a pattern of always giving in. The party that always accommodates to others may open itself to being taken advantage of. Particularly if the other is not monitoring the give-and-take in the relationship, he or she may take winning for granted. If this becomes a problem in an important relationship, the party who is disadvantaged should discuss the problem with the other person.

The Fine Art of Accommodation

In sum, accommodation is sometimes the best game to play. Let the other player win, and you save yourself a lot of trouble. A forfeit has its place in sports and in deal making. If you are teaching a child to play a game, you will often go easy, permitting the child to score. Similarly, you often need to permit the people with whom you have long-term negotiating relationships to win. Knowing which battles to fight and which to lose is part of the fine art of negotiation.

Avoidance

Now let's look at another game that is also appropriate when you don't want to pursue the outcome actively: avoidance.

THE MASTER NEGOTIATOR AVOIDS TROUBLE

Negotiations can be costly, and there are many cases where negotiators would have been better off to drop the matter entirely. In general, it makes sense to avoid the negotiation when neither outcome nor relationship concerns are important to you.

Another way to think about the avoidance option is to ask yourself if the likely costs of the negotiation outweigh the likely relationship and outcome returns. This return-on-investment perspective rules out a number of negotiations that have big potential outcomes but are likely to be messy and costly.

Yet another reason to avoid is if the other party is out of control and you cannot trust this person to engage in a proper negotiation. There are times when someone's behavior is motivated by anger, for instance, and you know that he will not be reasonable, at least until he has cooled down. Angry customers are not ready to negotiate, for example.

If you can't negotiate with an angry customer, what can you do? You don't want to hang up on her or throw her out of the store. But you can't expect her to agree to a reasonable compromise either. Nobody who is angry about how she has been treated will be reasonable, and a reasonable appeal from you will be met with anger. Instead, avoid negotiating terms, and focus on being empathetic and sympathetic. Listen to the person's complaints, ask questions to draw out more details, and agree that she has been treated badly. This empathetic listening often calms angry customers as they begin to realize that they now have someone's attention who thinks they and their problem are important.

Once the upset customer seems to be calmer, should you begin to get specific about how to solve the problem? Test her readiness to negotiate a solution by asking her what she'd like you to do. Note that this invites her to put an initial offer on the table and avoids your having to do it. The customer will respond in one of four ways:

• Continue to vent, rant, and rave. If she isn't ready to talk about it rationally, go back to empathetic listening until she has let off more steam. Then try again.

- Make a reasonable, even modest, request. Often all such a customer wants is just to get something simple that she ought to have had in the first place. You can now accommodate her.
- Make a difficult, less reasonable request. Sometimes the customer will take the tack that because she had been given poor service, she should be compensated with a free night at the hotel, a bigger discount, or something else of real value. Be prepared to agree in principle and then to steer her into your bargaining range. Tell her the sorts of things that you can do for her, and give her some choices. Often she will back down from her more outrageous opening demand and agree to one of your options.
- Walk away mad. Sometimes people are too upset and conflict averse to want to continue talking to you, even though you are trying to help. Remember that conflicts are stressful and unpleasant and that some people avoid them even when it's not to their advantage to do so. If the customer breaks away from your conversation, don't let this hurt your feelings or upset you. Remember that it's a natural emotional-level reaction to the stress of a difficult conversation. Let the customer go, but reach out to her in some other way right away, such as with a telephone call or a written note, apologizing for the inconvenience and offering some compensation. The goal is to win her back rather than lose her forever.

Depending on which of these four behaviors you see from the upset customer, you can react in somewhat different ways to patch things up and complete the process of service recovery.

Notice that the process always starts by avoiding a substantive negotiation until you have soothed the emotional storm enough that you think the customer is ready to have a level-headed negotiation with you. If you let this person enter into a shouted negotiation, she will escalate fast and will make perhaps loud and public commitments to extreme positions or threats that she won't easily be able to abandon later. Avoid letting her negotiate when she is upset.

When she calms down and responds to your empathetic listening, accommodate her as far as you can afford to, or compromise with her if she makes demands that are too costly. Be prepared to negotiate in this calmer stage of service recovery. Know what you can put on the table and what your walkaway points are. For example, would you replace a costly diesel generator for a client who claimed that your firm's mechanic ruined it by leaving a hose clamp loose so that coolant leaked out and it overheated? Your answer would depend on how valuable that customer's continued business was to your company.

Perhaps you would replace that burned-out generator for free if the customer's maintenance contract is worth a lot more than a generator. But if it was a one-time job, you might be tempted to point out that it should be up to the operator to keep an eye on the temperature gauge or at least to respond to the warning beeper alarm that signaled it was overheating. If you took this tack, you might then offer to provide a new generator at your wholesale cost and install it for free—a reasonable compromise the customer will probably agree to if she concedes your point that the operator should take at least some of the responsibility. Or she might disagree and refuse to deal with you again—always a risk if you don't accommodate the customer completely.

USING THE WITHDRAWAL-THREAT TACTIC

Sometimes you try to negotiate, but the other party acts as if he doesn't care. If your analysis of his position suggests that he ought to care (for instance, your business ought to be important to him because you are a big customer), then make it clear that you have very good alternatives and aren't locked into working with him, and you are considering withdrawing. Make these points unemotionally; don't get angry or sound disappointed.

Then wait a bit. Give him enough time to make it clear you are waiting for a response. If he values the outcome or relationship at all, he should signal his desire to keep you at the table. He'll do so by offering a concession, or at least by telling you the deal matters to him (in which case, you ask for a concession). In the worst case, he says he doesn't care either. But that's okay, since you were at that point before using the tactic, so at least it didn't hurt your position. Either way, it's often worthwhile to test his commitment by making him question yours.

> ### Let's Not Make a Deal
>
> A chronic borrower begged an old friend to lend him a hundred dollars. "I'll pay it back the minute I return from Chicago," he promised. "Exactly what day are you returning?" the friend asked. The man shrugged. "Who's going?"
>
> Myron Cohen quoted in R. L. Smith, *The Comedy Quote Dictionary* (New York: Bantam Doubleday Dell, 1992), p. 49.

Use avoidance when you see negotiation as a waste of time. You may feel that your needs can be met without negotiating, or you may decide that the outcome has very low value and the relationship is not important enough to develop through the negotiation. Sometimes it's more personal too, as when you don't want to do business with someone because you think he is unethical or you don't like his style.

Whatever your reasons, you feel that the relationship and the outcome are not sufficiently important (at least compared with the costs) and so take no action or simply refuse to negotiate.

END-RUNNING THE RISKS OF AVOIDANCE

Sometimes it's hard to avoid, particularly when the other players are eager to negotiate with you. If the avoider refuses to negotiate when the other party wants to, this may have a negative effect on the relationship. Even when the outcome is unimportant, many people prefer to avoid angering the other party, and so a more moderate method of avoidance may be desirable. For example, participate minimally without raising any objections to the proceedings, or just don't show up. If the other party insists on negotiations and it is important to preserve the relationship, then you might switch to accommodation.

OPTIONS MAKE AVOIDANCE MORE APPEALING

Avoiding is an especially viable game when you can pursue a strong alternative outcome. If a strong alternative is available, you may choose not to negotiate. For example, if you are looking at two houses to buy and both meet your needs, you may choose not to negotiate with one seller because you feel the price is too high and the person is inflexible. You simply select your alternative, and use avoidance in the first negotiation.

AVOIDING AN UNDESIRABLE CUSTOMER

A builder specializing in country homes in New England was approached by an eager buyer. The property was a new spec house the builder had designed and was framing on a pretty piece of land in a quiet town. The buyer was from the city and wanted a weekend house where he and his friends could pursue their favorite outdoor sports, principally target practice in the back yard. He was so eager to buy that he offered to purchase before the house was completed, at an above-market price, and entirely in cash.

The builder was uneasy about this offer. He had hoped to sell the house to a young family who would fit into the neighborhood. He also wondered where that cash had come from and wanted to avoid being part of any suspicious money-laundering activities. Moreover, he didn't usually set a price on the house before he was far enough along to be sure of his costs. What to do?

Although his realtor urged him to close the deal, he decided to try an avoidance strategy instead. He sent word that he would need another month to consider the offer since he had decided not to sell the house to anyone until then. A week later, he learned that the eager cash buyer had purchased another property in a different town. And in another week, he was approached by a young family eager to move into the house.

By refusing to act prematurely, this contractor ended up getting just what he wanted and avoiding a deal that didn't feel right to him. It took some courage to wait it out, but evidently his design and location were right for the market, which meant that more options were likely to arise over time. It is often that way in deal making. If you are in the right place and have the fortitude to wait out unappealing options, you should eventually find the deal that's right for you.

PICK YOUR BATTLES

If you get good at avoiding undesirable or suboptimal negotiating situations, you will be better equipped to win in the long run. The idea is that those who pick the time and place for battles generally win the war. Apply this thinking to a difficult business associate or boss, and you will see a big difference over several months.

Sun-Tzu was the first, and perhaps is still the most important, military strategist, hailing from China around 500 B.C. He advised, "When the strike of a hawk breaks the body of its prey, it is because of timing."[5] The point is important, even where a collaborative situation makes the predatory analogy completely inappropriate. Winning is often a matter of timing.

If you lack the power and position to obtain a desirable relationship or outcome result right now, temporary withdrawal is the best alternative. Negotiators rarely have such overwhelming strength of position that they can take the risks of negotiation for granted.

The strategist's approach to battles also applies to our personal conflict situations. And by picking our battles (and avoiding some of them), we become strategists as well as negotiators. Another metaphor—one we find very helpful—comes from the world of investments. You can think of yourself as managing a portfolio of investments in negotiations. To have a winning portfolio, you need to pick the ones you want in the portfolio. Pick winners, and reject losers. Then it's easy to win at negotiations.

In managing your portfolio of negotiations, you may want to prioritize negotiations based on their likelihood of success. And where success is unlikely at the moment, a temporary withdrawal is the best alternative. At worst, "temporary" will turn into "permanent," and you will have lost the outcome or relationship result you did not think you could achieve anyway. But in many cases, the other party will still view the negotiation as of potential value, and will permit you to reinstate the negotiation—when *you* decide the time is right to strike.

"If weaker numerically, be capable of withdrawing."—Sun-Tzu

S. B. Griffith, *Sun-Tzu: The Art of War* (New York: Oxford University Press, 1963), p. 80.

PASSIVE OR ACTIVE AVOIDANCE?

There are two ways to use this strategy: *active avoidance* and *passive* avoidance. In active avoidance, the party refuses to negotiate at all. In passive avoidance, the party does not show up for the negotiation or shows up but voices no objections during the negotiation. The other party and the conflict can thus be put off until some future time or permanently ended. Often passive avoidance is easier to get away with. You can delay and delay without actually saying you refuse to make a deal, and if you are lucky, the other party will get distracted or find an alternative and you will never have to actively refuse.

However, even with passive avoidance, the other party may be frustrated because efforts to initiate a serious negotiation are stopped or delayed. That is why avoidance is most appropriate where the relationship is not important. If the relationship is important in the long term, then use avoidance only as a short-term strategy. And remember you will have to put effort into overcoming the other party's frustration and rebuilding the relationship before reopening the negotiation in another style (accommodation, compromise, or collaboration).

Avoidance can benefit you in the following ways:

• You may be able to have your needs met without negotiation. If you really do not need to negotiate, it makes sense not to spend the time doing so. This would be the case if you have some other way of meeting your needs.

• You have strong alternatives or BATNAs that you can pursue. If you have strong BATNAs, then you may not need to negotiate. For example, if you can do just as well by switching to one of your alternatives, then the negotiation is not necessary. Thus, a strong alternative is like a trump card that you can play to maintain power and control in the negotiation.

• You have no interest in negotiating on the outcome, and you are concerned that if you try to negotiate, you will damage the relationship.

• Someone else on your negotiating team needs the experience. If this is the case, you may choose not to negotiate so the other person can have the learning experience. You may, however, assist the person in negotiating. "Not negotiating" with an opponent whom you want to develop may not be a good choice, though, since your refusal to engage may not be the best approach for helping your colleague to learn how to be more effective.

WRAPPING UP ON AVOIDANCE

As with accommodation, avoidance sidelines you, keeping you out of a game you don't want to play. But avoidance keeps the other party from playing too, so avoidance is likely to meet with more resistance than accommodation. That's okay if it is important to you to avoid entanglements with the other party. Sometimes the wisest way to negotiate is not to negotiate at all.

Avoiding is used infrequently but has merit in certain situations. In fact, we feel it ought to be used more often. It is termed "lose-lose" because it often results in both parties' sacrificing whatever gains they could have achieved from the negotiation. Unless they compete, neither can win. And unless they collaborate, they can't both win.

However, an active choice to avoid is not necessarily a loss on either the relationship or the outcome. Sometimes the costs (in time, stress, and lost opportunities) outweigh the possible gains of a deal, in which case you win in the bigger sense by withdrawing from the game. "Lose a battle to win the war," the old saying goes.

Notes

1. C. G. McClintock and W. B. Liebrand, "Role of Interdependence Structure, Individual Value Orientation and Another's Strategy in Social Decision Making: A Transformation Analysis," *Journal of Personality and Social Psychology*, 1988, *55*, 396–409. C. de Dreu, L. Weingart, and S. Kwon, "Influence of Social Motives on Integrative Negotiation: A Meta-Analytic Review and Test of Two Theories," *Journal of Personality and Social Psychology*, 2000, *78*, 899–905.
2. D. Goleman, *Emotional Intelligence* (New York: Bantam Books, 1995).
3. T. A. Warschaw, *Winning by Negotiation* (New York: McGraw-Hill, 1980).
4. Warschaw, *Winning by Negotiation*.
5. S. B. Griffith, *Sun-Tzu: The Art of War* (New York: Oxford University Press, 1963), p. 80.

CHAPTER NINE

THREE (OR MORE) IS A CROWD

Mastering Multiparty Negotiations

Negotiating is a challenge when there are just two parties. Add a third or fourth party with interests of their own, and things become even more complicated in a hurry. Two may agree, only to find the third upset and feeling that he is being ganged up against. Or one of the parties may be hard to bring to the table, preferring to stay disengaged and avoid conflict—which holds up the parties who want to resolve the conflict. These are just two of the many special problems that arise in a group negotiation. Group dynamics come into play, interweaving with the already complex dynamics of conflict and negotiation.

There are two forms of multiparty negotiations. In the first type, all the parties are at the table at the same time. This kind of a negotiation might occur in a team, task force, committee, or decision-making group where there are different interests present, and all must converge on a collective decision or agreement. In the second type, there are several parties, each of whom has different interests, but you deal with them separately and sequentially. Because the parties often find that they can gain strength in dealing with Y by forming an alliance with Z, these negotiations tend to be about forming and sustaining coalitions. This chapter focuses on the second type of negotiation.

Another wrinkle arises when you want to use different styles with different parties to the negotiation. For instance, two law firms and an accounting firm shared space in an older office building in downtown Boston. All were doing well and wanted to expand their offices. Another tenant, an office of a large brokerage firm, was planning to leave when its lease ended in a year or so. Could they work out an agreement with the landlord to share that space among them?

One of the law firms and the accounting firm got together and proposed this idea to the other law firm, suggesting that all three approach the landlord together with a proposal. It was a good idea, except that the second law firm had already begun its own negotiations with the landlord and didn't want to derail those talks quite yet because they were going well.

Why didn't this firm want to let the others join the negotiations? Because the landlord did not yet know that there was so much interest in the space and was in fact worrying that this older building would be difficult to rent. As a result, the landlord was on the verge of signing a low-priced lease with that law firm—we'll call it Crewel, Tough and McRuthless LLP (CRM).

The other law firm, Settle and Friendly LLP, was unaware of this side deal, and its representative, Sharon Smiley, was busy working up a proposed plan for the three firms, with the help of the accounting firm's representative, James Bean. Sharon and Jim felt it would make sense to agree among themselves how best to divide and share the space, so that each firm's offices could have a convenient layout and not have to be broken up between multiple floors or ends of halls. They had discussed this concept with Clint McRuthless from CRM and were waiting for information from him about the amount of floor space his firm wanted. As the largest of the three, CRM was going to have a significant impact on their plan.

Imagine their surprise when they heard that CRM was instead trying to lease the entire vacant space with the intent of turning around and subleasing part of it to them at a higher price! Upset, the two of them demanded a meeting with Anne Middlespot, the landlord's representative, insisted that they were unwilling to deal indirectly through subleases, and wanted to have their own leases instead. Anne was sympathetic and agreed that since they were both long-term and important tenants, they ought to be included in the discussions. She suggested that they all meet the next week to iron things out. Then she called Clint at CRM and told him she would need to wait on signing that lease until she'd reevaluated the pricing, since she was now aware of more tenants with an interest in the space.

When Clint bumped into Sharon in the lobby later that day, he took her aside and said, "You really messed this up, you know. I was about to get them to sign an incredibly cheap lease for us, and of course we would have passed some of the savings on to both of your firms. But now Anne thinks she's got us in a bidding war, and she's going to hold out for a higher price."

"Now wait a minute!" Sharon objected. "That's not how Jim and I see it. It seems to me that you went behind our backs and tried to strike a secret deal, while keeping us sidelined by making us wait for your information. I think you were trying to get a good deal for yourself and were hoping to make a big profit off our subleases."

"You're way too suspicious, Sharon," Clint objected with a hard smile. "Would I ever try to outsmart a clever lawyer like you?"

"If you're referring to that case in which you represented a litigant who sued my client, let me remind you that our appeal is going forward, and we'll be meeting in appellate court. We'll see who outsmarts who then."

"Whom, not who. But let's not let grammar, or our professional rivalries, get in the way of our mutual pursuit of a good deal on office space. What do you say to a strategy that cuts those boring accountants out of the negotiations and secures a favorable deal for both of our firms? We can always sublet to them later on at a modest profit."

"You're incorrigible," Sharon said in disgust. "What's wrong with just playing this one straight for a change?"

"Not a thing . . . unless that Bean counter is working a deal behind *your* back. Did that ever occur to you?

The two parted on less than perfect terms, and Sharon went home wondering how to handle the upcoming meeting. Would it still be possible to work out a collaborative proposal and negotiate with the landlord as a block? Or was Clint's shark-like style going to make it impossible to do it this way? She wasn't sure. But she did know it was going to be a difficult multiparty negotiation. What could she do to increase the chances of success?

Sharon has a good relationship with Jim, the accountant, but a poor one with Clint, the representative of the other law firm in her building. As these three parties explore their options and prepare to negotiate with the landlord, it would be natural for Sharon to form a coalition with Jim. Together, they control more space than Clint's firm and are therefore more powerful in negotiations with the landlord. But on their own, each is vulnerable to Clint's aggressive tactics.

As you can see, the example shows the importance of considering when you should form an alliance or coalition with someone else in order to strengthen your ability to achieve your objectives in a negotiation. This chapter is about how to form a coalition and use that advantage to maximize your negotiation gains.

COALITIONS

There is a classic research experiment used to study what determines the coalitions people are likely to form. In the study, three people are asked to play a game; each is trying to form an alliance with another in order to win prize money. Each person starts with a different number of votes: one party has two votes, one has three, and one has four votes. To win, a coalition needs to get together to pool at least five votes. They can't divide their votes. Can you predict which two will most likely combine to form a winning coalition?[1]

In this game, the most common coalition is between the person with two votes and the person with three votes. These less powerful parties join forces against the party with four votes because when they talk with each other about how to divide the prize money if they win, the person with the most votes (four) often argues that he should get a larger share of the prize money. The others feel that this demand is excessive and see the person as greedy. The smaller-vote parties often feel that they are being badly treated by the player with the most votes. They realize that by combining their votes, they can still win while shutting the greedy party out, and so they cut a deal and either split the prize money equally or sixty-forty.

Just as this coalition emerges most commonly in the research laboratory, this same coalition of the underdogs might develop in the case of the three parties negotiating for additional space in their office building. Sharon and James may feel that Clint is treating them poorly and trying to take too much for his firm at their expense. If they form a coalition, they are more likely to be able to prevail over him and could even consider negotiating a deal without him. It might be a good idea for Sharon to work with James and cut Clint out of the deal since she doesn't find Clint trustworthy.

Entering into a coalition with others can yield several advantages:

- Coalitions can give you more power and leverage in a group. If several members band together, they may be able to push through a plan or program that no one member could gain individually.
- Coalition partners can sometimes bring strengths to the negotiation that balances your weaknesses. Coalitions can pool all kinds of resources: different skills, different ideas, different past experiences, contacts with different people. Voting coalitions emerge in government bodies all the time to support or defeat proposed legislation and policies, for example.
- You can probably be more collaborative with your coalition members, which permits you to do more creative problem solving than you could if you competed with every other party to the negotiation.

FORMING A COALITION

Forming a coalition isn't difficult. Negotiators often find themselves in a situation where they need some kind of help: money, information, advice, or support, for example. So they approach someone else who might offer that help and propose a deal: if you give me this kind of help, I will offer you X in return. The other party either accepts the deal, counteroffers, or refuses to enter into negotiation at all. For example, in order to start a new business, an entrepreneur has to negotiate with a financial backer. In exchange for using the backer's money, the entrepreneur usually has to offer part ownership, stock, or a financial stream in the future. As the business develops, other financial backers might be added, as well as partners and stockholders. Because new business start-ups don't have more than an idea to prove their future success, they are in a weak bargaining position so they often have to give a sizable chunk of ownership in the business away to the early backers in order to get support. Once the business becomes successful and proven, additional backers may be offered a smaller share or may even have to buy in to join the new venture.[2]

Not all coalitions are this permanent and long lasting. In politics (at any level—community, state, or national, for example), coalitions form and disband quickly as individuals and groups work together to argue for a new initiative (or resist it), get legislation passed (or block it), or push for a change (or resist it). The Internet has become a huge vehicle for mobilizing interests of all kinds: environmental, educational, community, and others. Moreover, as people become more sophisticated in understanding coalitions, they also understand that different goals require different organizing principles. For example, while it may take a coalition of 51 percent to get a vote passed in a large decision-making body, it may take a far smaller coalition to block that vote by using a variety of tactics to disrupt, postpone, or delay action. Thus, there can actually be strength in weakness, because smaller parties can form a coalition that is large enough to overcome any individual larger party.[3] Keep this in mind. You may want to use the strategy yourself if you are a weaker party. And if you don't want it to happen to you, you should avoid alienating the smaller groups or parties in a negotiation to such an extent that they join forces against you.

There are three forms of power that can be gained by forming a coalition. First, you can gain *strategic power* by developing alternative coalition partners. Master negotiators bridge to as many of the participants in a multiparty negotiation as they can and try to keep doors open in case they need to make a shift in the way the coalition gets assembled. They also keep an eye on this kind of behavior on the part of others and try to prevent a rival from outmaneuvering them. Keep communicating with all the parties in order to stay in the loop, and reduce the chances of their realigning behind your back.[4] Be open to a switch from a competitive to a collaborative style of negotiation with coalition partners, since this is often necessary in order to create and sustain a coalition. It's harder to hold a coalition together if there is a lack of information sharing and cooperation in the coalition.

A second form of power is *normative power.* This power is gained by being the most reasonable voice in your coalition and in the negotiation as a whole. Normative power is negotiating power that derives from what the parties consider to be fair and just.[5] If you are the voice of reason or make the most reasonable and fairest proposal, the other parties may fall in line with it simply because it is fair. This is a good way to deal with a difficult party who is making unreasonable demands or a coalition that is trying to exercise its power to cut others out. When you are the most reasonable voice, others tend to be attracted to you and may prefer to form a coalition with you instead of parties who appear to be more extreme or selfish.

The third form of power is *relationship-based power.* This power is used by looking for shared or compatible interests with other parties to the negotiation and collaborating with them. Relationship-based power comes from the natural cooperation that flows from compatibility of interests. But to take advantage of it, you need to find those who have compatible interests, reach out to them to let them know your interests are compatible with theirs, and make an effort to collaborate consistently over time. In other words, it's beneficial to form working relationships with other parties who have something in common with you or your organization.

Let's say you are working on a budget for your project, department, division, or team—and so are a lot of other managers in your organization for their projects. In order to get the funding you feel you need, you must convince your senior executives that your projects are more worthy of funding than some of the others. This scenario is played out millions of times a year in organizations across the world. And often people feel that they don't get what their project or department deserved. How could you use all of the above strategies to give your budget proposal the best possible shot at acceptance?

Often the most powerful strategy is to learn as much as you can about competing groups and their budgets, with the goal of identifying one or more with the potential for collaboration. If you can find common or compatible interests, these may be very helpful in securing the full funding you want for your budget proposal. For example, if another project manager wants to buy a similar type of equipment, you could agree to share one piece of equipment that would meet both your needs and submit a combined request for it. Now your investment request is cut by half, and the potential payoff is spread over two projects instead of just one, making this seem a more profitable capital investment to the executives reviewing the budget requests. Not unsurprisingly, studies of the three forms of power tend to indicate that relationship-based power tends to dominate the reasons that people form coalitions and remain in them.[6]

How to Interact with Coalition Members

To form durable coalitions, keep in mind the following tactics. These are considered helpful rules of conduct for interacting with your coalition members:

- *Be honest about saying no if that's what you really mean.* Coalition members need to be clear about their concerns and objections rather than hedging. By making an objection known right away, you save the coalition from going down some path that will not be right for you, and you may save the coalition from falling apart as a result.
- *Share your information; don't horde or conceal it.* The best coalitions use the rules of collaborative negotiation: each partner trusts the other with information about their needs, strengths and weaknesses. If you don't want your partners to let this information get beyond the immediate coalition, tell them your expectations. And don't let their information go too far either. You need to act trustworthy in order to generate trustworthy behavior in others.
- *Speak clearly and honestly.* Avoid political double-talk with your partners. Too often in multiparty negotiations, politics rules the day and nobody speaks clearly or tells it like it is. This may be okay in competitive dealings, but it won't help you form or maintain a coalition.
- *Don't take a new position or say yes just to be accepted in the coalition.* It takes real compatibility to form a good coalition. If you have to shift your position too much in order to agree with your coalition partners, you won't find it easy to sustain the coalition. It will probably fall apart; many of them do when internal differences

come to the surface. So look for solid, realistic reasons to agree, and avoid flimsy coalitions. They usually end up being more trouble than they are worth.

• *Try to find a common vision that unifies your coalition.* If there isn't one already, see if you can provide it. If everyone gets excited about a good overarching goal, the coalition will set aside minor differences in order to achieve it.[7]

• *Don't bad-mouth other parties.* In spite of the fact that you may think what you say will be kept a secret, it always seems to get back to the other parties and cause you problems later. Have you ever noticed how people tend to court others in a multiparty negotiation by complaining about a third party? It's natural to side with someone and share an adversary, but this kind of alliance is fundamentally negative in nature and tends to produce negative results in the long run. It is better to agree on something positive, like a shared goal, than on a negative view of another party. Try to find constructive reasons to form coalitions, and avoid the shared-enemy approach if you can.

MANAGING GROUP NEGOTIATIONS

We now turn to the second type of multiparty negotiation: how to manage a group of people who have to work together to reach a collective decision. While many of the subgroup coalition dynamics might occur as part of these meetings, managing a group negotiation also requires the same skills as is necessary to lead an effective team or task force.

WHAT ROLE SHOULD YOU PLAY?

One of the first decisions you must face as you enter a multiparty negotiation is what role to play. There are three main roles that tend to emerge in multiparty negotiations: the task-oriented role, the relationship-oriented role, and the self-oriented role. In the chapter opening example of the multiparty negotiation for office space, Clint, the competitive lawyer, is playing a self-oriented role by trying to cut out one or both of the other tenants in order to win the best possible lease for his firm.

Should you play a self-oriented role? In some negotiations, this is the wisest strategy, because if you don't and the others do, you may end up being taken advantage of. Nevertheless, although the following tactics are often seen in multiparty negotiations, many are counterproductive:

- *Blocking,* by frequently holding things up and acting negatively
- *Recognition seeking,* by drawing group attention to self and often seeking the group's approval
- *Dominating,* by trying to dominate the discussions and manipulate the group toward your desired outcome[8]

Sometimes when you are pursuing a competitive goal in a multiparty negotiation, you may want to use one or more of these self-oriented tactics. For instance, you might feel that other parties are weak and disorganized and that if you quickly advance a strong and appealing proposal, you can dominate the discussion and get your proposal accepted. But if you try too hard to dominate, you may inadvertently alienate other parties, who might then form a coalition against you. This is the mistake Clint is making in the story earlier in this chapter.

What about playing a relationship-oriented role? Sometimes this is best, especially when the parties are having difficulty getting along or don't know each other enough to work well together yet. Here are some of the specific tactics often used in relationship-oriented multiparty negotiations:

- *Offering encouragement.* Support others by agreeing with their statements and contributions.
- *Harmonizing.* Smooth things over, help others get along, and emphasize shared identity or goals to try to create a sense of teamwork in the group.
- *Compromising.* Shift your position in a search for middle ground. Compromises are often necessary in multiparty negotiations.
- *Facilitating or gatekeeping.* Manage the contributions of others to make sure that one party doesn't dominate and to hear from those who are hesitant to speak up.
- *Setting standards.* Ask for or tell the others the rules of conduct that will help keep the negotiations on track and reduce problematic behavior. Seek agreement on how the group is going to negotiate.[9]

By thinking about your relationship-oriented role and behavior, you can take care of the human element in the negotiations and reduce problems arising from group dynamics or poor behavior by other parties.

Finally, you may want to think about your task-oriented role in the group negotiation. Task-oriented behavior focuses on what the group is trying to accomplish and moves it ahead—for example, you might:

- Suggest new ideas.
- Ask others for information that might help the group move ahead.
- Ask others for their opinions as a way to clarify their positions.
- Elaborate on a topic to clarify it.
- Coordinate the group's discussion by pulling together ideas offered by others.
- Energize by sharing your enthusiasm or motivation.[10]

All of these behaviors can help move the group forward toward constructive agreement. If that's your goal, it often helps to be task oriented by trying to get the rest of the parties to focus constructively on the desired outcomes too. Multiparty negotiations can get bogged down and fail to move forward because of the complexity of the group dynamics. Your task orientation can serve to remind the group of the need for progress and motivate them to move ahead.

Strategic Concerns in Group Negotiations

One helpful way to think about a multiparty negotiation is as having three stages, each with specific strategic issues you need to be aware of and plan for (also refer back to Chapter Three):

Stage One: Prenegotiation. Plan your strategy, set the agenda, and explore possibilities for coalitions.

Stage Two: Negotiation. Select a chair, negotiate the agenda, and conduct the talks.

Stage Three: Agreement. Firm up and document the solution.

In some ways, the multiparty negotiation is no different from a two-party negotiation. Most of the tactics and strategies of two-party negotiations apply, and you may use many of them in your discussions with the various parties to a multiparty negotiation. As in any other negotiation, you need to think about your interests, do your homework, study the other parties, and use effective listening and communication skills.

And as in other negotiations, you need to select your strategy. Sometimes you should walk away, avoiding multiparty negotiations that threaten to become ugly and destructive or that are highly unlikely to be productive for you. At other times, you may feel the negotiation is not worth a lot of trouble on your part but is still important enough to warrant your joining in. If so, you may decide to offer a reasonable compromise in the hope of reducing the time and trouble involved. And there will also be times when you are not too concerned about the outcome and are instead focused on supporting one or more of the other parties as they pursue their outcomes. In this case, you may wish to use a variant of the accommodate strategy. Enter the negotiation assertively, representing your party and making sure its power or influence is apparent to the entire group. Then form a coalition with the party you wish to support, and make it clear to the group that you will drop your demands as long as this party's needs are met. It is often an attractive offer to the rest of the group. In essence, you are giving your negotiating power to another party to help them gain strength in the multiparty negotiation.

If you have strong working relationships with all of the parties, then you need to champion a collaborative style and encourage all of them to put aside their differences and work together to find a win-win-win solution. This means you need to encourage everyone to share their information and put their problems on the table for the entire group to solve.

You may be competitive with some of the parties because they are untrustworthy but collaborative with others. If so, then your negotiation will have to use two styles. Collaborate with your coalition, but join forces with them to compete against the other parties. Since these two styles are so different, you'll need to meet separately with your coalition and formulate your strategy for

competing with the others. When you enter the multiparty negotiations again, make sure that all coalition members know the strategy and nobody makes unilateral concessions or unplanned
disclosures. It can be difficult to maintain a disciplined approach
to negotiating when you have a coalition involved. Discuss the
ground rules of how to negotiate, and make sure the coalition
members are aware of the importance of planning your strategy
and using agreed-on tactics.

If you are the most experienced or educated negotiator in your
coalition, suggest that the other members let you be their spokesperson during discussions with the other parties.

How to Move Through the Stages of a Multiparty Negotiation

There are a number of strategic issues to consider at each stage of
the multiparty negotiation. Table 9.1 summarizes many of the
strategic concerns to think about during the three stages. As this
table indicates, there are quite a few unique issues that reflect the
dynamics of having more than one other party with which to negotiate. One party can block the others or disrupt the proceedings,
for example. And coalitions can form or break down, changing the
balance of power and direction of the negotiation.

Additional Thoughts on Multiparty Tactics

In addition to the unique dynamics of the three stages of multiparty negotiations, there is the simple fact that more parties mean
longer talks and more complexity to the discussions. The process
of exchanging information and positions, and exploring concessions and trade-offs, takes a lot longer because of the complexity
of dealing with multiple parties and their concerns. Perhaps the
most important quality in a multiparty negotiator is persistence.

Be prepared to invest time and energy in discussions that can
seem to go nowhere for many hours, days, or even months. And
also be prepared for false progress. Two or more parties may feel
they are moving ahead nicely, but their progress may seem counter
to the interests of another party, who gets upset and steps in with
a major objection or threat—forcing the others to back up and

seek another path toward resolution. Patience is often the key to success.

If you feel frustrated and are considering walking away, make sure you are clear on the costs of failing to negotiate. Can you truly afford to abandon this negotiation? Or do you need to stick it out and invest the extra time needed to bring the various parties together and form agreement?

In multiparty negotiations, the costs of failure may be higher for some parties than others. Think about this possibility, and assess your costs of failing to agree. Compared to other parties, is it easier for you to walk away without an agreement? If you are less dependent on this multiparty negotiation and have less at stake than one or more other parties, you may be able to turn their dependence into your negotiating power—but only if they too recognize that you have the option of walking and leaving them to bear the costs of a failed agreement. If you have this advantage, find subtle ways of signaling your lack of concern.

If you would suffer more than others by a failure to agree, try not to let your concern be too apparent. You may not want to expose this weakness, for fear that another party will threaten to withdraw unless you go along with them.

We also think that the impression of having strong relationships with other parties can confer some advantage in a multiparty negotiation. It is not always clear who is in what coalition and which parties are supporting each other. If you make a point of cultivating polite relationships with other parties and are seen talking with them in a friendly manner outside the negotiations, others may assume you are in a coalition with them—even if you are not. The most personable negotiator may be perceived as having the most power simply by virtue of knowing all the parties and being able to talk with them.

In multiparty negotiations, where some or all of the parties are unsure of the others' relationships and strategies, everyone looks for subtle cues. Manage the subtle cues to your advantage as best you can.

A final thought is whether you ever want to be left out of a multiparty negotiation that could concern you. Often in workplaces, we are aware of negotiations going on around us that may not include us directly. It can be a good idea to ask to be included in

TABLE 9.1. STRATEGIC CONCERNS DURING A MULTIPARTY NEGOTIATION

Stage	Key Issues
Prenegotiation	Who should be included? Should anyone be excluded? Do you want to form a coalition? What roles do you plan to play? Who can you collaborate with by sharing goals, information, and ideas, and who do you need to be careful of and treat more competitively? What should the agenda be, and how should you negotiate the agenda? What are your costs of not agreeing, and do you have viable alternatives? What is your bargaining range and BATNA?
Negotiation	Who should be appointed chair, and how should this be decided? (Try to influence this decision so as to avoid someone with a bias against your party or position.) Do you accept the agenda, or do you need to let other parties know you plan to challenge it? What do you plan to say, and are you well prepared to say it? Do you understand the other parties' positions? If not, it will be hard to negotiate with them, so plan to ask them for more information. Is your coalition (if you formed one) still intact, or do you need to seek a realignment? What strategy or strategies should you use with each party? Do you need to reexamine your assumptions about how you will negotiate based on how they are behaving? (For instance, if a coalition partner is behaving competitively, then you may need to stop collaborating with this partner and switch to a competitive style too.)
Agreement	Is there a solution you like that the rest of the group will probably accept too? If so, advocate for it by presenting reasonable arguments and showing others how it benefits them. Do you want to close the negotiation in a collaborative manner by helping others get what they want, or do you need to compete to make the solution more favorable for you by nibbling for small concessions from one or more other parties?

Stage	Key Issues
Agreement *(continued)*	Could you achieve a significantly better end result if you disrupted the agreement stage (for example, by forming a new coalition) and pushed the other parties back into the negotiation stage for an additional round? This is a risky strategy as it can anger the others, but if you are unhappy with the direction the agreement is moving, it is sometimes worth the risk.
	Is this agreement premature and poorly thought out? Groups sometimes rush toward a premature judgment; if this has happened, it's best to point out the flaws and ask them to work on it some more.
	What form should the agreement take? Do you need a legal document, a handshake, or something in between?
	Are there any hidden errors, misrepresentations, or unsatisfied demands that may make the agreement impractical? If so, suggest that the group deal with these issues before finalizing the agreement. Loose ends should be tied up.
	Did the group forget to include someone who can block them by vetoing or sabotaging the agreement? Sometimes it becomes apparent that you need to include another party only when you see the form the agreement takes. If so, take the time to involve them now and get their approval, so that the agreement can be implemented.
	What time lines, responsibilities, measures, or other forms of structure are needed to make the agreement stick? Make sure you deal with these specifics of implementation, and include as many of them as you can in the agreement itself.
	What recourse do the parties have if someone violates the agreement? Discuss this with the group, and try to get them to include answers in the agreement itself.

these discussions. If you don't get a seat at the table, you won't know if there are decisions that hurt you until too late. Even if the issues are not of great concern to you, you may want to be included because of the politics involved. If coalitions are forming and re-forming, for example, you may need to be because they can have an impact on working relationships outside the negotiation.

Multiparty negotiations are usually important on many levels. Give them careful attention, and make sure you have a seat at the table whenever possible.

Notes

1. K. Murnighan, "Organizational Coalitions: Structural Contingencies and the Formation Process," R. J. Lewicki, B. H. Sheppard, and M. H. Bazerman (eds.), *Research on Negotiation in Organizations,* Vol. 1 (Greenwich, Conn.: JAI Publishers, 1986). Also see K. Murnighan, *The Dynamics of Bargaining Games* (Upper Saddle River, N.J.: Prentice Hall, 1991).
2. K. Murnighan and D. Brass, "Intraorganizational Coalitions," in M. H. Bazerman, R. J. Lewicki, and B. H. Sheppard (eds.), *Research on Negotiation in Organizations,* Vol. 3 (Greenwich, Conn.: JAI Publishers, 1991).
3. K. Murnighan, "Models of Coalition Behavior: Game Theoretic, Social Psychological and Political Perspectives," *Psychological Bulletin,* 1978, *85,* 1130–1153.
4. J. Polzer, B. Mannix, and M. Neale, "Multiparty Negotiations in a Social Context," in R. Kramer and D. Messick (eds.), *Negotiation as a Social Process* (Thousand Oaks, Calif.: Sage, 1995). J. Polzer, B. Mannix, and M. Neale, "Interest Alignment and Coalitions in Multiparty Negotiation," *Academy of Management Journal,* 1998, *41*(1), 42–54.
5. Polzer, Mannix, and Neale, "Multiparty Negotiations in a Social Context"; Polzer, Mannix, and Neale, "Interest Alignment and Coalitions in Multiparty Negotiation."
6. Polzer, Mannix, and Neale, "Multiparty Negotiations in a Social Context"; Polzer, Mannix, and Neale, "Interest Alignment and Coalitions in Multiparty Negotiation."
7. P. Block, *The Empowered Manager: Positive Political Skills at Work* (San Francisco: Jossey-Bass, 1987).
8. K. D. Benne and P. Sheats, "Functional Roles of Group Members," *Journal of Social Issues,* 1948, *4,* 41–49.
9. Benne and Sheats, "Functional Roles of Group Members."
10. Benne and Sheats, "Functional Roles of Group Members."

CHAPTER TEN

MASTERING THE FRAMING PROCESS IN NEGOTIATION

Phoebe joined Dan for lunch in a more agitated mood than usual. Her normal professional demeanor was replaced by a worried frown and a nervousness Dan was not accustomed to. She looked as if she hadn't slept much. Naturally, he postponed their business topic and asked what was on her mind.

Soon the whole stressful story came tumbling out. Several months ago, she'd rented a condo she really liked. The owners, a wealthy couple, were spending most of their time in a home in another city and told her they weren't going to be using the condo for a year or two and would like her to settle in and fix it up. She had just about finished the settling-in and fixing-up stage: fresh paint and repairs completed and comfortable furniture that suited the unusual architecture of the condo. Imagine her dismay when one of the owners called her last weekend and casually announced that they'd like to bring a couple of potential buyers to see it.

"Are you selling it?" she'd asked, stunned by the sudden change of direction. "Yes," she'd been told. "We've decided to put it on the market and sell it as soon as possible. We want to buy a condo in Florida for this coming winter instead."

Dan asked, rather tactlessly, if she had begun to look for another place herself.

"No," Phoebe said, "I haven't. I really had my heart set on spending a year or two in this place, I really love it. Besides, I've spent a lot of time and money fixing it up. I suppose that will make it more sellable, won't it? I'm just so upset, and I really feel like the owners are taking advantage of me."

Dan agreed and asked about her lease. She couldn't remember the particulars, but it was a standard rental agreement.

STOP ACTION! ASSESS.

What's going on here? This scenario (which is a real-life incident) is just one of millions of conflicts arising every day all across the country. To understand it better and to help Phoebe find a good, negotiated resolution, we need to think about how all the parties are framing this conflict. By *framing*, we mean how the parties are defining what the conflict is about or what is most important to them.[1]

Phoebe's viewpoint can be summarized as follows:

- The landlords deceived her and violated her trust. They are inconsiderate and not nearly as nice as she thought they were. They will benefit from the hard work she put into cleaning up, painting, and repairing the condo, and she won't.
- Now she'll have to leave her lovely new home in a hurry and start all over again, something she doesn't want to have to do right away.
- She has other priorities now, and it will be inconvenient to have to search for a new place in the next few months. Besides, it's a college town, and most condos are occupied through the winter, so she'll have less choice if she has to search for a new place before late spring or early summer. It's now early fall. She really wants to stay in her current place through the winter.

Dan's viewpoint is somewhat different, as he soon explained to her:

- They haven't given her an eviction notice yet, so the clock hasn't even started ticking on her having to move.
- Even if they do, the law in their state is protective of tenants' rights and it takes quite a while to evict someone, especially a good tenant like she is.
- If the owners are eager to sell, they may find having a tenant with a lease is a barrier to selling. Most buyers are going to

want the condo vacant before they'll close the deal. This, Dan pointed out, might put Phoebe in a position of some power when she negotiates with the landlords.

Dan suggested to Phoebe that she not worry about moving in the next few months, because she could safely assume it would take close to six months for them to evict her, at the least, and more likely that she would be able to stay until the end of the year-long lease, late next spring. In other words, he suggested, she need not trouble herself about it. Let the landlords show the property if they wished, but she had no urgent need to move. In fact, he suggested she not even think about it for now and that she continue to assume she could stay through the winter, as she had been planning, and move when she was ready.

Phoebe listened with interest to Dan's perspective and found herself calming down and beginning to agree with him. Normally very professional in her approach, Phoebe realized she had reacted emotionally to the situation. It is easy to get emotional about your home. But that way of framing the situation wasn't helpful; it only made her upset and led to feelings of helplessness.

How are the landlords framing this situation? Their perspective is yet a third view:

- They thought it would be nice to rent the place out to someone responsible while they decided whether to sell it, so that it would be in good condition.
- They liked Phoebe, and she seemed an ideal tenant. But it never occurred to them she might object if they decided to sell instead of holding the property. After all, *they* are the owners, aren't they? And people who rent must move fairly often anyway, right?
- They had come across a new building they loved in Miami and wanted to get the capital out of the old condo and buy a condo in this new building before all the units were sold to other people.
- Several friends and acquaintances had expressed interest in the old condo, so they thought they might be able to sell it quickly without the added costs of a realtor.
- Phoebe seems helpful and easy to deal with, and she agreed to

let them show the condo last weekend without complaint, so they assume she'll move without a fuss when they find a buyer.

Clearly, the landlords' frame is different from Phoebe's. They don't realize that she might be attached to her home and might not want to move out right away.

And the landlords' view is also different from Dan's. They haven't thought about tenants' rights or looked into the legalities of handling the sale when a tenant is involved. Since they are trying to sell the condo themselves, they have not benefited from the professional perspective a realtor would have on this subject. Their lack of awareness of this issue is perhaps naive, but it is real, and to understand their actions, we need to realize that they didn't include much thought about Phoebe in their framing of the situation.

WHAT SHOULD PHOEBE DO NEXT?

Phoebe asked a number of people for advice that day, including Dan, her friends at the office, and a boyfriend who is a lawyer. Each offered a different perspective. She was surprised at how many ways there seemed to be to frame this conflict.

And the odd thing about it, she realized, was that the landlords didn't even seem to see it as a conflict yet. They seemed oblivious to her perspective; they were simply assuming she'd accommodate them with whatever plans they made. Both Dan and her lawyer friend pointed out that if the landlords were thinking about evicting her, they would certainly have given her written notice already. Until they did that, the clock couldn't start to tick on their effort to move her out and sell the place. If they were assuming that just mentioning it in passing on the telephone was sufficient, they were wrong.

That's why Phoebe decided not to do what her friends at the office suggested. They urged her to write an angry letter to the landlords right away, letting them know she was upset that they wanted her to move. If she did that, then their frame would change and they would begin to worry about evicting her. That no doubt would lead to their visiting their lawyer, who would quickly begin the formal eviction process, thus starting the clock ticking on her move. She needed to be careful not to hasten the very thing she feared through a lack of understanding of the landlords' frame of view. So Phoebe decided to go with Dan's advice and do nothing about it right now.

What about the inconsiderate landlords? They continued to bring the occasional shopper through the condo but got no firm offers in the next few months, so they eventually listed it with a realty firm. The real estate agent looked at the lease, which now had only six months left on it, and suggested the owners ask Phoebe if she was willing to move out right away. She said no; she'd like to stay until the end of her lease. The realtor advised the owners not to bother trying to evict her, since it would take at least six months to do that.

They finally sold the condo the next spring, and Phoebe moved on to another place she liked even better. The new owners insisted on closing the deal a month before Phoebe's lease was up, because they had to move out of their old place then. So the landlords came back to Phoebe and begged her to move. After consulting with her legal-eagle boyfriend and with Dan and her other friends from work, she made them an offer: give her an extra thousand dollars plus her full security deposit and the last month's rent back, and she'd move a month early. By then, she'd found a good place and didn't mind moving.

As for the landlords, they didn't end up buying a condo in that new building in Miami. I think they got excited about some development at a ski resort in Colorado instead, and last we heard, they were making an offer out there.

And the conflict? It ran its course without causing any serious problems for Phoebe or the others involved. In fact, Phoebe ended up feeling pleased about how things worked out. As Dan had predicted, she ended up with some bargaining power and came away with some extra cash she used to decorate the new place to her liking. But it might have gone worse if she hadn't stopped to analyze her own and the landlords' frames and make sure she didn't do anything to escalate the conflict.

WHAT FRAMING CAN DO

It's easy to make things worse when you are looking at a situation from different viewpoints. In Phoebe's case, the fact that the landlords were very casual about the whole matter worked to her advantage; it would have been a mistake to change their frame by bringing in lawyers and escalating the conflict early on. Nevertheless, it would have been a very understandable and human mistake, because we usually want to act based on our own frame of the conflict, not on the other party's. Instead, try to step back, describe each party's frame, and then choose a course of action that is based on their frame, not just your own.

When you act based on a good understanding of the other party's framing of the conflict, then you are more likely to understand where the other party is coming from and communicate effectively with the other party. Framing is often the first thing to think about at the beginning of a conflict (although in many cases, you are thinking about how you want to frame the conflict, not how the other might be framing it). But if you take care to try to understand the other party's frame, you can often manage the conflict more effectively.

Then there is your frame. How do you see the conflict? What is most important to you? Are you overreacting? Perhaps you are if the conflict has hooked you emotionally. Are you misinterpreting the other party's moves? These were problems Phoebe had at first, and her lunch with her calm, level-headed friend Dan helped her reframe her own perspective on the conflict.

You might say that Phoebe's experience of conflict, and her approach to negotiating with her landlords, was all about framing: how she interpreted what the major issues were for each of these parties, what the major issues were for her, and how she was going to choose to respond in a way that would gain her some tactical advantage, address the other party's concerns, or move toward a resolution. As in many other conflicts, attention to each party's frames of view proved very valuable as she navigated successfully through what proved to be a minor and easily resolved conflict.

FRAMING IN BUSINESS NEGOTIATIONS

Framing affects business conflicts and negotiations. Every time two negotiators define a problem or issue—in a similar or a different way—they have enacted frames that may make resolution easier or more difficult. And when a negotiator shifts his own or the other person's frame, negotiations may move forward or may deadlock and stalemate. Negotiators who master the art of framing are better at handling all sorts of business conflicts and come out ahead in negotiations.

George, the sales manager for a company that does commercial property management and renovations, found it necessary to change the frame in a negotiation with Francine, the newly appointed manager of a large apartment building. Francine's predecessor had closed a deal with George's firm to maintain the apartments in "good, rentable condition." George's firm handles repairs and minor complaints from tenants and sends a monthly bill to the manager of the apartment building. And in the past when a tenant has moved out, the manager of the building has asked George to send in a crew to paint the apartment before the next tenant moves in.

Last week, however, Francine told George that some of the long-term tenants had complained that their apartments needed painting and that it wasn't fair to ignore them and paint apartments only when they are vacant. Francine agreed with them and promised to have their apartments painted when they went on summer vacation. So far, so good. However, when she gave the schedule to George, he was shocked.

"But Francine, I normally paint a few apartments for you each summer, and now you're asking me to paint fourteen in the space of a month and a half. I don't have the staff; my crew is already fully committed for most of the summer. How am I going to do this?"

Francine pulled out a copy of their contract and pointed to the part where it said George's firm would maintain the apartments in "good, rentable condition." "That's what you said you would do when you signed this," she pointed out. "It looks to me as if you haven't been fulfilling this contract. Some of those apartments are disgusting; they haven't been painted for five or ten years. If you can't live up to this contract, I'll put it out to bid again. Is that what you want me to do?"

"No," George said; that wasn't what he wanted Francine to do. He promised to think about it and get back to her the next day. Now he wondered what he ought to say to her. She was expecting his call.

To resolve this dilemma, George needs to change Francine's frame. The frame Francine has chosen, like all other negotiating frames, has a powerful effect on the way she defines the issue and on what her goals are for the negotiation. Those who study perception and communication in conflict have defined a number of frames that commonly arise in conflict situations.[2]

CHARACTERIZATION

Characterization refers to the way parties define other parties in the conflict. In conflict situations, characterization frames are usually negative: the other party is seen in weak, bad, or otherwise unfavorable terms. Francine is characterizing George, whom she met only recently and doesn't know well, as a slacker who hasn't kept the apartments in good order.

George may need to counter this frame with some information about himself in order to overcome Francine's negative attitude. For example, he may want to explain to her that her predecessor gave him access to apartments only when she wanted him to work on them; his firm has never had the authority or power to inspect apartments and maintain them at will. He could also point out that if she doesn't fully trust him yet, she may not want to give him this authority either and may instead want to continue to be in charge of the maintenance schedule. If he explains what normal operating procedure has been, Francine may come to realize she can't blame George for those apartments' not having fresh paint on their walls.

IDENTITY

Identity frames are the ways that parties define themselves. In conflict situations, identity frames are often the reverse or opposite of a characterization frame. Thus, while Francine sees George in a bad light, she is likely to characterize herself as virtuous, innocent, or even a victim of circumstances out of her own control. People usually define their identity in terms of membership in a variety of social groups: gender, religion, ethnic origin, place of birth, occupation or profession, or college attended, for example. Many long-standing conflicts can be traced to the positive identities groups hold for themselves and the negative characterizations they hold of others who are not like them. Religious conflicts, ethnic conflicts, and territorial disputes are some examples.

Outcome

This frame refers to what the parties prefer as the specific outcome or resolution of their differences. Francine is focusing strongly on how to achieve a specific outcome: getting all those apartments painted. She has this focus because she promised her tenants she would paint their apartments. As a new manager, she was probably trying to do the right thing, without thinking through how she would accomplish so much work in a short period of time. Now she may feel committed and strongly focused on accomplishing the outcome she promised.

George may need to help Francine think about alternative ways of achieving her desired outcome. Perhaps if he promised to paint two extra apartments a month for the next seven months, she could get tenants to agree to schedule these painting sessions over a longer period of time. It might inconvenience them more than having it done over their summer vacations, but they may well understand that the maintenance crew can't paint every apartment at once. Alternatively, George might suggest to Francine that he help her find other contractors who could help and that he manage their work for a fee in order to make sure it is up to his firm's level of quality.

Interests

A fourth frame is to focus on the parties' underlying interests. Focusing on interests versus positions (that is, outcomes) was one of the basic differences we identified when we discussed the difference between competitive and collaborative negotiations in Chapters Four and Six. Interests are sometimes called *aspirations,* in that the party focuses on attempting to satisfy his or her basic needs and concerns rather than push hard on obtaining a particular outcome. As we noted about collaborative negotiation, parties who frame conflicts in terms of interests are most likely more able to find a common resolution to their conflict.

RIGHTS

Some people frame conflicts in terms of right and wrong—or whose rights were upheld or violated. Whereas conflicts over interests are often resolved by negotiation, conflicts over rights are usually resolved by efforts to determine whose side is favored by the law, regulations, or policies. Francine's quoting of the contract suggests she is using a rights frame. Conflicts about rights usually go to a judge or arbitrator who interprets the law or regulations determines who is right or whose view is correct or appropriate.

If George can shift Francine from her focus on the contract to a deeper discussion of interests, he may make some progress. For example, George could ask Francine about the various tenants whose apartments need painting. How many of these paint jobs are in really bad shape right now, and how many of them are just jumping on the bandwagon and could probably wait six months or even a year without any real inconvenience? George could also ask Francine about her budget. How much is she willing or able to spend this summer on painting? She may have some financial constraints and may not yet be fully aware of how expensive it is to paint an apartment. Perhaps he could get her to focus on a broad view of all the interests at stake, so that they could have a productive problem-solving session.

POWER

Some people frame conflicts in terms of power: who is the stronger, who has more resources, or who is able to force the other to back down or accept a dictated solution to the conflict. People who are frustrated in their efforts to try to resolve a conflict by focusing on interests or rights often escalate to a power frame; those who have the power to enforce their will and make the other party do it their way will win the conflict.

Francine may be on the path toward a power frame. Her waving of the contract might go this way: George needs to be concerned about her threat to put the maintenance contract out to bid again. This threat represents Francine's power as the apartment building manager. George might be tempted to flex his power as a key supplier and refuse to meet what he views as an unreasonable demand. But if he does, their negotiation will degenerate into a power struggle. The power frame will become dominant, and the resolution will involve finding out who has more power. Conflicts resolved by power yield clear winners and losers, but as determined by who is the stronger, not by who has the better ideas or the more reasonable solution, or who "deserves" to win the conflict.[3]

Process

Parties often adopt different process frames in conflict. A process frame is the way each party prefers to work the conflict out or resolve it. One party may choose to strong-arm the other into a resolution; the other may prefer to negotiate or find a compromise solution. Others may want to take it to court and have a judge decide. Still others may choose to take it to a neutral third party, who might tell them what to do or help them discover a good solution. The parties may agree on what the conflict is about but still disagree about the best process for resolving their differences and spend much of their energy talking about finding a way to create a resolution.

The Importance of Frames

This list is not exhaustive. Other frames may be active that divide the parties: what the conflict is about, how the parties interpret past events, or how the parties perceive the risks associated with actions in the future. The important message about frames is to encourage the master negotiator to understand the frames he or she is using and the frames others are using. When the parties are consistently not communicating, talking past each other, or find their conflict escalating from simple differences to an angry confrontation, the chances are that differences in some key frames are part of the problem.

Changing the Frame

Frames are shaped and affected by perceptions of what is going on in the current dispute, past experience in similar situations, attitudes and prejudices, emotions, and also by information, setting, and context. Sometimes you can control these influences over the other party's frame, and you can get them to think about and perhaps moderate the impact of other influences. You are not helpless in the face of someone else's frame, particularly if you are able to understand how different frames are affecting you and your miscommunication with the other (and this is no easy process). One thing you can do is to identify clearly how you see these differences and try to negotiate the frame. In fact, if their frame is inconsistent with yours, you should try to agree on the best way to frame the issues before you negotiate about the actual issues or interests at stake. That's what George did in his conflict with Francine. As you read the narrative, see if you can identify the ways that George worked to reframe his perceptions of Francine and their conflict to move toward a more effective resolution.

First, George thought that Francine needed to know more about how Francine's predecessor had used his firm. He hoped that giving her some information might help change her frame. So he prepared a background briefing for her, which he dropped by her office that day. It showed a history of all the work they'd done, by month and year, for the past three years. He wrote a polite cover letter explaining that as they were now working together, he thought it might be helpful for her to have this information. In the cover letter, he also mentioned that the previous manager had always taken charge of deciding what apartments to paint and had scheduled painting well in advance and generally never given him more than two or three apartments to paint in any single month. Nevertheless, he said in the letter that he would be happy to talk with her about changing the approach and hoped to be able to sit down and work out a plan of action at her convenience.

Next, George called around town and located several painting contractors who might have some extra capacity over the coming months. He gave them the dimensions of the typical apartment in Francine's building and asked them to give him bids as soon as possible.

Then he talked with some of his other customers to see if any of them would be willing to push their work back a month or two in order to make more room for Francine's job. One couple said that was fine; they were a little short of money this year anyway and wouldn't mind waiting until fall to have their building painted. This meant George could put two crews onto Francine's building all summer if necessary instead of only one.

George made a follow-up call to the manager of another large apartment building in a nearby town. This manager had called to request information about George's firm's maintenance services. They were thinking of laying off their maintenance staff and contracting out for the work, and wanted to know if George's firm had the capacity to handle their building. Right now, George didn't think he could take on another large client. But if Francine was going to threaten to pull the plug on his contract with her firm, then he might indeed have some extra capacity to fill. He decided to warm up this new lead and see if he could develop a good alternative to working with Francine. Having an alternative always helps in a negotiation, after all.

When Francine called him and scheduled a meeting two days later, George was ready with the details on a number of options for her. She opened the meeting by asking him to present these options, and so he laid out the alternatives, which included having him put a double crew on the building and paint eight apartments this summer. Or, he explained, he could bring in subcontractors and do all the apartments, but it would cost her about 20 percent more per apartment because the painting contractors in the area charge more than his company does.

Francine listened and nodded and, much to George's surprise, thanked him for coming up with these ideas so quickly. Then she surprised George even more by saying, "I happened to run into my friend Larry last night, who manages the Sutton Estates building, and he told me you'd met with him yesterday and discussed taking his building on. I thought you didn't have the capacity to do any major new projects. How are you planning to handle his building too?"

Wow, small world, George thought. *I better handle this one with tact.* To Francine, George replied, "Well, to be completely honest, I had been stringing Larry along for a couple of months because I didn't think I had the capacity. But when you said to me the other day that you might replace us and terminate our contract, I thought I might find myself with a lot of extra capacity in a hurry, so I kind of reactivated my conversations with some other prospective customers. Of course, I'd much rather continue to work on your building; we've had a good history, and it's a profitable piece of business for us. But you know how it goes. It's good to be covered in case the worst were to happen."

George had not intended to mention his work on finding an alternative, but since Francine brought it up, he felt it was best to be honest with her and explain his position. He didn't want it to sound as if he was making a threat. But he didn't mind her realizing that he might have alternatives. That could help him shift Francine away from framing the negotiation around her use of power.

Hoping to shift the frame toward interests, George quickly added, "What I'd like to accomplish in this meeting, if it's all right with you, is to learn more about how you'd like us to work with you and what your goals are for building maintenance. For example, do you have any budget constraints I need to know about? Because if I ramp up our painting schedule this summer, it will of course raise your maintenance expenses. The previous management tried to keep our costs from rising more than 2 percent a year. Do you have any goal like that I need to know about?"

Francine gave him a long, penetrating look, as if trying to decide if he was trustworthy enough to discuss such matters with. Then she said, "The fact of the matter is, our vacancy rates are above the industry norm, and we aren't getting as high rents as we ought to. I'd like you to keep this between us, but I was brought in to turn this building around and make it more popular and appealing to tenants. That's why I'm concerned about maintenance. Many of our units are run down, and the overall feel of the place is out of date and a bit faded. I want to make some upgrades, and I have authority from the owners to spend whatever I think it takes to do so. I still will be watching the bills closely, of course, and I don't want to be overcharged for work. But if I need to spend something extra to improve the building, I'm prepared to do so."

"Well," George said, surprised. "I guess that explains a lot of things. And I appreciate your being so frank with me. I agree that the building is not the fanciest one in town by any means. We've been keeping everything in working order, but there's been no effort to update or remodel it for a long time. Are you planning to use other contractors to do the remodeling work?"

Francine leaned back and crossed her legs. "Honestly," she said, "at first I assumed your firm was not up to anything but the basics you already were doing. After all, you've been part of the problem here for several years. But that may have been because you were only doing what the previous manager asked you to do. I'm impressed by your preparation for this meeting and the options you presented, and I did a little research on your company yesterday. You also do remodeling and new construction, right?"

George nodded. He didn't interrupt, however, because he realized Francine was shifting her own frame, from the original negative characterization she had of him, and he didn't want to break the flow.

"So," Francine, concluded, "I'd be willing to let you have a crack at any improvements we decide to do for the building. If you have the capacity and can present a convincing and economically reasonable proposal, I'd probably be willing to let you have the work instead of putting it out to competitive bid—that is, assuming this first project to upgrade the apartments goes well."

"What else do you think you might want to do?" George asked, remembering a tip he'd read in a book on negotiation—that it is best to be the one who asks the most questions in a negotiation.

"The entryway and lobby need a facelift," Francine said, "and the elevators work fine but I'd like to replace their walls with some nice wood panels. First impressions make all the difference, and right now, the building makes a poor first impression."

"When do you think you might want to do that work?"

"Oh, probably in the fall or early winter. As soon as I get the apartments painted."

George thought for a moment. "If you're talking about wood paneling, mirrors, new flooring, that kind of thing, it would involve one of our carpentry crews," he said. "I've got more capacity for carpentry right now than I do painting because our painting crews get booked up with exterior painting jobs in the summer months. I'm not trying to rush you or anything, but realistically, it would be easier for us to do the lobby this summer and spread the painting over a longer span of time, say from now to the end of fall. Just to let you know what your options are."

Francine thought again, then asked, "If we stretch the painting out over a longer time, you can do it without hiring subs, right?" George nodded. "So that makes the painting more economical," she continued. "I'd rather splurge on the lobby than overspend on the painting. The extra money will make a bigger impact there. I was thinking of using some kind of fancy tropical wood paneling and a marble tile floor. With big mirrors and palm trees. I actually have a rough plan already. Would you like to see it?"

"Sure," George said, "and if you like, I can have our estimating department work up some numbers for you based on the plan."

"That would be good," Francine said. "I'll send it right over. And I like your idea of stretching the painting out a bit longer to avoid using subs. Did you say you could put a second painting crew on the job this summer?"

"Yes," George said. "I expect we can get through all those apartments by the end of September. And I could probably get a carpentry crew on site at the beginning of next month if you decide to go ahead with the work on the lobby right away. You might want to pick out the marble tile you want, however, because usually those have to be special ordered and that can take a month or two in some cases. I can measure the lobby and give you a count for the order, or if you prefer, you can pick out the tile you want and let me know, and our company will order it for you."

"Okay," Francine said. "I'll give you the name and order number of the tile I want when I send over those plans. Get me a price on the tile, and I'll let you know if I want to order it by the end of the week."

"Good, then, I guess that's settled," George said, standing and offering his hand. "I'll scramble a second crew and get the painting going as fast as we can. And I'll get you an estimate for the lobby remodeling by the end of the week and warn the construction department that I may need a crew for that job next month."

"I'm looking forward to working with you," Francine said. "This building deserves some love and care, and it's going to be fun bringing it back to peak condition."

"The pleasure will be mutual," George said with a smile.

ANALYZING GEORGE'S TACTICS

George's reframing of the negotiation was successful. Francine at first saw him and his firm as part of the problem. By the end of their meeting, she saw him as a key part of the solution. Francine stopped characterizing him negatively and began to listen to his suggestions and view him as a helpful resource. She also backed off her aggressive use of a rights frame and stopped threatening to exert the power she had to give the work to other firms.

There is a simple, big-picture plot to this story about Francine and George and their negotiations. Along with all the other more specific frames involved, there is a fundamental shift toward an interests or aspiration frame. An interests frame creates a predisposition toward satisfying a broader set of interests or needs through the negotiation. It asks, "What do we aspire to achieve, and how can we achieve it?" When Francine stopped seeing George as part of the problem, she opened up and began sharing her aspirations for updating and improving the building. George was quick to adopt this aspiration frame too. He rightly recognized it as a great way to reframe their negotiation, so that they were talking together about their collective interest in how to improve the building so that Francine can reduce vacancy rates and raise rents. With both of them operating out of this frame, George's firm can provide solutions that help Francine accomplish her business objectives.

The negotiation George engaged in with Francine is a great example of transformation of the frame, leading to win-win outcomes that made both parties happier. Framing is a powerful technique, and it always is part of the subtext of a negotiation. By attending to it as George did, you can often find ways to manage frames to your advantage and to the advantage of the other party as well. This process is often integral to moving negotiators from a competitive to a collaborative strategy for settling the negotiation.

TIPS FOR MANAGING FRAMES

Here are some general tips and techniques to help you manage frames during negotiations:

- *Stop. Assess. Figure out what the frames are.* Everyone uses frames. By thinking about them before you make any moves or demands, you may be able to come up with a better approach or strategy. If the other party's frame is negative or a barrier to your progress, work on shifting it first. Or it may be that your own frame is negative, blaming, accusatory, and characterizing. In this case, you may be the one who has to approach the conflict differently. Chances are that if the conflict has threatened some important part of your identity, you are already hooked, and it is going to be difficult for you to stand away from your own frame.

• *Don't talk issues if the other party is focused on process.* Some people have a strong process frame, meaning they focus on how the parties should go about resolving their dispute. Who should meet, and when and where? Should we trade concessions or present our demands in entirety? Should we use a neutral third party? Should we find out what the precedents or rules and regulations are first? These are process questions. If someone asks about them repeatedly, stop talking about issues and outcomes, and take the time to agree with them on the process—or agree to come back to them after the issues are defined. People with a process frame need to settle the matter of how to negotiate before they can begin the negotiation itself. You won't get anywhere until you help them meet this need.

• *Careful; you may be a victim of characterization.* Does the other party have a prejudice or negative assumption about you? Do you have one about him or her? Negative characterizations are common and tend to strengthen as a conflict escalates. They don't help; they hinder. So stop and check for them, and if they seem to be getting in the way, address them firmly but politely. Suggest a clean slate approach in which the parties agree to give each other a fresh start, and discuss the conflict objectively—that is, without prejudice and without dragging in who did what in the past.

• *Share personal feelings and pressures leading to past behaviors.* Empathy (emotional understanding) is a powerful weapon against negative characterizations. If the other party understands the factors leading you to act the way you did, he or she is less likely to blame you or be mad at you. The same is true with your perspective. So it is helpful to ask about and share the reasons and pressures behind each side's past actions. Perhaps everybody was acting reasonably given the circumstances at the time. When you realize this, it's easier to overcome negative characterizations and communicate well with each other about what the problem is and how to resolve it.

Empathizing is a great way to overcome identity frames too. Identity frames emerge when people disagree and begin to categorize each other. Are we disagreeing because I'm black and you're white, or I'm French and you're British? The possibilities are endless: when people want to find ways to group as self versus other, it's always easy to do, but not very productive in negotiations. So share the personal information that helps each side appreciate the other side's position and reactions. We're all human, and we can understand and empathize with the other side in every negotiation if we make an effort to do so.

Notes

1. R. J. Lewicki, D. M. Saunders, and B. Barry, *Negotiation*, 5th ed. (Burr Ridge, Ill.: McGraw-Hill/Irwin, 2006).
2. Lewicki, Saunders, and Barry, *Negotiation;* R. Lewicki, B. Gray, and M. Elliott, *Making Sense of Intractable Environmental Conflicts* (Washington, D.C.: Island Press, 2003).
3. W. Ury, J. Brett, and S. Goldberg, *Getting Disputes Resolved,* 2nd ed. (San Francisco: Jossey-Bass, 1993).

CHAPTER ELEVEN

MASTERING THE POWER AND INFLUENCE PROCESS

This chapter could be titled, "How to Win Friends and Influence People in Negotiations." The premise is that you as a negotiator may wish to influence other people by swaying their opinions, convincing them to make concessions, or preventing them from engaging in difficult or conflict-oriented behaviors. And you also want to avoid being overly influenced by others simply because they know how to use influence tactics to their advantage on you.

What are the ethics or the appropriateness of seeking to influence others? Clearly, if your goal is to be manipulative and get them to do things that are good for you but bad for them, and you and they will regret it later, then that's taking influence too far. And clearly, if you seek to influence someone's behavior or decision by concealing important information, lying, or otherwise deceiving this person, you are taking influence too far. That's not what this chapter is about. But you might think that's what this chapter is about, particularly if you've encountered manipulative, deceitful, or overly dominating behavior in other negotiators in the past.

We find that negotiators are often more ethical and feel better about the process when they understand the uses of power and influence more fully. There are many appropriate ways to exercise influence. The more mastery you achieve in this area, the less tempting those unethical and deceitful tactics will be because you won't need them to achieve your results.

We're starting this chapter with a look at the ethics of the topic because there is something off-putting about the study of influence to many of the people we encounter in workshops and classes. If you feel that way, then think about the reality that this is what this entire book is about. Fundamentally, negotiation is all about each party's efforts to influence the other. Social interactions are all about influence. No person is an island. Yet most people never study influence in depth, and so they go through life, and negotiations, in constant ignorance of the forces of influence at work around and on them.

Your mastery of the arts of power and influence not only puts you in control of your negotiations; it can also help inoculate you against a great many ploys and tactics that will be used against you. While most negotiators don't know all the tricks in the influence book, many have perfected two or three of them and will use their special weapons on every unsuspecting negotiator they encounter. These tactics are surprisingly effective and subtle. Some negotiators have won over and over by using just one or two of the more potent techniques—but not against you; *you* at least will be prepared to identify and counter their influence moves.

We'll start by reviewing some of the defensive tactics you can use to protect yourself and then move on to consider other influence tactics you can use to persuade and influence others.

FOUR EASY DEFENSE MOVES

There are several major tactics you should be aware of and protect yourself against.

WATCH OUT FOR CASCADING YESES

Many salespeople, and some of the savvier negotiators, frame their exchanges with you in such a manner that they get you saying yes early on by asking you simple, easy-to-agree-to questions. They ask, you say yes, and a nice, friendly pattern is established. You're comfortable and so are they because everybody is agreeing and things are going along smoothly. Before long, you begin to feel less comfortable, because the questions are not as easy to say yes to. Sometimes the other party will leave the problematic issue or concession to the very end and disguise it as just one more minor detail. At that point, it's socially awkward to switch gears and jettison all that nice agreement you'd been forging together. You may accommodate and give in. Or you may object, but not as strongly as you would have otherwise, and end up compromising in a way that you'll view as unfavorable in hindsight.[1]

Obviously a Con

Here's a letter that came unsolicited by e-mail to one of us recently:

Hello,

My name is XXXX XXXXXX and this e-mail is sent to you from the Philippines. You get e-mails every day, offering to show you how to make money. Most of these e-mails are from people who are NOT making any money. And they expect you to listen to them? I'm sure there has been a time in your life when you thought about starting your own company and or work while staying home. This is now possible with this online business.

Don't worry, I'm not trying to sell you anything . . . but I'd like to ask you a question.

If I offered you my help and support to start your own home-based business with the opportunity to earn more than you ever did in less than two years, will you send me a "thank you" card???

If your answer is YES, e-mail me back for more information. It won't cost you a thing but little time to read and understand and decide whether or not you want a change in your life.

This is so obviously a con that 99 percent of those receiving it will delete it. But it is a great example of the cascading yeses tactic: "Don't worry, I'm not trying to sell you anything, but I'd like to ask you a question." You will encounter far more sophisticated versions of this influence tactic as you engage in business negotiations. But they all at some point reveal the same message by reassuring you they aren't asking for a commitment on your part, they just want to ask you a question. And let *us* ask *you* a question: If someone asks you an obvious question that he or she knows you agree with, and you say yes, does this now earn the other person any special influence over you?

"No" is the right answer! Whenever you detect a variant of the "let me ask you a question" tactic, refuse to be drawn in. It's going to be an influence game. Even if it isn't as obvious as the one in the letter above, it's the same wolf in sheep's clothing.

Defend against cascading yeses by recognizing this tactic. If you are being maneuvered into agreeing repeatedly, recognize that the other party is herding you in his or her desired direction. And a good rule for negotiators (if not sheep) is, *Never let yourself be herded.* Break the pattern by saying, "Okay, you've asked a number of questions; now it's my turn. I'd like to ask for some more information. Are you willing to answer my questions?" This can put you back in control of the interaction and allow you to manage the negotiation according to your agenda. Alternatively, if you are already sure you don't want to agree with the other party, you can just say, "I could say yes again, but I know where this is going, and when you get around to asking me to . . . , I'm going to say no. So it will speed things up for me to say no right now." By putting your firm objection clearly on the table, you give the other person the option of addressing it, for example, by offering a concession or making some more attractive offer. Or the other party may prove to be inflexible, in which case you can terminate the negotiation.

WATCH OUT FOR POWER PLAYS

Businesses and other workplaces are hierarchical: some people have more positional power than others. Those with more power due to rank are in the habit of telling the less powerful what to do. They do not negotiate. And business-to-business relations can be hierarchical too if one company is far larger or more prestigious than the other. For example, a small business selling services to the federal government finds itself being told how it will do business and how long it will wait for payment rather than being asked. When one party assumes it can roll over the other because of its size, rank, expertise, or position, its power play is often accommodated. But do you always have to accommodate more powerful players?

You can defend against power plays by recognizing that you do have control over the outcome in every negotiation or interaction. You always have the choice of saying no. It may not be the most pleasant choice, but the choice *is* yours. Yes, you are probably trying to think of exceptions to this rule right now. This isn't a hostage situation at gunpoint; you have a lot more choice than you think. We know the example is extreme and we aren't planning to train you to negotiate at gunpoint, but the point is that you want to look for and take advantage of any openings to negotiate with someone who is making a power play.

Your boss isn't armed. You can negotiate with him, even if he doesn't invite you to. A good way to deal with power plays by bosses and other very powerful people is to reframe the discussion by bringing up the various trade-offs involved in doing what they want. (Refer back to Chapter Seven on compromise for a detailed discussion of how to do this with your boss.) Another related tactic is to frame the discussion in a collaborative style by sharing information about what you'll need to do in order to accomplish this person's goal (refer back to Chapter Ten). In this tactic, you shift the discussion around to what he can do to help you accomplish his goal by helping you overcome the barriers to complying with the request. You are talking about how to do what he wants, so he won't view you as resisting his power play. But when you engage him in a discussion of how you are bringing him into your world, he will usually begin to negotiate in a more open, even-handed manner and stop barking out absolute orders.

Another approach to these negotiations is to say "yes and . . ." rather than "no, because . . ." We find this to be true in our work as consultants. To counter power plays by clients without driving their business away, we try to say, "yes, and . . . " instead of "we can't do that," "that's not in the contract," or "yes, but that will cost extra." For instance, you could say, "*Yes,* we could expand the workshop to cover those additional topics *and* we could deliver it to first-line supervisors as well as middle managers, *and* we could give you a very favorable price on the additional development costs because we already have a lot of the needed content, *plus* we could probably discount the per capita rate for the added participants since we'll be there anyway and it will only involve adding a couple more of our staff to help facilitate the larger group." Everything you've said is positive, not negative. But you've managed to lay out your parameters and educate your clients that you can't accommodate every request they may have for free.

WATCH OUT FOR STRANGE REQUESTS

It may be a strange request to ask you to watch out for strange requests, but we have our reasons. Research shows (and experience reveals) that an unexpected request has considerable persuasive power when used in certain ways. If a poorly dressed person asks you for a quarter in Times Square, you will not be surprised—and you probably won't even break stride for long enough to think about whether it's a good idea to grant the request. But what if the same person came up to you in the lobby of a well-secured office building and asked for $1.50 to buy a copy of the *Wall Street Journal?* This unexpected request, in an unusual context, demands your attention. You would probably ask, "Why?"—or even give it to the person to reward the creativity of the request. And if there is any plausible explanation at all, you would probably do your best to provide the needed money. (In fact, in experiments, people usually gave the money no matter how poor the explanation.) You might even give the person a five dollar bill if you lacked change and suggest he or she go somewhere and make change. In other words, you'd be much more compliant and accommodating than usual simply because the request was packaged in an unusual way.

Negotiators who have been tough in earlier interactions may take advantage of this influence tactic by switching to a friendly, helpful style that is at odds with your previous expectations. It is easy to say no to someone who acts consistently negative or rude. But it is a lot harder to say no if the person is acting in a surprisingly pleasant, polite manner. For one thing, you don't want to be responsible for returning relations to the bad old days of unpleasant argument.[2] (By the way, con men often use this tactic by approaching their mark with an unusual business opportunity or request for help. But that's a topic for another book.) Many business negotiations will start out in a formal manner and create a stiff, arm's-length pattern of exchanges about the contract. Then, when the parties are fairly close but there are a few more details to resolve, they may suddenly warm up to you and begin to socialize with you. They may take you to an expensive restaurant for dinner with fine wine or offer expensive front-row seats to a sports event or show. It's amazing how those final objections will often melt away when these master influencers switch styles on you.

Defend against strange requests and unexpected behavior by focusing away from the behavior and evaluating the substance of the request or position instead. By violating your expectations, the other party has forced you to attend to the influence-seeking message more closely than you would have otherwise. But stop as soon as you realize that the "something strange" tactic has drawn you in.

Ask yourself, "Is there any good reason from my perspective to be in this negotiation in the first place, or is it just the oddness of it that got my attention?" If it's the latter, use the avoid tactic right away. But if you still want to stay engaged in the negotiation, next ask yourself, "Ignoring their behavior and the context, what is the substance of their offer or position? Is it reasonable and attractive? Would I accept it if it were delivered in a more ordinary manner?" Often the answer is no, and you need to come back with a strong counteroffer instead of being seduced by a well-packaged but unfavorable proposal.

NEVER LET SOMEONE GET YOU INTOXICATED DURING A NEGOTIATION

Don't try to negotiate over a lunch or dinner where alcohol is being served. Drinking and negotiating don't mix; in fact, they produce a doubly toxic cocktail. You will probably be more agreeable after three glasses of wine than you are right now (unless you find it necessary to drink in order to get through our chapters; if so, please don't tell us). It's amazing how many times someone makes a concession while engaged in social drinking. We don't like to admit the next day that those concessions or agreements were perhaps a bit rash, but if we are honest with ourselves, they usually were. Research has shown that negotiators under the influence think they are doing better in a negotiation when in fact they are doing considerably worse.[3]

If you find yourself in a situation where drinking and business seem to be mixing, it may be impolite to refuse to socialize; in fact, it may be bad for business. But you don't have to drink. Order a nonalcoholic beverage and resist efforts to get you drinking. Or make sure that once you engage, any business discussions are deferred until later. This is particularly a problem in non-American cultures, and you should be prepared to socialize as necessary while politely deflecting their offer to drink. Those who don't normally drink at all already have lots of experience in handling such social drinking situations.

Influence tactics and ploys all have in common the quality of trying to herd us in a direction that doesn't usually feel all that good if we think hard enough about it. Whether someone is trying to get you to say yes to an unreasonable request or is offering you a drink you don't want, it's important to recognize the influence ploy and formulate your countermove before reacting.

HOW TO USE POWER

Now that you've inoculated yourself against some of the more common ways in which negotiators will try to exert influence over you, we will turn to the proper use of power and influence in your own negotiating tactics.

TAPPING INTO FREE SOURCES OF POWER

Negotiators often approach power as if it is something they have no control over: either they outrank the other party, for example, or the other party outranks them. Not so. It is possible, even essential, to manage power throughout the negotiation. Sometimes you may need to maximize your coercive power in order to try to tip the balance in your favor during a distributive tug of war on an issue of importance to you. Other times, you may want to balance the power and reduce its importance in order to create a comfortable, open environment for collaborative problem solving. But whichever way you want to shift it, the power dimension is always there and must always be part of your master negotiating strategy. Here are some ways you can increase your power by using "free," no-cost approaches to framing the offer or the deal:

- *Offer a reasonable, fair position.* The more reasonable party gains power by virtue of his or her position. Reasonableness and high-mindedness tap into a limitless source of power, one we might best call moral authority. Reasonableness knows no rank and is independent of the size of your organization. It doesn't correlate with age or who is taller or better dressed. If an objective third party would agree that you are being reasonable and fair and have right on your side, then your position has the negotiating power of reasonableness. The high road is the powerful road in most negotiations. Conducting yourself with dignity and offering reasonable proposals gives you some power over less reasonable and less well-behaved negotiators.

• *Ideas are powerful.* If you offer a fresh idea or approach, ask an insightful or helpful question, or are viewed as a helpful problem solver, you will gain the power of ideas. Creativity taps into the power of problem solving. Innovative thinking is extremely powerful.

• *Technique* is powerful—perhaps more powerful than anything else in negotiating. One of us (Alex) plays a lot of racquet sports and is part of a loose group of racquetball players who meet weekly at the University of Massachusetts to duke it out. Among the group, two retired professors are usually the winners. They have managed to fend off younger, fitter players for many years, including some graduate students who are less than half their age. How? Their technique is superior. They may not be able to outrun Alex, but they don't have to, because they make him run twice as much as they do. You can't assess the relative power of two players or two negotiators until you see them in action.

• *You can gain power through persistence.* If you work harder to find a solution, persist longer in your efforts to win concessions, and generally seem to care more and be willing to invest more in the negotiation, you often gain power over less committed and persistent parties. Motivation matters. The person who cares most will, all else equal, always win more at the table. So don't overlook the power of persistence. Persistence seems to work for a number of reasons. Persistent people are comfortable being in a contentious mode with others, they don't fear or avoid the conflict, and they are flexible as well as determined. They redefine their strategy and approach as the situation changes.[4]

Testing Power

Power may be implied but not stated or acted on. If one party has much more power than the other and both recognize this, then the less powerful party may act accommodating in order to avoid a test of power. Watch pedestrians and automobiles interact to see this principle at work. Most pedestrians gladly cross at a crosswalk or light if they see that the cars are stopping. But if the cars don't seem to be willing to stop, the pedestrians step back onto the side of the road and let them pass. Most pedestrians don't want to risk a head-on collision with a car. There are also many times in a negotiation in which the party perceived to be more powerful (such as a senior executive) is simply accommodated, as if the others were fearful of being run over by him or her.

Rather than assuming that the more powerful party will use force to get his way, we recommend testing this person's resolve. It's far less risky to find out how determined he is than to find out whether oncoming cars will stop to let you walk across the road. Simply put your own concerns, position, or suggested solution forward in a polite but clear way, and see what the response is. Does the more powerful party resort to a threat based on his power? He may, but in the majority of instances, he will not. Instead, he may go ahead and negotiate with you in an orderly manner. In that case, you've eliminated the advantage of power, at least for now, because you've gotten him to negotiate without flexing that power. Don't assume you'll lose the negotiation just because the other party has more power. It is not always advisable, or comfortable, to exercise power, so test to see if he really intends to do that.

Understanding Your Own Power Choices

Why don't more powerful negotiating parties always use their power? To understand why restraint is often advisable, think about how you might use your own power in a negotiation. What could you actually do with it?

For instance, perhaps you are negotiating with someone who reports to you. Or maybe you are representing a large company that buys from a smaller one and could do without the relationship. How might you use that power to get your way? If you are in a position of power, you have a choice of strategic approaches. First, you may choose to exercise that power in the negotiation in one of two ways: by being directive or by making threats.

Directive: Giving Orders or Instructions

The directive approach presumes the other party will do as you say. This approach works well if she accommodates you or follows your orders. But what if she doesn't? You now have a choice of escalating to try to enforce your orders or of switching to a different style. For instance, you might now say (if she refuses or objects), "I didn't realize you'd have an issue with this. What's your concern?" That would be an invitation to a collaborative sharing of information followed by joint problem solving. Or you might invite her to compromise by saying something like, "What did you have in mind?" to draw out a position or offer from her, to which you could suggest a reasonable compromise. (In this case, *reasonable* means something that gives in partially but does not go as far as halfway, since you can hope reasonably to use your greater power to sway the compromise in your favor.) Whichever style you switch to will provide you an out and allow you to avoid escalating to an enforcer role—unless you really want to, in which case, you will use threats and ultimatums.

Threats and Ultimatums

You may "show your sword" by letting the other party know what costs you will exact if he does not comply. For example, a manager might say to an employee, "Sam, you've skipped the last four team meetings, and you are behind on your share of the work. I need you to catch up by next Friday and to attend all team meetings for the rest of this month. If you don't do this, I will initiate disciplinary action by writing the problem up for your employment file." In this case, it may be appropriate and necessary to pull rank and issue a well-thought-out ultimatum to this employee. Some things are nonnegotiable. In fact, many managers and supervisors make the mistake of being too flexible and accommodating about poor behavior; they fail to reprimand the employee and document the problem according to the employment policies of their organization.

The problem with threats and ultimatums is that people often use them without having thought them through completely. The assumption is that you'll prevail by threatening to exercise power and won't actually have to do anything. But what happens when someone calls your bluff and dares you to make good on your threat? Often we find that we aren't comfortable executing what we said we would do. Even if our position of power makes it possible for us to fire an employee who has missed four meetings in a row, it might not be practical or easy to do so, or we really don't want to endure this person's wrath when we carry out the threat. If the employee says, "I think you are out of line to fire me over this. As you know, I'm having some health problems right now, but

other than that I've been a model employee. In fact, your performance review of me last year was favorable. So go ahead and try to
fire me, but I don't think you'll get very far." And the employee is
probably right. This manager spoke without thinking and should
have either avoided an ultimatum or made a more conservative
and careful one (such as explaining the formal procedures for taking disciplinary action, which no doubt go through many earlier
stages before reaching the point of firing).

TAMER POWER CHOICES

There are a number of ways we can use power to have less dramatic, but perhaps equally significant, effects.

Reframing Around Interests

Instead of pulling rank and trying to prevail because of your
greater power in the negotiation, you could shift away from the
power dimension and instead use your influence to initiate a discussion of needs and an effort to problem-solve. Interest-oriented
negotiating is at the heart of the collaborative style and often
informs compromises as well.

It can be difficult to get the other party to open up and engage
in the honest exchange of information and ideas needed to pursue interest-based solutions. Pushing the other party away from a
distributive (competitive) approach and toward an interest-based
discussion is a more benign use of your power. In the case of the
employee who isn't coming to team meetings, for instance, you
might say, "As your manager, I could of course write up these performance problems and treat this as a disciplinary matter; however,
I don't want to do that. Instead, I'd like to see if I can help you balance your team duties with your other work. What's going on right
now? Why is it difficult for you to attend these team meetings? Or
is there some other reason that you haven't been going?" This
approach starts with a reminder of your positional power and the
responsibility it brings with it to manage the employee's performance. But it then shifts the frame by showing that you are interested in helping the employee solve this problem rather than in
disciplining this person. If you persist in asking open-ended questions and seeking information about the causes of the problem,

most employees will eventually open up and engage in a problem-solving discussion with you.

Reframing Around Rights

Another way to avoid having to use your power is to reframe the negotiation in terms of rights. The rights approach makes reference to obligations, rules, conventions, precedents, or prior agreements. It seeks a solution based on what the parties agree is right or correct. For example, you might ask a vendor you think is late on shipments if he or she is complying with the terms of the contract. If the vendor is in fact so late as to be out of compliance with the contract, your question will remind him or her that you could take recourse by canceling. But you didn't have to say that, and you won't feel obligated to carry through on a threat if the vendor continues to run late. It keeps your options open to avoid threats and instead discuss the rights of the situation. And if you are in fact in the right, this moral authority gives you a different sort of power that may be even more useful in persuading the vendor.[5]

ACCESSING SOURCES OF POWER

What if you are negotiating with someone (or some organization) that is particularly difficult or powerful and you feel you need to seek additional power to counter their's? Here are some sources of power that you may be able to tap into (in addition to the "free" sources of power we already discussed: reasonableness, fresh ideas, negotiating technique, and persistence).

Information

Buy some time in a difficult negotiation by avoiding or postponing for long enough to do additional research. Seek information about the other party, about options, and about precedents, procedures, or rules that might be favorable to you. Do research: find data, statistics, history, and background to support your arguments. And if you are dealing with technical or complex issues such as foreign currency fluctuations and their effect on price over time, become expert in these topics or find a helpful expert to advise you. Information is power. Yet most negotiators shortchange the research phase and rush into engagement with the other party or parties.

Often the party who appears better informed wins simply on the strength of the arguments.

Position Power

Ally with someone in a position of power. Even if you aren't in a powerful position yourself, you may be able to find a champion who is. This is where a deep network comes into play. If you are already known and trusted by senior executives, you can now go to them and ask for help with your problem. If you have not built these relationships, it will be harder to build a personal relationship, but you may still be able to find someone in a position of power who has an alignment of interests with you. For example, if you work for a small importer that sells to a large retail chain, you could go to larger vendors or your trade association for help in resolving a dispute with the retailer. Others may share your interests and be willing to lend some of their weight to your argument.

Control over Resources

In some offices, the most powerful person is the one who controls the purchasing of basic supplies. You don't want to get on the wrong side of the person in purchasing who decides whether you can get an upgraded computer this year. Negotiations are often over disputes about resources. Perhaps the oldest and most classic example of a resource dispute is the one that arises between those who live upstream and downstream on a river. Those on the downstream side always feel that they aren't getting their fair share, but it's hard for them to do anything about the problem since their upstream neighbors are in a geographical position of control.

At the same time, even if you can control some resources the other party needs, it's usually wise to avoid rash threats and ultimatums. Usually you want to let your resource control power be implied and avoid having your bluff called and being stuck between backing down or escalating. Resources of importance in business negotiations can include human capital, supplies, money, equipment, and services. When resources are widely disbursed, as they tend to be in organizations today, the individual who makes the effort to gain control over them has a significant power advantage that can be used to punish or reward others or simply to enter into reciprocal exchanges of favors.[6]

Time

Time is an especially powerful resource and can often be controlled through negotiating tactics. Whenever you negotiate, work hard to buy yourself as much time as you can. For example, never make unnecessary time-based promises to your constituencies. (Don't tell your boss that you plan to come back from the next meeting with a closed deal, for example.) Also, seek ways to turn up the time pressure on the other party. If you have the ability to impose a deadline directly, consider doing so. Or if you know that there are deadlines affecting the other party, slow the pace and let the clock run down until those on the other side become more eager to do a deal with you. The party without a deadline in negotiation usually has an advantage, because they can put pressure on the other party to agree before the deadline.

Having a Seat at the Table

Another form of power derives from having a seat at the table during negotiations. Researchers have experimented with situations in which one party (out of multiple parties) was not included at some of the negotiations. Even if that person controlled resources and had some power as a result, she tended to get the short end of the deal if she wasn't able to participate in all the discussions.[7] This may be news to researchers, but it's an old tactic to negotiators who are masters at scheduling and locating meetings so as to make it difficult for someone they don't want there or to hold the meeting when they know key people are unavailable. Groups often make decisions when an opposing member is absent. The crafty negotiator occasionally uses this tactic to get around a difficult person.

USING POWER BY FRAMING A STRONG INFLUENCE MESSAGE

Perhaps the preeminent way to influence others is to deliver a compelling or convincing message. As long as you can get your message to the other party, you have a chance to exert this influence, even if he or she is a lot more powerful than you are. Here are some things that have been learned from the study of persuasion and advertising about how to frame a strong and persuasive message.

Plan Your Message Structure and Style

Often what matters is when and how you say something, not so much what you say. You may, for example, have multiple points or concerns to raise. Which should go first, which in the middle, and which last? Research is consistent in showing that anything buried in the middle is going to get short shrift. It may be forgotten, and it won't be taken as seriously.[8] So put the important stuff at the front or back end of your message (or both, to reinforce the point).

Is there a rule for when to put a key point at the start versus at the end? The first thing we hear in a list is often memorable; this is called the *primacy effect*. Negotiators can increase their influence using the primacy effect by starting with something the other party wants to hear. It will be memorable and may give a more positive feeling to their memory of the entire presentation, even if followed by a number of points that they view as negative. Sometimes master negotiators open with supportive, relationship-oriented comments or thanks, followed by statements of their commitment to work together and build a profitable relationship. These positives tend to have more impact when said first and help make the others more receptive to requests or demands that follow.

But if your goal is to make sure the other party remembers an important but complex or unfamiliar point, put it at the end to take advantage of the *recency effect*—that is, we tend to remember the last thing we heard, especially when the list is hard to recall. Master negotiators may use this technique when dealing with complex technical issues or multistep projects. In these sorts of deals, you may get the other party to agree to do something, but will they remember to do it later or even recall the details of exactly what they said they'd do? Maximize the odds of their following through by going into the details of what to do at the end, so they walk away with a clear recall of these important instructions.

One of us has a colleague who does a popular two-day workshop on customer service. She approached us about the idea of collaborating to turn her workshop into a book and training manual. We offered to provide some help and advice, since we have a lot of experience in creating written materials. In a wide-ranging discussion of a number of topics, we told her to make sure she captured the content of her workshop by bringing a tape or video recorder with her next time she presented and recording both days. Then, we told her, she could have it transcribed to create a written text of the workshop. Once it was captured in a word processing file, we said we'd show her how to edit and format it into a manual and might even help her publish it. Then we talked about a lot of other things, like how to publish books and workbooks and where to sell them.

Two months later, we received a video from her. It was not the video we'd suggested she make. Instead, she'd gone into a studio and shot some footage of her presenting a fifteen-minute summary of the workshop. "Could you help me market this video," she said, "and by the way, when are you going to help me write up my workshop in book form?" Well, no time soon. Not without a transcript or something to look at. We still had no idea what she actually did in that two-day workshop.

What had gone wrong with our agreed-on plan? She'd remembered that she was "making a video for us" but had gotten confused about the specifics of it and what it was for. Since she doesn't usually write things down, the importance of a transcript had escaped her, and in her mind the project had gradually evolved into something else. We had to tell her that although we still liked the idea of working with her in principle, we were in fact no further along than last time we met and were not going to do anything to help her until she captured her workshop in written form for us to review. The disappointment and wasted time could have been avoided with a clearer delivery of our instructions, which were in essence the terms of our offer. We should have delivered these terms at the end and reviewed them carefully, so that they would have been remembered accurately. Even better, we should have summarized the discussion in a short e-mail or note so that it would be clear what we explained to her. *Make sure the first and last thing they hear or see is your key point or most important requirement.* (Notice that we structured this paragraph to illustrate the advice it gives.)

PUT YOURSELF IN THEIR SHOES BEFORE TRYING TO MAKE THEM WALK YOUR WAY

What is the best way to formulate a proposal or argument? You will be most persuasive if you have thought about the other party's perspective first and can ground your argument in an understanding of those priorities and concerns. For example, if you are presenting a proposal for funding a new product, ask yourself if the decision makers are more interested in making big returns or in reducing financial risks. If they are risk averse and you keep talking about the great possibilities but never explain how to avoid a loss if the product fails, you won't get their vote. Understanding their concerns and shaping your argument toward them is the key to persuasiveness in many business negotiations.

Sometimes you don't fully understand the other party's concerns and interests until you listen to their questions and objections. If you had assumed those executives were interested in maximizing future sales but all their questions are about reducing risks of failure, then you will realize that your presentation was off target. In that situation, you might want to tell them the truth, saying something like, "I can see from your questions that you are particularly concerned about ways of minimizing the risks of new product failure. As I didn't know that in advance, I think it might be best for me to go back to the drawing board and prepare some projections and strategies based on the goal of minimizing risks. Would you like me to do that, and give you a modified proposal next week?"

By anticipating their rejection and offering to revise your approach before they can say no, you keep the door open and prevent yourself from being shot down right away. And now you know a lot more about this group's concerns and interests, since you've been beaten up by their questions once already. Modify your proposal if necessary, and then prepare carefully to handle their objections, so that you can be more persuasive the next time you present.

CHOOSE YOUR COMMUNICATION MEDIUM WISELY

Imagine you are negotiating the terms of a business-to-business agreement. Should you present your contract requirements verbally, in an e-mail, or in a formal, written draft of the contract? If you are negotiating a contract that will eventually take the form of a lengthy, detailed written document, it is often most persuasive to present your desired terms in a written form that looks and reads more like a finished contract than an informal negotiating point. The legal, written form tends to add credibility to the proposal.

But if you are involved in a collaborative negotiation and want to bounce some possible alternative solutions off the other party, a face-to-face discussion is probably the best choice. You don't want this person to think you are making a formal proposal, and you don't want a formal, guarded response in return. Make the message sound informal and off-the-record if that is the spirit in which you want it received. You can always use facial expressions and tone of voice to soften the impact of a tough message.

Always think about the medium in terms of the impression you want the receiver to get and the way you want him or her to respond. The more formal the medium (for example, a formal offer or proposal), the more you may want to send a registered letter or overnight mail package, but the more careful and stiff the reply. If you want to control a difficult negotiator who tends to get emotional and make threats or exaggerate points when speaking, you may shift to written communications to see if that person will be more disciplined and easy to deal with in this medium. But if you are engaged in e-mail discussions that are escalating and leading to misunderstandings and bad feelings, you may want to switch to a telephone call to iron things out.

Always remember that the medium is a variable, and you can control it. If the negotiation isn't going well, try changing the medium of communication. Maybe your message will work better and be more influential in a different medium.[9]

ONE-SIDED OR TWO-SIDED MESSAGE?

Think about the form your arguments take. For example, let's say you are trying to win a contract to supply business services to a large company. You have made the short list and are invited to make a presentation in its boardroom. In planning your message, you have to decide if you will focus only on your proposal and its merits or also on other approaches and why you believe they won't work as well. Should you use a one-sided message that is only about your proposal, or should you explore the other side by showing the cons of other approaches you know your competitors will propose?

In this situation, the two-sided approach is usually more influential. You probably don't want to say bad things about specific competitors, since this seems tacky, but you do want to compare

Conducting Negotiations by E-Mail

Since there is an increasing tendency to use e-mail for all kinds of communication, we should briefly comment about negotiating over e-mail. It has distinct advantages: you can write out exactly what you want to say. You can take time to consider an offer and respond when you are ready rather than having to respond immediately to a verbal offer on the telephone or in person. You also have a record of who says what that can be tracked over time. And it is possible that your opponent will fly off the handle and overreact to a situation, saying all sorts of wild things in e-mail. She will exaggerate accusations, make extreme threats she can't or won't want to make good on later, or state outright lies. You can print them out and wave them around. Usually this is not a constructive game to play, but sometimes you are looking for any way to gain some influence over a difficult negotiator, and this ploy can be tried.

The major liability of e-mail is that people often communicate thoughtlessly and emotionally in this medium. They don't take the time to consider what to say or how to say it. Instead, they bang off a message and hit the Send button before editing it or thinking about the consequences. And you can't reach through the screen and pull back an angry e-mail or easily apologize for it if you find out that the other party took it the wrong way. In addition, you may be held accountable for promises or commitments you made earlier but really didn't think you would have to carry out.

Use e-mail negotiations to your advantage by being slow and reasoned in the way you respond; watch out for the urge to send an intemperate message, because the consequences are never good.

your proposal and approach to other possible approaches and show why yours is superior. After all, this is what your potential clients are trying to do: they have to compare all the proposals and pick the best one, so why not help them figure out how to do the comparison? It would be a mistake to present your argument in a vacuum as if there were no other options.

The two-sided message is usually more persuasive than a one-sided message when dealing with thoughtful, well-educated negotiators (we hope that's who you'll usually encounter in business) and also when you know the other party will be exposed to counterarguments and alternatives. And if the issue or topic is already familiar to the other party, you can anticipate that they will form counterarguments in their mind as they listen to you, so you might as well acknowledge and address those counterarguments.[10]

If you are going to present two or three alternatives and recommend one of them, put your favored alternative at the end. The recency effect is helpful here, and your final option will usually be more influential than the others. For example, you might present three new product ideas to the executive committee, giving pros and cons of each, but placing the one you personally favor last in the sequence to give it the best chance.[11]

Be Prepared to Handle Questions and Objections

Many times in negotiations, you will find you need to respond to an attack or refute a point. For example, you may present a detailed growth plan and budget in a staff meeting, only to have an associate at the other end of the table say something like, "Well, I don't know about the specific numbers, but it seems to me we tried something like that years ago and it didn't work."

What should you say? If you have not thought about possible arguments against your plan, you may not have any idea as to what this colleague is referring. But if you are prepared for this objection, you might counter with something like, "Well, if you are referring to the expansion project of 2003, I've reviewed that file and it's nothing like this. It had the same goal of growing our West Coast revenues, but it relied on a partnership with X-Y Company, which as you know went out of business later that year, so we never got a chance to test our products in the West Coast market. Our new plan uses only internal resources so we aren't vulnerable to that kind of risk."

It's fair to say that many business proposals sink or swim on the strength of the presenter's handling of questions and objections after the initial presentation. The presentation itself is often treated as informative, a briefing that gets the group up to speed so that it can debate the proposal intelligently. If you are presenting a plan within your own company, this collegial spirit of debate will probably be the rule. Be prepared to handle questions and enter into the debate.

How best to prepare to handle questions and counterarguments? Many negotiators prepare by focusing on their own arguments and the facts that support them. This is a good start, but it is insufficient. A better preparation strategy is to anticipate counterarguments and be prepared to debate them. For example, you might brainstorm a list of all possible objections and counterarguments. Make as long a list as you can, seeking help from others if necessary to make sure you anticipate as many counterarguments as possible. Then prepare your responses to each objection or argument. The combination of preparing to support your own arguments and preparing to debate other arguments makes the best preparation. Develop arguments both for and against your position, plus the arguments to counter those arguments that go against you.[12] Make separate lists or a big table for pro arguments, con arguments, and counters to con arguments to make sure you are fully prepared.

Reducing Anticipation of Counterarguments

As you make an argument or present a proposal, those listening will be thinking about their counterarguments. In fact, the better portion of their attention often goes to what they are going to say, not what you are saying now.[13] Their focus on counterarguments reduces the effectiveness of your arguments. How can you reduce this tendency of them to listen with only one ear?

One strategy is to distract the other party or, perhaps more accurately, use more of their mental processing power so that they are not as able to think about counterarguments and instead have to give you their full attention.[14] For example, if you prepare a series of detailed exhibits and charts, hand one out as you make a key point. Then hand out another as you make your next key point. The physical activities of handing the charts around the table, plus the mental activities involved in figuring them out, keep the other side busy. Your words plus the chart-related activity add up to a rich enough message that you capture the bulk of their attention and they don't think as hard about counterarguments.[15]

Should you present PowerPoint slides along with your verbal argument, or speak without audiovisual aids? Should you hand out a written report or a set of graphs, tables, or charts to go with your presentation? Should you provide slides on a screen, plus a handout, as you talk? Normally in speaking before business audiences, we think about clarity and professionalism as we address such questions, but in a negotiation, it may make more sense to think about the level of distraction you want to provide. If you think a point will be particularly appealing to the other party or parties, reduce the amount of distraction through multichannel message delivery. Let the receivers' subvocalizations (their self-talk) go on without distraction if you think this will be positive. But when you get to points you expect will generate resistance and negative subvocalizations, maximize the number and variety of forms your message takes to keep them so busy that they cannot generate strong counterarguments while you are presenting.

Summary

Power and influence are important in every negotiation, but not necessarily in the expected ways. Raw exercise of power is rarely constructive. Negotiators who make threats or give ultimatums often regret it later when they find they've put themselves in the position of having to do something unpleasant or having to back down and look foolish. And the most persuasive and influential negotiators often avoid loud, overbearing, or overly colorful styles and instead rely on careful preparation, sound arguments, and subtle tactics to win others over. As you negotiate, always keep one eye on the balance of power and the uses of influence. Defend yourself against being herded by someone who uses strong-arm influence tactics. And make good use of those tactics you feel comfortable using, such as the presentation of a well-structured, well-argued message.

If you find yourself outinfluenced and outpowered, stop and seek sources of additional power and influence for your side. We hope this chapter has convinced you that power and influence can be developed and used as need requires. Your negotiating skills and knowledge of technique are valuable sources of influence and power, as are your abilities to manage your own emotions and take the high road of reasoned, reasonable positions in any negotiation. The master negotiator is always mindful of power and careful to create sufficient influence to press his or her agenda forward.

Notes

1. E. F. Fern, K. B. Monroe, and R. A. Avila, "Effectiveness of Multiple Request Strategies: A Synthesis of Research Results," *Journal of Marketing Research,* 1986, *23,* 144–152; J. L. Freedman and S. C. Fraser, "Compliance Without Pressure: The Foot in the Door Technique," *Journal of Personality and Social Psychology,* 1966, *4,* 195–202; C. Seligman, M. Bush, and K. Kirsch, "Relationship Between Compliance in the Foot in the Door Paradigm and Size of First Request," *Journal of Personality and Social Psychology,* 1976, *33,* 514–520.

2. S. K. Miller and M. Burgoon, "The Relationship Between Violations of Expectations and the Induction of the Resistance to Persuasion," *Human Communication Research,* 1979, *5,* 301–313; B. Barry, "Influence Tactics in Organizations from a Social Expectancy Perspective," in A. Y. Lee-Chai and J. A. Bargh (eds.), *The Use and Abuse of Power.* Philadelphia: Psychology Press, 2001.

3. M. Schweitzer and J. L. Kerr, "Bargaining Under the Influence: The Role of Alcohol in Negotiations," *Academy of Management Executive,* 2000, *14,* 47–57.

4. R. J. Lewicki, D. M. Saunders, and B. Barry, *Negotiation,* 5th ed. (Burr Ridge, Ill.: McGraw-Hill/Irwin, 2006).

5. The distinctions between power, interests, and rights strategies are based on W. Ury, J. Brett, and S. Goldberg, *Getting Disputes Resolved,* 2nd ed. (San Francisco: Jossey-Bass, 1993).

6. J. Pfeffer and G. R. Salancik, "Organizational Decision Making as a Political Process: The Case of a University Budget," *Administrative Science Quarterly,* 1974, *19,* 135–151. J. Pfeffer, *Managing with Power* (Boston: Harvard Business School Press, 1992).

7. P. H. Kim, "Strategic Timing in Group Negotiations: The Implications of Forced Entry and Forced Exit for Negotiators with Unequal Power," *Organizational Behavior and Human Decision Processes,* 1997, *71,* 263–286.

8. E. P. Bettinghaus, *Persuasive Communication,* 2nd ed. (New York: Holt, 1966).

9. R. Lewicki and B. Dineen, "Negotiation," in R. Heneman and D. Greenberger (eds.), *Human Resource Management in Virtual Organizations* (Hoboken, N.J.: Wiley, 2002).

10. S. Jackson and M. Allen, "Meta-Analysis of the Effectiveness of

One-Sided and Two-Sided Argumentation" (paper presented at the annual meeting of the International Communication Association, 1987).

11. P. G. Zimbardo, E. B. Ebbesen, and C. Maslach, *Influencing Attitudes and Changing Behavior* (Reading, Mass.: Addison-Wesley, 1977).

12. W. McGuire, "Inducing Resistance to Persuasion: Some Contemporary Approaches," in L. Berkowitz (ed.), *Advances in Experimental Social Psychology* (Orlando, Fla.: Academic Press, 1964).

13. T. C. Brock, "Effects of Prior Dishonesty on Post-Decision Dissonance," *Journal of Abnormal and Social Psychology,* 1963, *66,* 325–331.

14. K. K. Reardon, *Persuasion Theory and Context* (Thousand Oaks, Calif.: Sage, 1981).

15. R. E. Petty, G. Wells, and T. Brock, "Distraction Can Enhance or Reduce Yielding to Propaganda: Thought Disruption vs. Effort Justification," *Journal of Personality and Social Psychology,* 1976, *34,* 874–884.

CHAPTER TWELVE

MASTERING PERSONAL NEGOTIATIONS

In this book, we have focused on your role as a business negotiator. Your negotiations with coworkers, suppliers, customers, regulators, landlords, employees, unions, the media, and others have been pursued with the best interests of you and your employer in mind.

But what about you?

One of the most remarkable and pleasant things we've learned from teaching business negotiation skills is that they translate so easily into personal life. Your approach to negotiating with your teenager about when he can and can't borrow the car may be different in tone, but it is not different in principle from your negotiations at work. You have a long-term relationship. Your goals are to avoid tickets and injuries, and you are willing to be assertive about these goals. Add up a concern for the outcome with an abiding concern for the other party—your son—and you have a classic case for the use of the collaborative style. Engage your son in conversation about his interests and feelings (even if he is at first reluctant to talk), let him know you are on his side, but also make your needs clear and don't be afraid to provide clear structure.

Above all, explain and share both information and feelings. Model the open, mature, adult conversation style you want your children to use, even when they get mad and act competitively or slam doors or stomp up the stairs. You are teaching them not only how to survive teenage driving, but also how to negotiate well with others.

That's an example of negotiating from a parent's point of view. We often work with parents, and we also work with younger adults who are concerned about negotiating to buy their first car or to work out the details of their wedding or their first serious job offer. Whether you're haggling with the classic used-car salesman (perhaps the prototypical competitive negotiation to American readers) or worrying about blowing your salary negotiations with a desirable potential employer, you can apply what you know of business negotiations. In fact, you had better do so.

In the job context, salary is usually most negotiable at the beginning of your relationship with an employer, before you have accepted an offer and inked the deal. From then on, your salary will tend to grow roughly in relationship to the rate at which other salaries grow in that organization. If you get a promotion or an offer from another company, then your good performance will earn you a pay raise—but the old pay level will still influence the new pay level. Similarly, if you get bonuses or merit raises, they will be based on the initial base. So that first negotiation (or lack of negotiation) carries forward economically, determining things like whether you can afford a Caribbean vacation five years from now and what kind of house you'll end up owning.

LEAVING TOO MUCH ON YOUR PERSONAL TABLE

The first point we made in this book was that people often fail to recognize negotiating situations and thereby leave too much on the table. Don't make this mistake in business, and certainly don't make this mistake in your personal affairs either. Negotiate job offers and pay raises appropriately (we'll go into the details in a few pages). And negotiate appropriately with lovers, spouses, parents, children, friends, and even enemies.

The personal passion of one of us (Alex) is painting and photography. Alex recently learned about a new art gallery opening in a town near where he lives that he thought might want to show his work. Asking around, he found that the owner of the gallery was just one step removed from him; one of Alex's good friends had already met him. It was a great opportunity to ask for a small favor and arrange an introduction. However, it turns out that Alex's friend thought the gallery owner had snubbed him and wasn't talking to him any more.

Alex's friend Marc, the one who had met the new gallery owner, runs a nonprofit arts organization that, among other things, puts on outdoor fine arts shows in city parks. Marc had visited the new gallery shortly before a major outdoor show, and the gallery owner had expressed interest in bringing some of his artists' work to the show as a promotion for the gallery. He'd promised to call Marc to finalize the arrangements. Marc had tried to confirm several times by phone and e-mail, but with no luck. The guy "blew him off," as Marc saw it, leaving him scrambling for someone else to use the space he'd set aside. To add insult to injury, the owner had then showed up at the event and walked around talking to some of the artists but had consistently avoided eye contact with Marc and acted as if he didn't know him. Although Marc is normally a patient individual, the stress of staging a show with twenty-five artists, a half-dozen musicians, a dozen volunteers, and hundreds of visitors usually wears him a bit thin. He wrote the new gallery owner off in his mind. The guy was definitely in his "enemies" cubbyhole, if he remembered him at all.

Then along came Alex, asking for an introduction. Marc's first reaction was a definitive "no way," as he explained the snub and the strange behavior of the gallery owner. But Alex had just finished drafting a chapter on communications and wondered if this was really a substantive rift or simply a lack of clear communications. In fact, it sounded to Alex as if the gallery owner might simply be vague and had forgotten not only to call Marc back but also who Marc was and how he knew him. It was at least a possibility. And since nowhere in the story was there an affirmative communication from the gallery owner saying he didn't want to work with Marc, Alex asked Marc to come to the gallery with him and explore the situation.

As Alex had hoped, the gallery owner was affable, friendly, and completely unclear as to who Marc was and when and how they had met. "I've talked with so many people since I opened up," he explained apologetically. "I just can't recall who you are or when we met." When Marc explained again what he did and who he was, the gallery owner's face lit up. "Oh, that's right!" he said, "I went to your show last weekend. It was great! Sorry I didn't follow up, but I lost your contact information. Maybe we can do something in the future!" So take one person out of the enemies category and put him in the "future business friends" category instead. (And by the way, the introduction went well and the gallery owner invited Alex to show some work.)

This story illustrates a number of important principles of negotiating (which apply to both business and personal life), but the most striking lesson it offers is the tendency to ignore *people* by assuming they are "enemies" or "don't like us" and failing to negotiate with them.

This same author (Alex) had a similar experience years ago that taught us this lesson in a striking manner. Authors often offer cover quotes or testimonials for other authors, and one of us was looking for an appropriate person to provide a cover quote at the request of a publisher.

"Don't you know so-and-so [a best-selling author]?" one of our editors asked. "Why don't you get him to provide a cover quote?"

"Well, that's a long story," came our reply. "You see, several years ago, we worked on a project together and fell into a dispute. He had his lawyer write an extremely aggressive demand letter, and we'd decided to accommodate with a several thousand dollar settlement check to avoid having to hire a lawyer and go to court."

It was a ridiculous thing. He was way out of line, but we decided it was cheaper to settle than to litigate, even though we were sure we were right. So of course we assumed that relationship was toast and never talked with the guy again. But was it? In fact, *he* was probably pleased with the outcome, since he'd gotten a nice check. And authors like to give cover quotes because it promotes their own name and work. Obviously we would have to be careful to make the ground rules clear and get everything in writing to avoid another messy dispute. But why not ask? We did and got a glowing quote that helped make our book a success. Perhaps he felt a little remorse, and maybe he really liked the book, but for whatever reason, he did the job quickly and well. We still don't hang out together, but we have learned an important lesson about assumptions from this experience. There was no good reason to leave that relationship on the table forever by assuming we were enemies and couldn't work together again.

Does this lesson apply in personal life? For that matter, what's the difference, in both these stories, between personal and business life? When it comes to relationships with individuals in our networks, personal and business affairs intermingle, and our personal feelings can and often do determine who we work with and how we pursue our business interests.

DEALS OF A LIFETIME

Business and personal negotiations sometimes have a broad boarder of overlap. They certainly do in most of the negotiating situations we address in the rest of this chapter: buying a car, negotiating a salary, planning (and paying for) a wedding. These selections include many of the most common negotiation situations that people find themselves in during their adult lifetime and show how you can use the principles of negotiation that we have explored in the previous chapters. While you will probably encounter many other negotiating situations too, we are confident that they will have much in common with the ones that we address here. We have ordered them in the sequence one might usually encounter them in one's life: from buying one's first car (usually a used one), to making other major purchases (new car and house), getting married (a major multiparty negotiation), getting a job, negotiating for a salary increase in a job, and having the house repaired. We hope that our advice is helpful to you and allows you to achieve your objectives while still maintaining a strong, positive relationship with those you love, live with, and work with on a regular basis.

BUYING A USED CAR

One of the first "big deals" in a lifetime is buying your first car. Some people get to relive this joy when you help a child or relative buy their first used car. Here's a checklist of things you should remember when you go out to buy that car:

1. Figure out your requirements for the car. How are you going to use it? Getting back and forth to work or school? Transporting just you or several other people as well? Putting on lots of miles or just a few each day? Maybe hauling tools or equipment? Thinking this out should let you define the current mileage level, the size (compact, midsize, SUV, pickup truck), the style (sporty model or more conventional sedan), and other distinctive features

required such as four-wheel drive, trunk size, or ski or luggage rack. These are your interests.

Define these interests clearly and don't waver from them unless you have a chance at some amazing deal on a car that does not fit this profile. When you are looking at cars, it is easy to get distracted by models and types that don't meet these interests. Define what you want, and don't budge unless you have a good reason to do so.

This tendency to forget our own interests and get distracted by features and benefits is a problem in all consumer purchases, and sometimes in personal relationships as well. What qualities do you value most in furniture, for instance? If comfort and lasting value are at the top of your list, avoid an overpriced, uncomfortable Italian designer couch even if all the cool people are buying them.

2. Figure out how much you can afford to spend. If you are paying in cash, can you pay it all now, or do you need to pay it in several payments? If you are thinking of borrowing money for a car loan, visit a bank before you start looking for a car and find out how much the bank will lend you and what the monthly payments will be. Have the bank help you think about what your budget should be and how much you can afford. These become your financial *targets* and *walkaways*.

3. Locate several cars that meet your specifications from one of these:

- Your local newspaper or auto trader, either in the classified ads for used cars or in the used car ads placed by dealerships
- Car dealer Web sites
- Car lots (new and used)
- Word of mouth, friends, bulletin boards at work or school
- "Drive-bys"—cars sitting in yards or empty lots that individuals are trying to sell

Car dealers make their money by buying cars at a low price and reselling them at a higher price. So when you deal with a dealer, you are paying more for the car than the dealer did. Sometimes this is good because dealers may give a warranty for ninety days against defects and mechanical work needed. Private sales from individuals may be cheaper to you, but you probably can't get any guarantee and don't have anyone to complain to if you discover problems.

Your objective is to find several cars that meet your interests. Your job now is to find out how to get the best deal on that make, model, and year of a car. For example, if you find a 2004 Honda Civic that you like, start looking for other 2004 Honda Civics so you can compare mileage, wear and tear, and quality of other features like the radio, tires, and cleanliness.

4. Research the "book" value of the car. There are many resources on the market that tell you what any car of a specific make, model, and year should be selling for. These "blue books" often list the average book value, what a car in very good condition might be worth, or what a car in poor condition might be worth. All banks, bookstores, and libraries have them as well. You can also find several Web sites with this information. We particularly like www.edmunds.com

5. Contact the owners of the cars you are interested in. Go to the used car lots or set aside a Saturday morning and call some of the numbers in the newspaper ads. You need to do the following:

- Find out the initial price.
- Look over the car. Take a friend with you who is not emotionally invested in the car to help you spot defects, damage, and wear and tear.
- Ask about the car history. Particularly if it is a private owner, ask how long the person has had it, whether the service records are available, and how and where it was driven.
- Test-drive it to get a sense of how it starts and runs.

6. Locate a mechanic who will inspect cars for you. Many gas stations or garages will perform an independent mechanical inspection of the car without pressuring you into buying their repair work. If you have doubts about the mechanical condition of the car, paying fifty dollars to have the car fully inspected is well worth the time and the satisfaction.

7. Begin the negotiation. Assuming you have decided to try to buy this car, here's where all your planning and preparation come into play. Make sure you have set your target price, based on what you can afford and what the industry standard says for the value of the car. Also know your walkaway point (the least you will pay) and a BATNA (what other similar car might be available in the neighborhood). Then ask the owner to name the price. Even if you are

in a dealership and there is a big price sticker in the window, ask whether that is the best price the owner can give you today.

How you negotiate depends on whom you are dealing with. If this is a private sale from a stranger, or a dealership, you are most likely in a competitive negotiation. If you are buying the car from a friend or relative, you will not want to bargain hard and make the person angry. You might make a little more but you must also worry about preserving your relationship with this person. Chances are he or she is going to be as worried about this as you are.

8. Make your counteroffer. You might want to start the bidding by making an offer. If you do, offer about 85 percent of what the owner is asking or a price that is 5 percent below the blue book value of the car. Some people suggest you should counteroffer even less just to find out how serious the owner is about the first offer. Be ready to justify your counteroffer with a list of arguments about why the car is not worth what the owner wants for it—or at least not worth it to you. This might include:

- High mileage
- Wear and tear on the paint, nicks and dents, upholstery, and unpleasant odors, for example
- The cost of immediate work you have to do to get the car in good condition (even if you never intend to spend that money)

9. Bargain hard until you get to your target. Be prepared to spend a lot of time at this. The longer you stay at it, the more likely the owner may be to make big concessions just to get the sale over with. If it is a private sale, ask how quickly the owner has to sell. The longer the person has had it or the more quickly he or she needs the cash, the more willing he or she may be to come down quickly. Make small concessions when you make them (say, in hundred dollar increments). Try to get the owner to give more and give more often. And be prepared to walk away if the counteroffers do not make significant movement toward your target.

In this step, you have to watch out for emotional decision making. Don't fall in love with the car or the seller unless you are willing to pay several hundred dollars more for that love affair. The more you fall in love with this car, this seller, or needing to "drive this car off the lot," the more likely you are to pay too much. Love affairs are never cost free.

Your mantra as you haggle over the car you've chosen should be, *There are always more cars on the market.* Eventually you'll find a similar car with similar mileage, even if you don't see an alternative on the market right now. So don't feel as if you have to close this deal no matter what. Patience is the most important quality of the used car shopper, and it gives you the upper hand in every negotiation.

In fact, patience and a level head are the most important qualities in any negotiation, whether business or personal. As we promised, the skills of the master business negotiation carry over easily into your personal deals of a lifetime too.

Buying a New Car

Many of the principles for buying a new car are the same as for buying a used car. We will repeat some of these major points here:

1. Figure out your requirements for the car. How are you going to use it? Getting back and forth to work or school? Transporting just you or several other people as well? Putting on lots of miles or just a few each day? Maybe hauling tools or equipment? Thinking this out should let you define the current mileage level, the size (compact, midsize, SUV, pickup truck), the style (sporty model or more conventional sedan), and other distinctive features required such as four-wheel drive, trunk size, or ski or luggage rack. These are your interests.

Define these interests clearly, and don't waver from them. When you get out looking at cars, it is very easy to get distracted by models and types that don't meet these interests. Define what you want, and don't budge unless you have a good reason to do so.

Make sure you also specify all of the options and features you want on the car (for example, quality of radio, special brakes, sun roof, heated seats). When you begin to get prices, you will want to find a car loaded with all the features you want, and then compare prices on that identical car. Car dealers often use a bait-and-switch strategy in which they advertise or tell you on the telephone about a low price, assuming they will move you to a more expensive purchase later when you realize you want a car with more features.

2. Figure out how much you can afford to spend. If you are paying in cash, can you pay it all now, or do you need to pay it in several payments? If you are thinking of borrowing money for a car loan, visit a bank before you start looking for a car and find out how much the bank will lend you and what the monthly payments will be. Have the bank help you think about what your budget should be and how much you can afford. These become your financial targets and walkaways. (Many new car dealers now have financing experts who can tell you who has the best loan or lease financial packages before you even begin talking about a specific car).

It is very important to know your target payment (total dollars or monthly payment) and your walkaway (the most you will pay) before you begin any discussions with car dealers. Walkaways can also be determined by understanding the dealer's costs.

It is helpful to know your BATNA. What will you do if you do not buy a new car at all? For example, can you drive your existing car for another year or lease a car for a year, or are there several dealerships in town offering the same makes and models?

3. Do your research. Information equals bargaining power. Places to look for information include:

- Books and magazines that describe the new makes and models
- Consumer guides that rate new cars on appearance, safety, performance, reliability, and other features
- Web sites for car manufacturers or consumer guides (again, we like www.edmunds.com)
- Annual auto shows, which are held in large cities
- Car dealerships

We do not recommend visiting car dealerships until you have decided on a few specific makes and models or you have a lot of time to kill. Otherwise, you will have high-pressure salespeople trying to talk you into something you may not need or want. If you do, insist that you are "just looking" and take home the dealer's literature on the cars you are evaluating.

4. Determine if the timing is right and how much time you have before you need the new car. Many dealers have end-of-year specials in late summer or the end of December or when the models change. However, the more that they discount the selling price automatically to get rid of the car, the less negotiating room you may have. One of us (Roy) bought his most recent car on Labor Day. There were six salesmen in the showroom and absolutely no customers—and the sales manager was anxious to sell something that day. (Roy got a great deal.)

Take time to shop. Don't be pressured by a dealer to make a quick decision. And be careful, because dealers are great at creating a false sense of urgency: "My manager doesn't normally let me sell this close to cost, but he has some new cars coming tomorrow and if I move this today . . ." Their sales pitch lines are endlessly creative and often quite plausible. But hold fast. Resist the pressure to reframe your month-long search into a two-day panic attack, and take the time to make a reasoned decision.

Sometimes it's necessary to state your ground rules to a salesperson: "I will not make a decision under extreme pressure, and if you keep coming up with short-term deals, I'm going to walk away. I expect you to give me a good price that you will stand by, not waffle on or take back tomorrow. Is that clear?" Then wait to see if it *is* clear. If not, say it again. Many salespeople will get away with whatever they think you'll let them get away with, but are quick to adjust their style if you make your preferences clear.

We know we're talking about buying a car here, but a quick story about a car repair is relevant. One of us had a lot of repair work commissioned by the service department of a large car dealership. The work was inadequate; in fact, some of the work on the bill evidently had not been done, and other work was done poorly. In the ensuing debate with the sales manager, the manager kept saying that he was new and would lose his job if he gave in too much. This is an example of an inappropriate framing that doesn't sound plausible and certainly shouldn't be the concern of the dissatisfied car owner. Appeals to charity are one thing, but let's not mix them with paying bills for bad work at car dealerships. It was helpful to explain, clearly and firmly, that if the service manager wanted advice about how to keep his job, that would be a matter for after-hours discussion but not for this discussion about a disputed bill. Set boundaries as needed to make sure the other party doesn't add inappropriate external pressures to the negotiation.

5. Locate several car dealerships that meet your specifications. Check the Yellow Pages, the Web, or your local newspaper (many papers have large auto advertising sections on Saturday or Sunday). It's a good idea to find several cars that meet your interests. Your job now is to find out how to get the best deal on that specific make, model, and collection of options.

6. If you are trading in an old car, check the "blue book" value of that car—what that particular make and model, in good or average condition, is now worth. You ought to get something close to this value, but you may not get full value because the dealer wants to make a little profit when it resells the car.

Decide whether you want to trade in or sell the car separately. Selling separately is more of a hassle, but you may get a few more dollars by doing it. Your research on the market value of your car will help you decide if the difference between the dealer's trade-in and the blue book value is big enough to make selling it yourself worth the hassle. If the difference is less than 15 percent, you probably don't want to bother. Trade it in and spend your weekends doing something more entertaining or profitable.

Tip: Always negotiate for the price of the new car separately from the value given on the trade-in. Many dealers will try to confuse you by giving some discount on the car combined with an offer on your car and will not clearly break it out separately. Watch out for these magically shifting numbers between new car price and value of your trade-in.

7. Go back to your information sources—the books, articles, or Web sites. Check out dealer cost on your specific targeted cars, including all of the options and add-ons. This is what the dealer pays the manufacturer for the car, although sometimes even this number is discounted because dealers get rebates on volume discounts or promotions from the manufacturers.

You probably should set your opening bid at dealer cost (or below, if there is reason to do so). The dealer will not be happy, but it is a fair opening. Try to set your walkaway at about five hundred dollars above dealer cost.

8. Consult at least two dealers, and ask them to give you a price on the outfitted car. Use one price as the BATNA and ask another dealer to beat it. "Whipsaw" them back and forth until they both have stopped at the same number. Variations of this process now exist on the Web, where you can indicate the car you want to buy, with the relevant features and add-ons, and wait for dealers to bid on the price they would be willing to accept.

Take your time, and don't agree on a deal until at least the second visit to the dealership. Get the salesperson to invest a lot of time in you; he or she will be more willing to try to help you get a good price. Make concessions slowly.

Decide whether you want to take a spouse or friend with you. If you and your friend don't agree or one of you is more impatient than the other, you may expose weakness that the dealer will exploit. In general, it is best to let the most experienced bargainer negotiate alone. Don't let yourself be distracted by others who need to leave early, go somewhere else, or are getting bored and pressuring you to give in quickly.

This advice is important in many negotiating contexts at work and beyond. We often see situations in which one side has created its own internal pressures and failed to negotiate a good outcome as a result. Most of your associates, friends, and loved ones are not master negotiators. Be politely firm with them. Don't let them determine the pace of your negotiations. You lose your mastery as soon as you lose control of the timing. If you can't explain at the moment (because you are in the presence of a salesperson or other representative of the opposite side), just tell them, "This is how we need to do it," or "You'll have to wait; sorry," and then add, "I'll explain later," and "thank you" as needed to keep them at least moderately happy while you take care of the negotiation. When you are alone, you can explain more fully what was going on and why you needed them to stop putting time pressure on you.

9. Ask lots of questions. Find out how the dealership determines price, markup, cost of extras, and so forth. In some dealerships now, the money issues are handled by a person separate from the car sale. You may want to talk to this person about financing packages and warranties before you finalize your negotiations with the salesperson. The knowledge you'll gain from the financial

person may help you structure your offer and close a better deal. But realize that the car dealership may have a preferred sequence for the sale and may at first resist your efforts to talk about financing before you have a firm deal. That's just one of the ways they try to control the negotiation. You can politely but firmly insist on doing it your way, not their's, and they will have to go along.

10. You might nibble at the end for extras such as undercoating, special molding or trip packages, extended warranty, or service packages. Think about the things you can probably win through nibbling, and plan your nibbles in advance. Anything that doesn't cost the dealer too much is a candidate. Nibbles are for small bites only, so don't expect to win a lot more this way.

Watch out for the dealer's attempts at nibbling by adding charges, costs, and options (paint sealer, undercoating, and others) at the end. Get all of this included in the price. If it is not clear whether something is included, ask lots of questions. And if despite your efforts to clarify the deal, you find the dealer is nibbling you at the end, consider having a controlled tantrum and insisting that this should have been included. If the dealer fears you are upset and are going to walk away, the sales rep may back down and throw it in for free. The trick is to do more of the nibbling than the other party.

We have found that when we negotiated really great deals on cars, the dealer often tried to change the price, value of the trade-in, or other components on the day we showed up to take delivery. But if the dealer committed, it has to stick to the deal. Make it clear that you are willing to walk out of the negotiation if you sense the dealer is trying to go back on the deal. Make it clear you view this as a matter of integrity, that you won't buy from anyone you don't trust, and so forth. A dealer who thinks he or she has bumped into your line in the sand will almost always make good on the initial deal. But dealers love to try to nibble you one more time, and you can't blame them for trying.

Also keep in mind that any reasonable-sized city has several dealerships that sell the same car, so if one dealer won't make good on the deal, say you are going to see if you can get another dealership to honor the deal instead. Often you can, but occasionally you can't. If that happens, you still have the option of returning to the first dealership and accepting the revised terms. You might be willing to if you are sure the first deal really was too good and nobody is willing to accept it. But that's a rare situation; usually you can close your preferred deal by letting them know you aren't going to let them play games.

PLANNING A WEDDING

Planning a wedding is one of the most stressful and complex negotiations most of us ever do. There are several reasons for this. First, it's a very emotional time. Everyone wants everything to "go just perfectly," but they all have different ideas of what "perfectly" means. People's choices and preferences are often based on sentimental reasons and logic. Hence it is hard to negotiate with those who feel most strongly about the way things should go. In addition, there are many people who have to be pleased. Certainly the event is for the bride and groom, but both sets of parents and relatives also have high expectations and may also be paying the bill. Remember that planning a wedding successfully is often a task worthy of an international peacekeeper. It requires great diplomatic skill and coordination to ensure that everyone is reasonably satisfied and still talking after the newlyweds head off for the honeymoon.

1. Issues. All kinds of things get negotiated in weddings. You probably should buy a bridal book or magazine that has a number of special checklists for all of the planning events. But here is a partial list:

Phase 1: Early Planning

- Date and time of wedding
- Location (near one or the other's parents or near where the engaged couple is currently living?)
- Number of guests (is this to be a big, moderate, or small wedding?)
- Location (church or other facility for ceremony and reception; destination wedding?)
- Religion (what kinds of prewedding coordination and education are required?)

- Responsibilities of others in the wedding party (ushers, bridesmaids, best man, maid of honor)
- Finances (how much is available to pay for everything and who
  will pay for it)

Phase 2: Sixty to Ninety Days Before the Wedding

- Guest list (who is invited)
- Bride's and bridesmaids' dresses
- Groom's and ushers' attire
- Honeymoon location and arrangements
- Bridal party (how many and who on each side)
- Rehearsal dinner and reception (alcohol, meal served, band
  or other music, seating)
- Picking out gifts (china pattern, silver pattern, and regis-
  tration)
- Transportation the day of the wedding

Phase 3: Within Thirty Days of the Wedding

- Menu (meal and cocktails)
- Music (band or DJ)
- Wedding rings

2. Planning and early discussion:

- Meet with the betrothed and with each set of parents to determine their primary interests and figure out what is most
  important for each set of parents in the wedding planning
  (location, church, reception, food, guest list)
- It's important to let the other loved one decide on those issues
  that are key to him or her—divide up the most important
  issues for each side.
- Pick your battles. Figure out what your personal interests really
  are and which interests are worth fighting over.
- Let each side decide the issues that are most important to
  them, and drop all further discussion of them.
- Meet with the bridesmaids to coordinate and agree on their
  dress colors.

It's also essential to decide whether the marrying couple makes
the decisions or whether their parents do. (If the parents are pay-

ing the bill, maybe they should have the final decision.) This is something to talk about early on, so that all constituents are clear on who is in the driver's seat how much of the time during the planning.

3. Let parents make decisions that are unimportant to either bride or groom, and vice versa. Everyone should feel as if they have had real input into planning. Involve them and invite people to take responsibility for making certain things happen. Share the responsibility and the decision-making power.

4. Do not hesitate to negotiate with the major service providers. Particularly if it is a large wedding, here are some of the key negotiables:

- Wedding ring. Look at several different rings based on amount of gold, size of stone, and design. Visit several shops. Make a counteroffer.
- Bride's and bridesmaids' dresses. Since you are buying several dresses for the wedding party, see if you can get a bulk price, or make sure all alterations are included in the price.
- Rental of tuxedos, limousines, and other equipment
- Price for flower arrangements (table decorations, bouquets)
- Reception. Negotiables include the prices of dinners and drinks, special arrangements for dancing and music, and table decorations. Once again, if you can specify what you want, get several bids on the entire package.

This is a good place to "rock" the parties' offers back and forth. Get a good offer from one, go back to the other and ask them to beat the offer, go back to the first and ask them to beat the second, until you get a deal you like.

NEGOTIATING A NEW JOB WITH A LARGE EMPLOYER

After buying a car, the next major life negotiation for many of us is to get hired by a company or other employer and negotiate our new salary. Many people do not even try to negotiate starting salary (they are happy just to have a job offer), and others assume that starting salary packages cannot be negotiated. This is definitely not true. Negotiables in this process may include:

- Salary
- Vacation time (and length)
- Incentive or signing bonus
- Moving and other relocation expenses
- Work schedule and job duties
- Starting date
- Work location

We have found that negotiating with bigger companies is somewhat different from trying to negotiate with a small business, so we will cover them separately. This section focuses on getting hired by a large company.

Unlike buying a car, which suggests a very short-term focus and limited discussion with the car dealer, negotiating a salary and job has long-term consequences for you and the relationship with the company. Therefore, a collaborative strategy is most desirable.

1. Do your homework on the company and the job you want. There is much that we could say here, but space limits the discussion. We are assuming that you know what kind of job and position you want and that you have interviewed several companies and received a formal offer for one or more or those jobs. If at all possible, generate more than one offer from more than one company. The power of a good BATNA is again obvious. It will be much harder to negotiate with only one company than if you have a BATNA offer.

2. Determine your target, walkaway, and opening. The target is what you think you should be paid. You may decide this on the basis of studying the pay and pay grades for certain jobs, gaining information from a career counselor, or reading the want ads. Gather information that will help you determine what a person with your skills, education, and experience should be paid. Be fair and reasonable, but try to benchmark yourself against similar people in the job market at this time.

The walkaway is the least you are willing to be paid for this job and still accept the position. You may decide this based on the same information gathered about the target, or your current needs and expenses, or how desperate you are.

Set the opening at least 10 percent above your target. If you get asked, you may need to justify this request based on research you have done about salaries in this industry. Although companies usually make an opening offer when they want to hire you, many ask in the interview, "What are your salary requirements?" or "What are you expecting?" State your opening number, not your target.

Don't Make Outrageous Demands: A True Story!

Reaching the end of a job interview, the recruiter asked the enthusiastic M.B.A., "And what starting salary were you looking for?"

The candidate said, "In the neighborhood of $125,000 a year, depending on the benefits package."

The recruiter said, "Well, what would you say to a package of five weeks vacation, fourteen paid holidays, full medical and dental, company matching retirement fund to 50 percent of salary, and a company car leased every two years—say, a red Corvette?"

The M.B.A. sat up straight and said, "WOW!!! Are you kidding?"

And the recruiter responded, "Certainly, but you started it."

---

3. Convey to the potential employer the need to weigh other options. Indicate that until the discussions are completed, you may continue to pursue other job interviews and options.

4. Ask questions about the opening offer. Ask if the offer is consistent with recent market offers and if it is consistent with offers given to others who have the same portfolio of skills, background, and experience. Then inquire, "How did you get that number [the opening offer]?" in an effort to discover the thinking and logic used to put together the offer.

The question, "How did you get that number?" is useful for uncovering the logic, thinking, analysis, and information of the other party. The more you understand their thinking and information, the more you will learn how to present counterinformation and logic to challenge their view and support your own!

5. Negotiate for base salary rate first. Try to get an agreement on the base salary first, and then negotiate the rest of the package. Many large companies fix their starting salaries based on internal salary grading systems (tying specific salary levels and ranges to specific entry level jobs). Therefore, you may not be able to negotiate starting salary, but you can often negotiate the add-ons. So if the company will not budge on the salary number, try negotiating on

the other items where there may be more flexibility and ability to make concessions.

6. Think about what add-ons are desirable to you, and try to negotiate these separately. These might include:

- A signing bonus
- Reimbursement for moving costs
- Assistance with making a down payment on a house or condo
- Reimbursement for extra trips to visit the company or look for housing
- An automatic cost-of-living increase
- Location of assignment (where you go to work)
- Benefit packages, including various health care options
- Payment into retirement and 401(k) plans
- Assistance in paying college or graduate school tuition
- Insurance packages
- When you start the job
- Vacation (when you get it, how long it is)
- A bonus or profit-sharing plan based on excellent individual or company performance
- A company car, uniform allowance, or other extras necessary to do the job
- Level of clerical and administrative help and assistance

7. Package and repackage until you get the deal you want. Combine and trade off the add-on elements to get the best deal you can. But remember the key trade-off here. Do not let this negotiation get competitive. Be honest, fair, and reasonable at all times, and treat the other kindly. Nevertheless, *do not* allow yourself to be talked into a salary or job requirements that you will come to dislike only in a few weeks.

NEGOTIATING A NEW JOB WITH A SMALLER EMPLOYER

There are several differences between negotiating with a big corporation or government organization and a small company:

- Small companies may have less of an idea of what you are worth in the market, and you may have to take greater initiative to educate them.

- Small companies may offer you less money but more opportunity to get good experience in a variety of jobs and situations.
- Small companies usually don't have fixed salary grades for starting positions, particularly entry-level management positions, so you have more freedom to negotiate salary as well as add-ons.

Plan to use a collaborative approach. Your reputation and relationship with key company officials is the most important thing. Don't push hard for money if it will make them angry or they wind up seeing you as greedy.

1. Research the company and the job. Ask lots of questions about the job, your duties and responsibilities, and people you will work with, for example. Find out what the company's interests are: ask questions about why they are hiring, what they are looking for, what potential they might see in you. Meet lots of people in the organization. Get a sense of who they are, what they are like, how you feel about them, whether you would like to work with them. Learn how they see the company and its future.

2. Define your interests and goals. Realize that your work (both positive and negative) is much more visible in a small firm than a large one, so both the risk and the reward could be greater. Then decide why a small company situation might be better for you (for example, you will probably learn more about the broad scope of the business, have a greater opportunity to do many jobs, learn new skills, show what you can do, and work directly with the key boss). Then determine your market value, and find out the average starting salary for your region given the industry, your level of work experience, and other qualifications.

3. Be ready to identify and discuss your strengths:

- Education, including graduate degrees
- Previous job experience
- Skills you have learned in previous jobs
- Your interests and career plans
- Particular skills or experiences you could apply to this job
- How you would add value to the company immediately

Be ready to offer examples of your previous work to show what you can do: reports, studies, projects, and testimonials, for example.

4. Have your walkaway, target, and opening salary numbers clearly identified. (Refer to the previous section on negotiating a job with a large company.)

5. If possible, create a BATNA, and have at least more than one offer on the table. It is tempting to invent or make up a BATNA to say you have another offer even if you don't have one. But be careful about being dishonest. While some negotiation experts say it is okay to do this, be aware that the company can always double-check, and then you will be caught telling a lie before you are even hired. If you don't have a BATNA, determine industry norms and standards for the specific kind of job you are being offered.

6. Try to build a relationship with the person who will be determining your salary. Find out his or her interests or needs. What is this person looking for? Why does the company want to hire someone like you? Be ready to talk about how your skills and qualifications match this organization's interests. Get to know this person. He or she is likely to be your boss or senior manager. Find out if you can work together successfully.

7. Don't hesitate to negotiate job add-ons. You want to achieve the best package, not necessarily the best starting salary. If the company will not negotiate salary now or increase its offer, ask whether you can obtain an early performance review. In most companies, performance gets reviewed once a year, and salaries are determined by the performance review. If you think you can make a quick and visible contribution, ask for a performance review after six or eight months.

Have a target for all negotiable elements of the deal, and rank them in order of importance—for example, (1) salary, (2) job duties and responsibilities, and (3) health care benefits. Know where you can make trade-offs (for example, when is one less week of vacation equivalent to getting a full-time secretary?).

8. Always have a walkaway point. Don't be pressured into accepting a job offer that you will dislike in a month and that will send you back into the job market. Even if you have no BATNA, you should seriously consider whether any job is better than no job.

NEGOTIATING A RAISE WITH YOUR CURRENT EMPLOYER

At some point, you will feel that you want to try to negotiate a raise, promotion, or change of responsibilities. You are not unhappy enough (yet) to leave the company, but you are certainly not feeling completely satisfied or well treated. So you decide to go to your boss and try to negotiate a promotion, a raise, or a change of responsibilities. This is another negotiation that must be kept at a professional level. Work toward collaboration or compromise at all times. Be clear about what you would like, but do not press too hard or use any competitive tactics. Here are the things you need to do to maintain control and focus in those negotiations:

1. Do research. Learn what the industry norms might be for a person of your current duties, job level, past education, and experience. Then try to benchmark yourself against comparable salaries for your kind of work in your region, territory, and type of industry. You can find these statistics on the Web or ask your local librarian to help you.

2. Make a complete list of your accomplishments. Have it typed and organized into a clear outline with bullet points:

- Be clear about what you have personally accomplished.
- Be clear about what improvements or changes have occurred during your tenure.
- Quantify the value, worth, and cost savings of these contributions.
- Focus on those things that were unique and hard to do, and ways you overcame major obstacles.

3. Ask around the company about raises. Find out if others have successfully negotiated a raise and, if so, how it was done. Talk to people who have negotiated with your boss, and find out how salary budgets are structured and how much discretion there is in them.

4. Know your walkaway and BATNA. Determine whether you will stay with the job or the company if you do not get what

you want. If you have decided to move, begin your job search now, because if the salary discussion turns ugly, you may wish you had a choice to move quickly. You may wish to interview with another company to determine how much interest there is in you and what another organization would offer to pay you. But this is risky. Do not use your BATNA as a threat in your negotiations. No one likes to be threatened. You may want to make it clear that if you do not get a raise or promotion, you may have to look at the market, but do not threaten to walk if you do not get your demands met. You may find yourself on the street sooner than you wanted to.

5. Make a clear, strong request:

- Quote your opening number.
- Tell the boss how you decided on that number—that is, tie your request to research you have done on job grades and levels, profitability of the work you have done, and other reasons.
- Justify it with the list of accomplishments you have prepared.
- Be able to point to the value of those contributions as a reward for your hard work.

Think about where you want to conduct this negotiation. Some negotiators suggest that you get the boss to a table where you can maintain level eye contact and fairly close distance.[1] Do not negotiate with him in his high leather chair behind the big desk. This is the power seat where he makes most of the "no" decisions. Taking him to lunch might also be a good idea.

Remember to keep your emotions in check. Do not get upset or afraid. If you are reading this, chances are that you are not in a minimum wage job. Do not talk about how you need a raise to pay your bills; your spending habits are your problem, not your company's.

6. Listen clearly to the boss's response. Find out what his interests and concerns are and how he evaluates your performance and accomplishments. If he refuses your request, ask questions in order to learn how you might qualify for a raise in the future. If you can do no more, negotiate a plan for how you can qualify for a raise, or when it might happen, or how you can improve your work in order to get a raise.

7. Close the deal. Ask your boss if it would help to write a memo summarizing what you have agreed to. This will allow you to put it in writing and be sure that the facts are remembered if your boss is transferred tomorrow or too much time passes.

Buying a House Through an Agent

Another major negotiation that we face in our lives is buying (and selling) one or more houses. Particularly if we are not familiar with an area or neighborhood or don't have the time to do all the leg-work on our own, most of us use professional real estate agents as intermediaries.

As we noted in Chapter Three, negotiating through an agent is significantly different from doing the deal yourself. Understand that you will be negotiating with someone who is doing the nego-tiating for you, but you can maintain an active role by giving instructions and directions, coaching, and calling the strategic shots.

1. Once again, everything starts with research. Find the neigh-borhood and type of housing that meets your needs. Talk with your spouse, and decide on the most important elements for a house. This might be location of schools, availability of public trans-portation, configuration and size of house, or size of lot. Rank-order these, and make sure you stick with them as you look at possible properties.

If you are unfamiliar with the area, contact a brokerage agency that has contacts throughout the city and ask to be given a general tour of neighborhoods, price ranges, quality of schools, etc.

Find a broker you like who understands what you are looking for. Don't hesitate to talk to several brokerages or agencies to find a person who is willing to work with you and understands your needs.

Decide whether you need your own broker. Agents usually rep-resent only the sellers. But you can hire a buyer's agent if you think that person has a unique set of skills, or you want someone loyal to you in the negotiations, or you will be out of the area and want someone local to handle it for you.

You may want to negotiate the agent's commission. A commission is normally 6 percent for the seller and 3 percent for the buyer. (Check on this; in some states, buyers do not pay any commission.) If there are unique circumstances—for example, you don't think the agent has worked very hard—try to negotiate the commission.

2. Get a general idea of the price range for houses or condos in the area you select. Then consult with a bank or mortgage company about the different kinds of mortgages available and what those will require in the amount of money down and your monthly payments. You don't have to commit to any company at this point, but you should try to understand financing options and costs before you start getting serious about a particular house. Also get an estimate of the closing costs in that area. Agents can supply this information.

3. Once you have decided on the amount you want to finance, you can apply for a loan. This will allow you to know whether you qualify for the requested loan amount before you find the house of your dreams and will allow you to move much more quickly if and when you find the place. Ask your agent for banks and mortgage companies offering the best rates, or check the Web or financial pages in the local newspaper.

4. Set your walkaway price. This is usually the price for the house plus the estimated cost of remodeling to make the house livable or up to your standards. The challenge is now to find a house that once repaired will cost you no more per month than you have allocated. Once you have found the house—even if it is brand new—make a list of all the things you think the house needs: cleaning, repainting, remodeling and repair, or new appliances, for example. Have the agent help you figure out approximate costs. This list will also be helpful to you as arguments for why the current asking price might be discounted.

5. Find your BATNA. Figure out comparable houses and prices in the same general neighborhood. Your agent can identify all the properties in the neighborhood that sold in the past year and the relevant details about those houses. Find another one on the market you would like to own.

6. Visit the house and tour the property. Try to talk to the owners about the house (and make an effort to identify which of the owners is the more conversational one):

- Why are they selling, and how quickly do they want to sell?
- What are the great things they have loved about the house, the neighborhood, schools, and other topics?
- Are there any problems or drawbacks that they know about?

7. Identify the strong and weak features of the house (maybe you love the yard but hate the kitchen). Consult with others who might be able to give you an objective assessment of the house, property, and neighborhood. For example, you could come back without the agent and talk with the neighbors. Go down the street several doors, and ask a neighbor if he or she is aware of any problems with the house or area. Ask other agents about the property. Consult public records to find out what the current owners paid for the house, and how long ago. If you have any doubts about the structural nature of the house, insist that it be inspected by a building inspector, pest control specialist, and others. There are other questions to consider too: How long has the house been on the market, and how desperate are the sellers to sell? These are critical questions to determine the sellers' willingness to negotiate. If they are moving out next week regardless of whether the house is sold and the house has been on the market for more than a few weeks, chances are you will have much more negotiating leverage.

8. The price will generally already be set. Be ready to make a counteroffer:

- Define whether the price covers any current repairs to the house (for example, painting, yard repair, fixing leaks or breaks).
- Offer about 90 percent of the asking price if the repairs are included and less if you have to pay for them yourself. Be ready to justify your offer.
- Have your priority list available. Define what you must have, what you would like, and what is truly optional relative to this house.
- Come up with possible options for settlement (no remodeling, remodeling done, some work done).
- Get the sellers' commitment to tell you if someone else is looking seriously at the house.
- Ask the sellers whether they will carry some of the mortgage

themselves. Then you can pay them directly, perhaps at a lower interest rate than what the bank will charge.

- Don't take the first counteroffer. Make a concession of 1 to 2 percent of the asking price and reoffer. Try packaging and repackaging with added options. This is a good place to try "throw-ins" (for example, "We'll pay that price, but you have to include the refrigerator, the deck furniture, and the pool table in the basement, and you agree to have the garage repainted when you leave").

- If it is important to you, one great throw-in is the closing date, when you sign and exchange money and paperwork. If you are preapproved for a loan, you could close quickly if that would help you, or postpone the closing if necessary.

If you are with your spouse, make sure only one of you does the talking. One spouse is usually more willing to compromise than the other; the "hard" one should do the talking, and you should talk between yourselves only out of earshot of the buyer and the agents.

Negotiating the Home Repair Contract

Now that you have bought that new house, it may be several weeks or several years before you have to have it fixed. Whether we are talking about a simple paint job, a complex kitchen remodeling, or doubling the entire square footage, you need your negotiation skills as much as you did when you bought the place. Here are a few pointers:

1. Figure out what changes you want to make. It might be wall-papering, changing some cabinets, redoing a room, or more. You can get good ideas from home repair contractors, home goods stores, and decorators who work on a fee basis. House and home magazines also offer lots of ideas.

2. Get at least two estimates for everything. Pick the contractors you call on the basis of personal referrals (talk to friends and neighbors). Look for trucks in your neighborhood working on local houses. Ask people in your church or club who they have used. If you recently bought the house, ask the real estate agent

for recommendations. If you have to pick a company blind from the telephone book, ask each contractor to give you references of work he or she has done in the area. Always check the references.

3. Most remodeling work is done by small contractors who are often not good businesspeople, so you need to monitor and check them more closely than if they were big and established:

- Get them to create an itemized estimate for the work you desire.
- Find out when they intend to start and complete the work. Also find out how busy they are and how long it will take before they can begin. Hold them to this schedule. Many contractors do 90 percent of the work quickly and then take forever to finish the job. Meanwhile, you live with the dust and mess.
- Ask about their promptness and craftsmanship when you do reference checks.
- Agree to a payment schedule. Offer them additional money or cash up front if they start and finish on time.
- Find out whether there will be one person on site to supervise the job, or whether there will be groups of workers without supervision.

4. Make sure each contractor submits a detailed written bid of the work to be done and a time line for when each piece will be completed. Agree that no charges will be assessed unless you sign off on them and that if either party changes the agreement (you make changes, or they suggest different equipment), "change work order" paperwork will be completed.

If you have two written estimates for the same work and they are quite different, find out why. There may be times when you care about high quality and craftsmanship, and there are other times where inexpensive alternatives will do.

5. Meet and talk with the contractor and workers regularly. Offering coffee or doughnuts in the morning is cheap compared to the cooperation and care you will receive from the crew working on your house.

6. Never pay the contractor in full until you have inspected the job and it meets all of your expectations. Again, be clear that if

there are significant delays in work completion, there will also be delays in payment. Also, never pay until the building inspector has signed off on the project.

PARTING THOUGHTS ABOUT NEGOTIATING AND LIFE

There may be other big negotiations in your life. Half of adults negotiate a divorce, for example. Whatever the conflict, however personal or difficult, the principles of negotiation apply. Do your research. Reach out to make sure you are communicating clearly and well. If things break down, take a break. Ask more questions. Propose using a mediator. And if it truly is impossible to negotiate in a friendly, collaborative way, hire a good lawyer and run a sound, competitive negotiation.

Any good divorce mediator or lawyer will tell you that in divorces, there are no winners. Even when the relationship is over, the objective is not to dominate the negotiation and take advantage of the other party. It's to achieve a fair, livable agreement. And divorce law (although it varies from state to state and country to country) is based on the principle of fairness, which is a good one to apply to your personal negotiations of all types. The best agreements are always reasonable and fair. Don't be taken advantage of. Do negotiate masterfully and energetically. But don't take advantage of other people; you are negotiating to achieve better, fairer, more livable outcomes, whether in business or in personal life. The master negotiator always takes the long view and always keeps the bigger picture in mind.

Our best wishes to you as you bring your mastery of negotiations to the important events and milestones of your personal life.

Good negotiating!

Note

1. M. C. Donaldson, M. Donaldson, and D. Frohnmayer, *Negotiating for Dummies* (Foster City, Calif.: IDG Books, 1996).

THE AUTHORS

Roy J. Lewicki is Dean's Distinguished Teaching Professor at the Max M. Fisher College of Business, The Ohio State University, where he teaches courses in negotiation, leadership, and management. He has previously served on the faculties at Duke University, Dartmouth College, and Yale University. Lewicki received his B.A. from Dartmouth College and Ph.D. in social psychology from Columbia University. He is the author of over thirty books, including *Negotiation, Negotiation: Readings, Exercises and Cases* and *Essentials of Negotiation,* which are the top-selling textbooks used to teach negotiation skills in business schools. Lewicki conducts numerous executive seminars in negotiation and leadership for companies such as Wells Fargo, Schlumberger, American Electric Power, Nationwide, Limited Stores, Eli Lilly, and Netjets and many government and nonprofit organizations. Among his many teaching awards is the Distinguished Educator Award from the Academy of Management.

This is the third book that Lewicki and Alex Hiam have coauthored; the others are *Think Before You Speak* and the *Fast Forward MBA in Negotiation and Deal Making.*

Alexander Hiam is the president of INSIGHTS, which provides leadership, conflict management, and negotiation programs and materials to managers in business and government for clients such as the FBI, U.S. Coast Guard, 3M, GM, Home Depot, Exxon-Mobil, AT&T, UPS, Kaiser Permanente, Royal Caribbean Cruise Lines, and the U.S. Navy and Army. He received his B.A. from Harvard College and his M.B.A. from the University of California, Berkeley, and served in management roles in high-tech and transportation companies before founding his own firm. He has also been on the faculties of the business schools at the University of Massachusetts at Amherst and American International College. His previous books include *The Vest-Pocket CEO, Marketing for Dummies, The Portable MBA in Marketing, Motivational Management, Making Horses Drink,* and *Taming the Conflict Dragon.* He is also the developer of Assessing Behavior in Conflict, a negotiation-style assessment instrument.

INDEX

A

Aaronson, K., 112–113

Accommodation, 186–193; with bosses, 190; as delaying tactic, 191–192; disadvantages of, 193; as negotiation style, 32, 36; reasons for using, 192–193; when to use, 185, 186, 189–191; why we use, 187–189

Acting upset: as coercive tactic, 79, 118, 123; example of, 13, 15; if information concealed, 123

"After you" tactic, 167

Agents, 47–50; defined, 47; disadvantages of using, 48–49; real estate purchase using, 287–290; tips on working with, 49–50; when to use, 48

Agreement, as stage of multiparty negotiations, 212, 216–217

Agreements, reaching into future, 30–31

Alcohol, negotiating while drinking, 244–245

Alliances, negotiating strategic, 153–154

Allies, used to manage impression of your concerns, 123

Alternatives: with avoidance, 197–198; in competitive negotiation, 80, 84–86; with compromise, 168; example of value of, 231–232; generating, in collaboration, 142–147; of other party, 63

Anger, 66, 117, 123

Antique dealer Web site, 163

Art gallery opening, negotiating showing at, 264–266

Aspirations. *See* Interests

Attorneys, when to consult, 79, 125

Authority: of agents, 50; giving impression of not having, 122; of other party, 64–65

Authority trap, 176–177

Avoidance, 193–201; active vs. passive, 200; examples of, with customers, 194–196, 198; moderate methods of, 197; as negotiation style, 32, 36; in order to pick time for battles, 199; potential benefits of, 200–201; by using withdrawal-threat tactic, 196–197; value of alternatives with, 197–198; when to use, 185–186, 194, 197, 201

B

Bait-and-switch tactic, 173–174

Bargaining, viii

Bargaining mix, 82

Bargaining range, 80–83

Bargaining stage, 44

Begin, M., 57

Better Business Bureau, 123

Bidding process, 44

Blocking, 211

Body language, 58–59, 63, 122

Bogey issue tactic, 116

Bosses: accommodation with, 190; collaborating with, 154–156; compromising with, 177–181; defending yourself against power plays by, 242; with poor negotiation skills, 73–75

Brainstorming, to generate alternative solutions, 145

Breakout groups, to generate alternative solutions, 146

Bridging solutions, 144

C

Cars: purchasing new, 271–277; purchasing used, 79–84, 85, 90–91, 99, 267–271; relationship and outcome concerns when buying, 26, 29–30; teenager wanting to borrow, 263

Carter, J., 57

Cascading yeses tactic, 239–241

Caving in, 10

Cell phone, bait-and-switch when purchasing, 174

Characterization, 226, 234, 236

Children, negotiation learned by, 7

Ciba Corning Diagnostics, 153–154

Ciba-Geigy, 153–154

Closing stage, 44–45; in competitive negotiation, 125–126; when compromising, 170

Coalitions, 202, 205–210; advantages of, 206; forming, 206–207; interacting with members of, 209–210; power gained from, 207–209

Coercive tactics, 118

Collaboration, 127–156; to achieve win-win solution, 16–17; with bosses, 154–156; commitment needed for, 136–137, 138, 151; focus on underlying interests in, 53–54; four-step process for, 140–150; goals in, 128–131, 137, 139, 150; in multiparty negotiations, 213–214; negative connotation of term, 127; as negotiation style, 32–33, 36–37; obstacles to, 137–139, 151–152; overcoming breakdown in, 152–153; problem-solving orientation of, 127–128; relationship building in, 131–133;

requirements for, 134–137, 139–140; suggested tactics for, 150–151; switching to competitive negotiation from, 152, 153; use of time in, 136, 140, 149; when to use, 133–134

Columbo, 104

Commitment, 107–111; final offers as statements of, 109–110; getting out of, 110–111; required for collaboration, 136–137, 138, 151; signals of, 107–108; types of statements of, 108–109

Commitment trap, 173–176

Communication: choosing medium for, 255–256, 257; example of need for planning, 4; of strong influence message, 252–260; when using agents, 49

Competitive negotiation, 92–126; closing in, 125–126; commitment in, 107–111; concessions in, 98–104; excitement and drama in, 90; general guidelines on, 105–107; haggling as form of, 181–183; how to cope with tough tactics in, 123–124; impact of, on relationships, 76–78; importance of mastering, 75–76; managing other party's impressions of your concerns in, 120–123; in multiparty negotiations, 213–214; as negotiation style, 32, 36–37; opening offers in, 79–80, 92–98; power of alternatives in, 84–86; preparing for, 79–84; self-fulfilling prophecies in, 89–90; tactics used in, 13, 14, 78–79, 111–118; time used tactically in, 13, 14, 107, 118–120; when not to use, 87–89; when to use, 77, 86–87; winning as goal of, 11–15

Compliance trap, 171–172

Compromise, 159–183; as blend of negotiating styles, 165–166; with bosses, 177–181; costs and benefits of, 166–167; dangers to avoid in, 171–177; example of, 163–165; haggling as form of, 181–183; making concessions in, 166–167, 168, 169, 170, 171; as negotiation style, 32, 33, 36–37; suggested tactics for, 167–171; value of spirit of, 159–160; when not to use, 162–163; when to use, 161–162

Concerns: in collaboration, 139, 140, 141–142; in compromise, 165, 170; managing other party's impression of your, 120–123; of other party, 106. *See also* Interests

Concessions, 98–104; defined, 98–99; irregular, 103–104; packaging, 101–102; pattern of, 102–103; rules on, 105–106; when collaborating, 140; when compromising, 166–167, 168, 169, 170, 171

Conflict management, viii, 34

Conflict resolution, viii

Consistency, in competitive negotiation, 98

Cooperative negotiation. *See* Collaboration

Corning, 153–154

Costs: of agents, 49, 50; cutting, as tactic for generating alternative solutions, 144; effect on, considered in choosing negotiation style, 30–31; of failure of multiparty negotiations, 215; fixed, importance of negotiating, 31; used to manage other party's impressions of your concerns, 122

Crucial conversations, 1–2

Cultural differences: in comfort with silence in negotiations, 113; in length of stages in negotiation, 45–46; in time for building support within organizations, 154; in time spent building relationship in

competitive negotiation, 96; in willingness to haggle, 182

Customers, using avoidance with, 194–196, 198

D

Deadlines: in collaboration, 136, 140; as source of power, 252; as tool in competitive negotiation, 13, 14, 119; when compromising, 168–169

Deception, in competitive negotiation, 79, 114–117

Dickering. *See* Haggling

Difficult conversations, 1–2

Digging in, 10

Directive approach, to power, 247–248

Divorce, negotiating, 292

Dominating, 211

Drinking, negotiating while, 244–245

E

E-mail, conducting negotiations by, 256, 257

Emotional goals, 5, 7

Emotional signaling, 13, 14

Emotional stupidity, 188–189

Emotions: escalated, in collaboration, 149; intangible goals and, 52; reacting with, 219, 221; used to manage other party's impression of your concerns, 122, 123

Empathy, 236–237

Employees: accommodation by, with bosses, 190; focuses of negotiations between managers and, 178–179; negotiating claim by former, 24–25; supervisor's time spent dealing with, 29; underlying interests in dispute between supervisor and, 53–54

Employers: current, negotiating raise with, 112–113, 285–287; negotiating new job with, 279–284

Ethics, of influence and power, 238–239

Excitement, in competitive negotiation, 90

Expand-the-pie tactic, to generate alternative solutions, 143

Expert proof, 175–176

F

Fairness, in collaboration, 148–149

Final offers, as commitment statements, 109–110

Formula-detail, 44

Frames: common types of, 226–229; tips for managing, 235–237; value of understanding, of other party, 223–224, 229

Framing, 219–237; defined, 220; example of transforming, to resolve conflict, 229–235; landlord-tenant conflict resolved by managing, 219–223; of strong influence message, 252–260. *See also* Reframing

G

Game, negotiation as, 8–9, 40–41, 46–51

Goals: in collaboration, 128–131, 137, 139, 150; of competitive negotiation, 11–15, 86, 87; as concern in negotiation, 5, 6, 7; inexperienced negotiators' mistakes with, 9–10; prioritizing, 52, 168; researching, of other party, 61–62; setting, 42–43, 51–52, 69. *See also* Outcomes

Goleman, D., 59, 188

Good cop–bad cop tactic, 114–115, 176

H

Haggling, viii, 181–183

Hardball bargaining. *See* Haggling

Hardball tactics, 111–118, 123–124

Having seat at table, as source of power, 252

"Helping the other party" tactic, 112–113

HFG Expansion Fund, 57

Highball-lowball tactic, 115

Highland Energy Group, 56–57

Home purchase, 287–290

Home repair contract, 290–292

Honesty, required for collaboration, 135–136

I

Ideas, fresh, as source of power, 246

Identity, as frame, 226–227, 236–237

"If . . . then" statements: as commitment signals, 108–109; when compromising, 156, 180; when making concessions, 100–101

Implementation stage, 45

Inexperienced negotiators: common errors made by, 9–10; competitive negotiation by, 88–89; examples of, 3–4, 73–75; extreme opening positions of, 92–94

Influence: delivering convincing message to gain, 252–260; ethics of, 238–239; tactics of, to protect yourself against, 239–245. *See also* Power

Information: concealing, 122–123; incomplete, suboptimal results due to, 3; listening to obtain, 106–107; misrepresenting, 122; as source of power, 250–251

Information gathering: on other party, 60–66; in preparation stage, 41–42, 43

Information sharing: with coalition members, 209; in collaboration, 137; with other parties, 59–60

Intangibles: in collaboration, 140, 148–149; in competitive negotiation, 86, 100; in compromise, 165–166; as concern in negotiation, 6; as consideration in planning, 51–52

Interests: determining underlying, 52–56, 69; differences in, in collaboration, 129–130; as frame, 227, 232, 235, 249–250; of other party, 62–63, 141–142. *See also* Concerns

Intimidation, 117–118

J

Job hunting, power of alternatives when, 85–86

Jobs, new, negotiating with employers about, 279–284

Joukowsky, T., 57

K

Kennedy, J. F., 190

Khrushchev, N., 66

L

Lauder, L., 164

Lawyers, when to consult, 79, 125

Learning how to negotiate, 7–8

Lease negotiations: misdirection used in, 121–122; multiparty, for office space, 203–205, 210

Likability trap, 176

Limits, identifying your, 69–70

Listening: in competitive negotiation, 107, 113–114; when asking questions, 63

Logrolling tactic, to generate alternative solutions, 143

Lose to win. *See* Accommodation

Lose-lose. *See* Avoidance

M

Master negotiators: example of skills of, 73–75; slow initial steps of, 10–11; style flexibility of, 17, 19–22

Misdirection, 121

Multiparty negotiations, 202–218; coalitions in, 202, 205–210; decid-

ing on role to play in, 210–212; negotiation styles used in, 203–205, 213–214; stages of, 212, 214, 216–217; types of, 202; unique aspects of, 214–215, 218

N

Needs, researching, of other party, 62–63

Negotiation: as daily activity, 2–4; by e-mail, 256, 257; five-stage model of, 41–46; as game, 8–9, 40–41, 46–51; learning, 7–8; main concerns in, 5–7; participants in, 46–51; prevalence of, 1–2; as stage of multiparty negotiations, 212, 216; terminology for, viii, 1; to win, 11–15. *See also* Multiparty negotiations; Negotiation styles; Personal negotiation

Negotiation strategies. *See* Negotiation styles; Tactics

Negotiation styles: compromise as blend of, 165–166; considerations in choosing, 22–31, 32, 33; determining your preferred, 17–18, 34–35, 38–39; interactions between negotiators of different, 35, 36–37; in multiparty negotiations, 203–205, 213–214; need for flexibility in use of, 17, 19–22; no-strategy approach to choosing, 35, 38; overview of types of, 32–33; researching other party's likely use of, 65–66. *See also* Accommodation; Avoidance; Collaboration; Competitive negotiation; Compromise

Negotiators: agents as, 47–50; interactions between, using different negotiation styles, 35, 36–37. *See also* Inexperienced negotiators; Master negotiators

New cars, purchasing, 271–277

New York City Landmarks Preservation Commission, 163–165

Nibble tactic, 14, 116, 124
Nixon, R., 66
No, saying, 172–173, 209
Nonverbal cues, 58–59, 122
Normative power, 208

O

Objections, handling, after presenting proposal, 258–259
Objectives. *See* Goals
Opening offers: in competitive negotiation, 79–80, 92–98; extreme, 92–94, 96; setting tone with, 97–98; who makes first, 94–96
Opening stage, in negotiation, 43
Opponents. *See* Other parties
Other parties, 56–67; considering concerns of, when formulating proposal, 254–255; considering relationship with, 60; dealing with tough tactics used by, 123–124; example of anger of, 66; face saving by, 111; importance of understanding, 56–57; information sharing with, 59–60; making opportunities to study, 57–58; managing impressions of, of your concerns, 120–123; nonverbal cues of, 58–59; planning negotiation based on needs of, 59; researching, 60–66, 68–69; role reversal with, 67; value of understanding frame of, 223–224. *See also* Multiparty negotiations
Outcomes: as concern in negotiation, 5, 7; as consideration when choosing negotiation style, 22–25, 28–31; as frame, 227. *See also* Goals

P

Participation, as source of power, 252
Payoff, offering, to generate alternative solutions, 143–144
Persistence: of multiparty negotiators, 214–215; as source of power, 246

Personal negotiation: of divorce, 292; example of, with suboptimal results, 3–4; of home repair contract, 290–292; of house purchase through agent, 287–290; leaving too much on table in, 264–267; for new job with employers, 279–284; of parents with teenagers, 263; prevalence of, 1–2; of raise with current employer, 112–113, 285–287; terminology for, 1; when buying new car, 271–277; when buying used car, 267–271; when planning wedding, 277–279
Piano, R., 163, 164–165
Piggybacking, to generate alternative solutions, 145–146
Planning, 40–71; analysis steps for, 68–70, 71; considering participants when, 46–51; determining underlying interests when, 52–56, 69; determining what other party wants when, 56–67; importance of, 43, 68; setting goals and, 42–43, 51–52, 69. *See also* Preparation
Playing chicken tactic, 117
Position, as source of power, 251
Power: choice of approaches to, 247–250; ethics of, 238–239; as frame, 228–229; sources of, 245–246, 250–252; testing, 246–247; types of, gained from coalitions, 207–209. *See also* Influence
Power plays, defending yourself against, 241–242
Prenegotiation, as stage of multiparty negotiations, 212, 216
Preparation: for competitive negotiation, 79–84; as stage in negotiation, 41–43. *See also* Planning
Primacy effect, 253
Prioritizing: alternative solutions, 146–147; goals, 52, 168
Problem solving: four-step collabora-

tive process for, 140–150; as orientation of collaboration, 127–128

Problems: generating alternative solutions to, 142–147; identifying, 141; selecting solution to, 147–150; understanding issues behind, 141–142

Process, as frame, 229, 236

Promises, as commitment statements, 108–109

Proposals: choosing communication medium for, 255–256, 257; considering other party's perspective when formulating, 254–255; handling questions and objections after presenting, 258–259; one-sided vs. two-sided approach to, 256–258; planning structure and style of, 253–254; reducing concentration on counterarguments to, 259–260

Pruitt, D., 143

Publishing: competition and collaboration required in, 16–17; negotiation of testimonial in, 266

Purchasing, negotiating per-unit costs in, 30

Q

Questions: for determining underlying interests, 55; handling, after presenting proposal, 258–259; in opening conversation of competitive negotiation, 96; for researching other party, 61–65; silence bracketing, 114

R

Real estate: avoiding selling, to undesirable customer, 198; competitive negotiation of sale of, 12–15; framing used in negotiating conflicts over, 219–223, 225–229, 230–235; multiparty negotiating leases for, 121–122, 203–205, 210; negotiating home repair contract for, 290–292; negotiating purchase of, through agent, 287–290; outcome and relationship concerns in negotiating rent for, 23–24

Reasonableness, as source of power, 245

Recency effect, 253

Reciprocity trap, 172

Recognition seeking, 211

Reframing: around interests, 249–250; around rights, 250; example of, to resolve conflict, 229–235

Rejecting offer, when compromising, 172–173

Relationship-based power, in coalitions, 208–209

Relationship-oriented role, in multiparty negotiations, 211–212

Relationships: accommodation for sake of, 190–191, 192, 193; avoidance and, 200; building, in collaboration, 131–133; competitive negotiation and, 76–78, 86; as concern in negotiation, 5–6, 7; as consideration when choosing negotiation style, 16, 23–28, 32, 60; extreme offers as risking destroying, 94; in multiparty negotiations, 215, 218; valued, tips on negotiation involving, 27–28

Rent negotiations, outcome and relationship as concerns in, 23–24

Resources: control over, as source of power, 251; as focus in employee-manager negotiations, 178–179

Rights, as frame, 228, 235, 250

Risk tolerance, in collaboration, 130

Rituals, closing, 45

Rogers, W., 191

Role reversal, with other parties, 67

Rubylane.com, 163

Rules: for competitive negotiation, 105–107; discussing, before negotiating, 78; written and unwritten, 40–41. *See also* Tactics

S

Sadat, A., 57

Salary negotiations: with new job, 279–284; outcome as concern in, 30; for raise from current employer, 112–113, 285–287

Saving face, helping other party with, 111

Saying no, 172–173, 209

Scarcity bias, when compromising, 177

Self-fulfilling prophecies, 89–90

Self-oriented role, in multiparty negotiations, 210–211

Silence, in competitive negotiation, 107, 113–114

Situation, as consideration when choosing negotiation style, 33

Skelton, R., 128

Small business owners, caution on competitive negotiation by, 89

Social proof, 175–176

Social value orientation, 187

Solutions: generating alternative, 142–147; selecting, 147–150; writing down, 150

Specifications, as focus in employee-manager negotiations, 178

Split the difference. *See* Compromise

Spokespersons, in team negotiations, 51

Stoner, T., 56–57

Strange requests tactic, defending yourself against, 242–244

Strategic power, 207

Strategies. *See* Negotiation styles; Tactics

Straw man tactic, 78–79, 116

Styles. *See* Negotiation styles

Summarizing, 152–153

Sun-Tzu, 199

Surveys, to generate alternative solutions, 146

T

Tactics: for collaborating, 150–151; for competitive negotiation, 13, 14, 78–79, 111–118; for compromising, 167–171; for generating alternative solutions, 143–146; hardball, 111–117, 123–124; of influence, protecting yourself against, 239–245; for interacting with coalition members, 209–210; in multiparty negotiations, 211, 212; to overcome breakdown in collaboration, 152–153; researching, likely to be used by other party, 65–66; time pressure as, 13, 14, 107, 118–120. *See also* Rules

Target point, 79, 105

Task-oriented role, in multiparty negotiations, 212

Team negotiation, 50–51

Technique, as source of power, 246

Threats: as commitment statements, 108, 109; as way of using power, 248–249

Time: accommodation to buy, 191–192; as focus in employee-manager negotiations, 178; future, agreements reaching into, 30–31; picking, for battles, 199; required for competitive negotiation, 87–88; required for multiparty negotiations, 214–215; required for negotiation stages, 45–46; as source of power, 252; used in collaboration, 130–131, 136, 140; used in competitive negotiation, 13, 14, 107, 118–120. *See also* Deadlines

Tone, setting, 97–98

Toughness, in competitive negotiation, 98

Trust: building, in negotiation, 135; possibility of destroying, 88; required for collaboration, 134–135

Trustworthiness: importance of, 41; researching, of other party, 64

U

Ultimatums, as way of using power, 248–249

Used cars, purchasing, 79–84, 85, 90–91, 99, 267–271

V

Vacation, collaboration to determine location for, 143, 144

W

Walkaway points: alternatives as, 85; concealing, 105; defined, 80, 83; indicators of proximity to, 83–84; knowing, when compromising, 168

Web service provider, "accidental" negotiation with, 107

Weddings, planning, 277–279

Whitney Museum of American Art, 163–165

Wiggle room, 97

Win-lose. *See* Competitive negotiation

Winning, as goal of negotiation, 11–15

Win-win. *See* Collaboration

Withdrawal-threat tactic, 196–197

Y

"Yes, and . . .," 180–181, 242

Yeses, cascading, 239–241

Z

Zigzagging, 10